IMAGES
of America

LAUDERDALE COUNTY

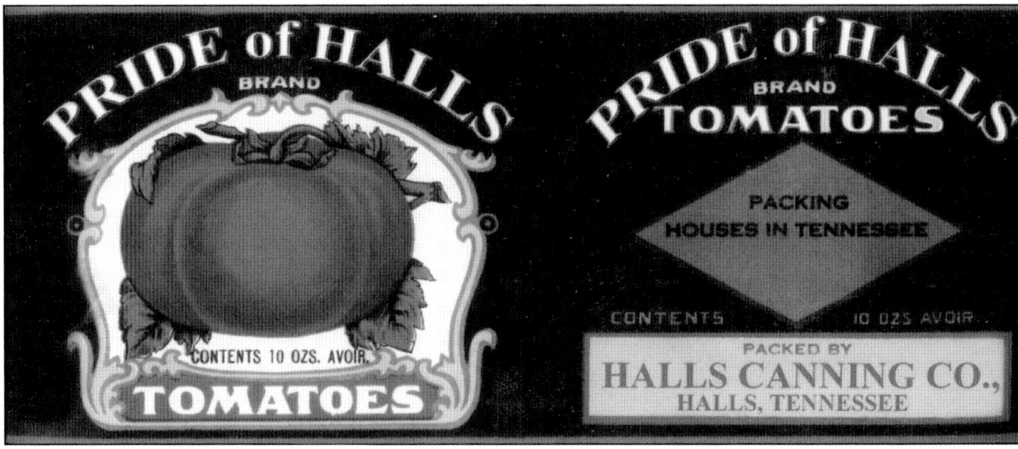

Tomato Can Labels. Tomato cans from the Halls Canning Company and Ripley Canning Company had many colorful labels and names, including Pride of Halls and Forked Deer brand. (Courtesy of Dot Craddock.)

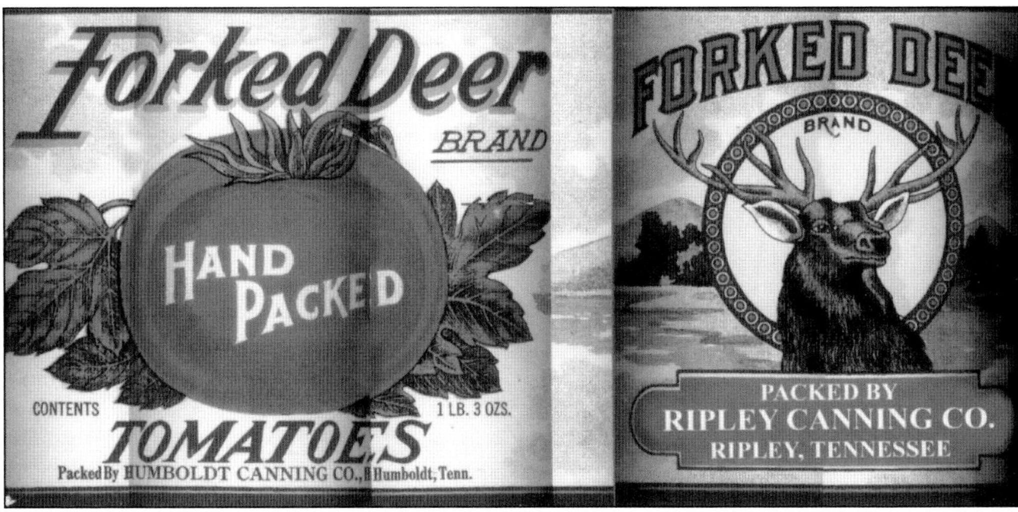

On the Cover: Ripley The Ripley Canning Company provided a ready market for the large tomato crop grown by Lauderdale County farmers. This factory, photographed in the 1930s, employed 250 people. The capacity of the plant was 2.5 train carloads per day or 4,000 cases with 24 cans to the case. Owned by the Robert Craddock family, these canning factories were operated in Humboldt, Halls, and Ripley, Tennessee, during the 1930s, 1940s, and early 1950s.

IMAGES
of America

LAUDERDALE COUNTY

Billie Morris

ARCADIA
PUBLISHING

ISBN 978-0-7385-8223-8

Published by Arcadia Publishing
Charleston, South Carolina

Printed in the United States of America

Library of Congress Control Number: 2010939087

For all general information, please contact Arcadia Publishing:
Telephone 843-853-2070
Fax 843-853-0044
E-mail sales@arcadiapublishing.com
For customer service and orders:
Toll-Free 1-888-313-2665

Visit us on the Internet at www.arcadiapublishing.com

This book is respectfully dedicated to the pioneers and early settlers who ventured to West Tennessee with their families to make their homes in the wilderness that would become Lauderdale County, Tennessee.

Contents

ACKNOWLEDGMENTS

Billie Morris wishes to express a special appreciation to the following people who preserved the histories and photographs of Lauderdale County: Bettie Brandon Davis, Lauderdale County archivist and historian; Terry Ford, executive editor of the *Lauderdale County Enterprise*; and Lisa Hankins, former executive director of the Lauderdale County Chamber/Economic and Community Development and currently director of REDI, a 12-county Regional Economic Development Initiative. Without them, time would have wiped away these historical photographs.

I also wish to thank the many staff members of the Lauderdale County Library, Halls Library, and the Lauderdale County Museum for opening their facilities to me.

Unless otherwise noted, all images are courtesy of author Billie Morris.

Introduction

The Tennessee General Assembly established Lauderdale County on November 24, 1835, and named it for Col. James Lauderdale, who died at the Battle of New Orleans. The new county was formed from the part of Tipton County that lay north of the Hatchie River, most of the part of Dyer County that lay south of the Forked Deer River, and a sliver from the western part of Haywood County. The Mississippi River flows along the entire western border of Lauderdale County except for Forked Deer Island (Island 26), which now abuts Arkansas, and the Obion River forms part of the county's northwestern border. The eastern part of the county is part of the Gulf Coastal Plain; the western portion is in the floodplain of the Mississippi River.

The act establishing the county had named a committee from Haywood County to choose a site for the county seat, which was to be named Ripley, after Gen. E.W. Ripley, another hero of the War of 1812. The committee chose 62.5 acres "on the waters of Cane Creek" donated by Thomas Brown of Lowndes County, Mississippi. It was part of a 5,000-acre Tennessee grant to Charles McDowell, who had been a major participant in the Revolutionary War's Battle of Kings Mountain. Brown was to have his choice of a lot in the town that would be built there.

During the antebellum period, cotton dominated the county's agriculture. Steamboats carried cotton from landings on the Forked Deer, Mississippi, and Hatchie Rivers. Cotton remained the primary money crop after the Civil War, and much of it was taken to Brownsville for shipment on the railroad there. However, with the coming of the railroad to Lauderdale County in 1882, fruit could be grown, and for years, many acres of strawberries were planted and picked for shipment to northern markets. In earlier days, the timber industry was concentrated in overflow areas of the county and on or near the county's streams from which logs could be floated downstream to market. Access to railroad transportation made shipment of timber and sawn lumber possible, and that industry began to flourish in the hills, as well. While corn, soybeans, cotton, and wheat are now the major crops grown in the county, tomatoes have become an important county crop, and "Ripley Tomatoes" are known and valued far and wide and celebrated with the annual Tomato Festival.

Lauderdale County has been valiantly represented in every war since its establishment. Fort Pillow, overlooking the Mississippi River near Fulton, was constructed by Confederate forces early in the War Between the States as part of the Confederate river defense system, but after the river fell to the Union army in 1862, it was abandoned and later occupied by Union troops. The most controversial engagement of that war took place at Fort Pillow on April 12, 1864. Fearful of the Union soldiers stationed there who were going about stealing livestock and poultry, the citizens of Lauderdale and surrounding counties appealed to Confederate general Nathan Bedford Forrest for relief. Soldiers under his command, many familiar with the terrain, attacked early on April 12 and quickly seized the high knolls around the fort from which rebel sharpshooters were able to wound and kill numbers of the Federals, including the commander of the fort. The major who took command ignored Forrest's demand for unconditional surrender, and the Confederates overran the fort. Casualties were high among the 295 white and 262 US Colored Troops that garrisoned the fort, and many accused General Forrest's troops of perpetrating a "massacre" of the black troops. "Remember Fort Pillow" became a rallying cry among colored troops and reinvigorated many whose interest in the war was beginning to flag. To this day, varying opinions of the action that took place that day still exist, as some refer to it as the "Massacre of Fort Pillow," while others maintain it was an honorable battle.

Union troops roved about the county during the Federal occupation, and there were skirmishes between them and the Confederate troops at Woodville on October 21, 1862, at Double Bridges on November 18, 1862, at Knob Creek in January 1863, and at Durhamville in September of that year.

A World War II facility, to be called the Dyersburg Army Air Field, was constructed in Halls in 1942 to train crews of B-17s. About 7,700 crewmen received training there before being sent to the European Theater or to other US bases to await overseas assignments. After the war, the base was deactivated, and the 2,451 acres were returned to agriculture and industry. The Veteran's Museum is located on the site.

One

The Early Years

Earliest settlements were located at Fulton in 1818, Key Corner in 1820, and Durhamville in 1826. Other early settlements were at Gold Dust, Nankipoo, and Hales Point. Lauderdale County's other cities, towns, and communities include Arp, Asbury, Ashport, Barr, Bexar, Campground, Cedar Grove, Central, Cherry, Chisholm Lake, Concord, Conner, Curve, Double Bridges, Dry Hill, Edith, Flippin, Forked Deer, Fort Pillow, Gates, Glimp, Greaves Chapel, Halls, Henning, Hurricane Hill, Knob Creek, Lightfoot, Luckett, Mack, Mary's Chapel, Open Lake, Orysa, Pleasant Hill, Plum Point, Poplar Grove, Porter's Gap, Ripley, Salem, Three Points, Walnut Grove, Whitefield, and Woodville.

The new county court met for the first time on May 2, 1836. At the second meeting of the county court, at the home of Jacob Byler, Henry Rutherford was elected entry taker—not county surveyor as he is often said to have been. It was Able H. Pope who was elected county surveyor, and with help from R.S. Byrn, R.C. Campbell, Henry Rutherford, and William Turner, he produced in 1838 perhaps the very first map of the county showing its civil districts. By the time of the county court meeting of February 1837, John and William Laird had finished the first courthouse, a temporary one of 22 feet by 26 feet and 17 feet high, built of logs on a reserved lot in Ripley for $174.74 ¾, which was more than $25 under contract. The county court members made plans for a jail later that year, and at their meeting in October 1839, they appointed a committee to make plans for a new courthouse on the Court Square after the trees and stumps were removed. The first courthouse built on the Court Square was destroyed by fire in 1867. The county court met at the Baptist church until the courthouse was replaced with a brick building in 1870. The contract for the present courthouse was let in late 1935 to the R.M. Condra Company of Nashville for $108,833; Marxs & Holman, also of Nashville, were the architects. A Public Works Administration grant of $45,000 and bonds issued by the county for $75,000 were used to pay for building and equipping it. It was ready for occupancy early in 1937. The present building is in the National Register of Historic Places and was refurbished in 2010.

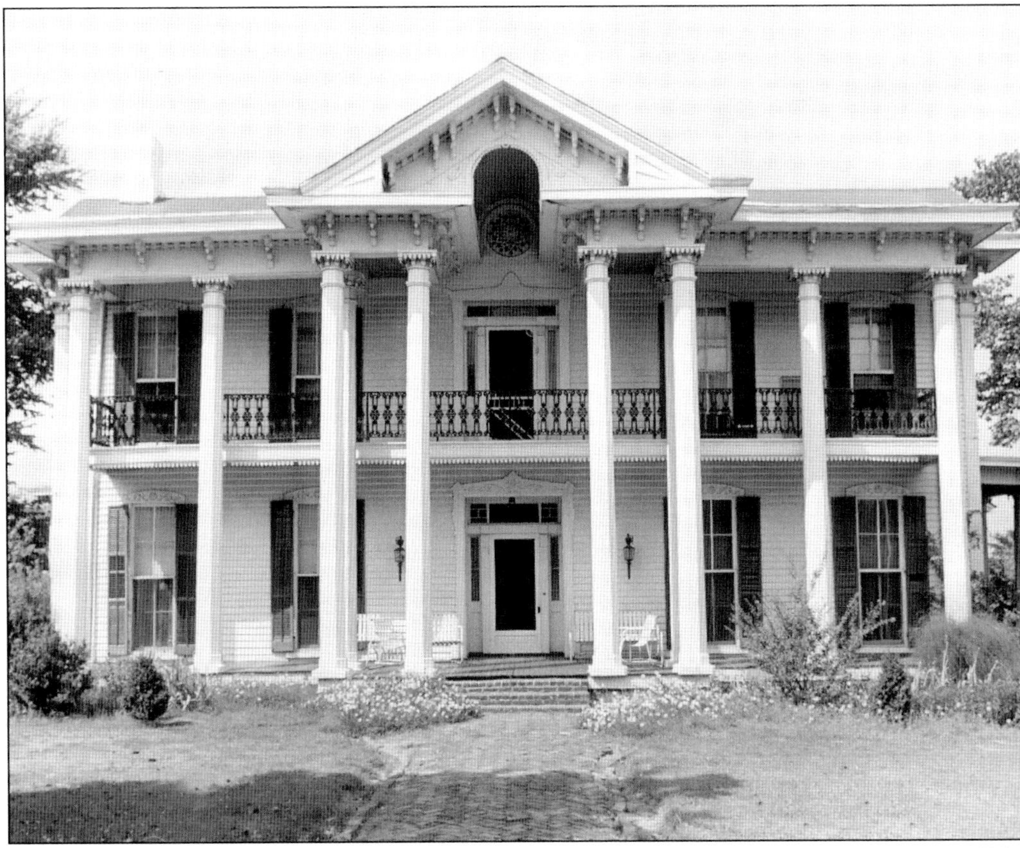

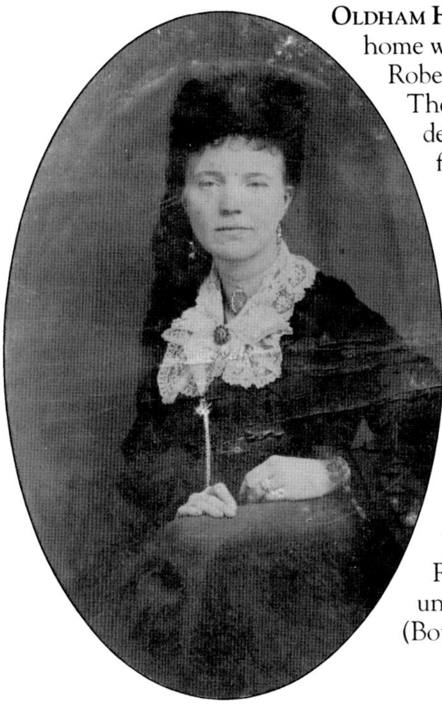

Oldham Home, Lafayette Street, Ripley, c. 1848–1851. This home was built by Dr. Samuel Oldham of Eylau for his son Dr. Robert Oldham and his bride, Laura Partee (pictured below). The home was Colonial in architecture and elaborate in detail, with beautiful iron grillwork across the upper gallery, four center columns that extended out over the front steps, and ornate wooden details under the eaves. The inside featured a beautiful curved stairway and plaster rosettes in the ceilings. In the back was an adjoining, covered walkway with the kitchen at the end. In the center of the walkway was a cistern. There were side porches on each side and a lovely formal garden on the east side. Because of family connections, many distinguished guests were entertained here, among them Pres. Andrew Johnson. Dr. Oldham died of a fever he contracted while attending to soldiers camped near the Hatchie River and left Mrs. Oldham with two small children. She moved to Eylau and sold the home to nephew Hiram Glass. He, in turn, sold it to R.C. Klutts. The home remained in the Klutts family until 1988, when it was sold to Ripley First Baptist Church. (Both images courtesy of Susan Partee Scott.)

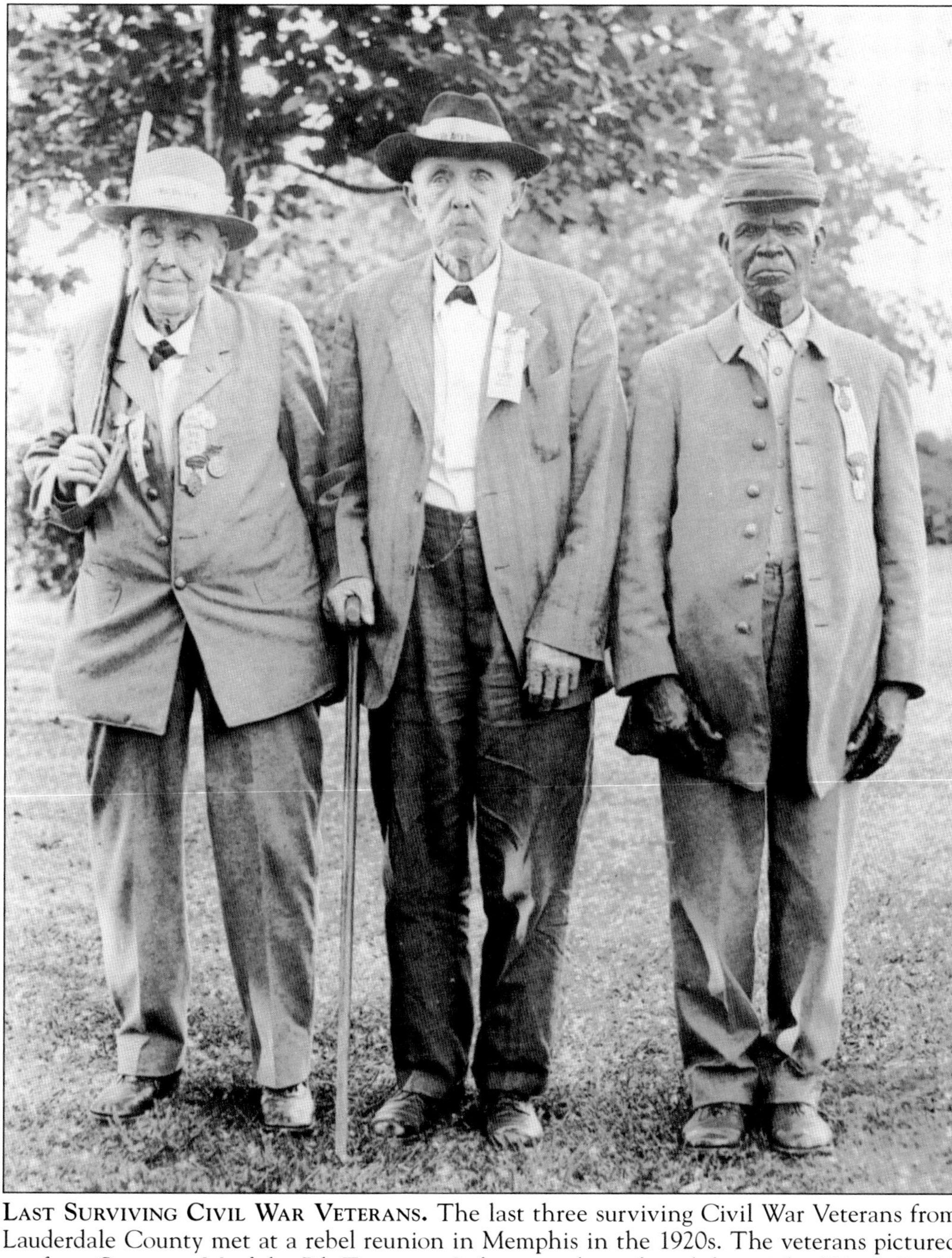

LAST SURVIVING CIVIL WAR VETERANS. The last three surviving Civil War Veterans from Lauderdale County met at a rebel reunion in Memphis in the 1920s. The veterans pictured are from Company M of the 7th Tennessee Infantry and are, from left to right, "Uncle Buck" Buchanan, William Ball Drake, and Louis N. Nelson. Though he was black, Nelson fought for the Confederacy at Shiloh, Lookout Mountain, and Vicksburg. After the war, he returned to the Oldham plantation for 12 years and was later a janitor at Ripley Grammar School. He attended 39 Confederate reunions. When he died in 1934, only two members of Company M, both white, survived. Both attended his funeral. He was buried in uniform, and his coffin was draped with the Confederate flag. (Courtesy of Terry Ford.)

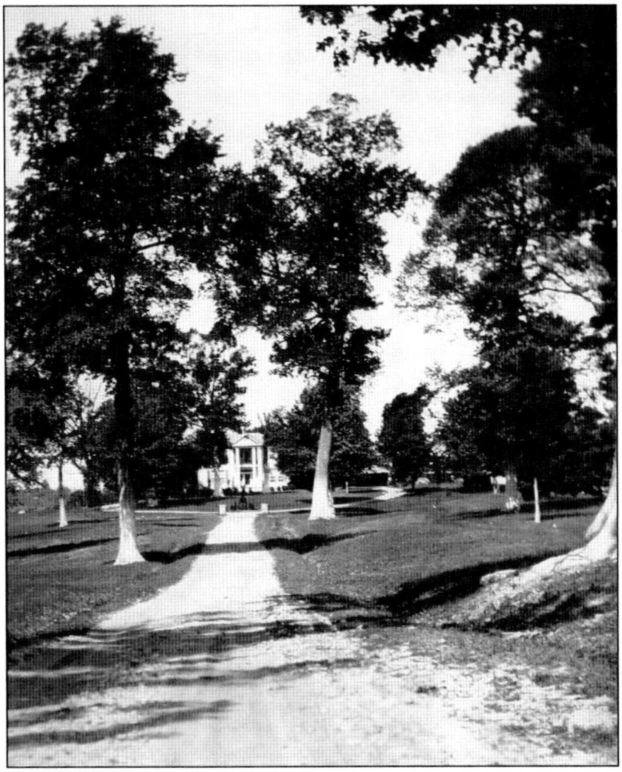

SCOTT LAWN, RIPLEY. This old home, first known as Shadow Lawn and today known as Scott Lawn, is possibly from as early as 1829. (Courtesy of Lauderdale County Library.)

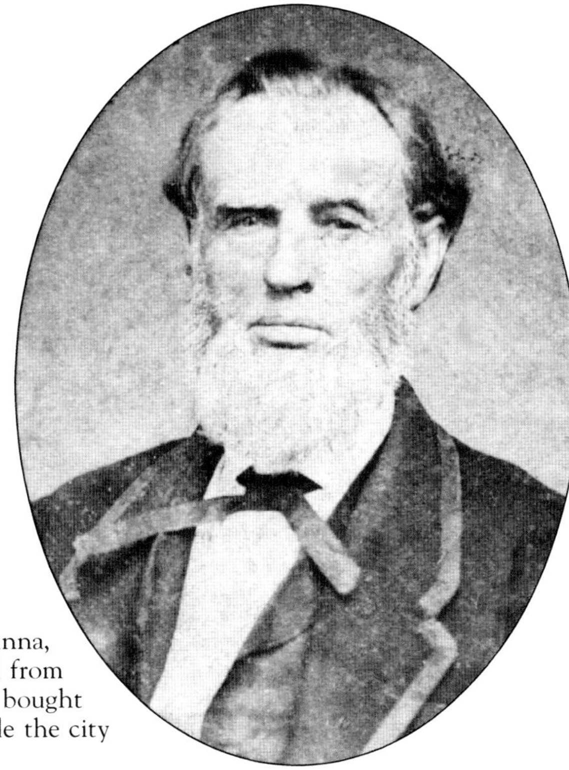

Hiram Partee (pictured) and his wife, Louanna, along with their six children, migrated from Gibson County to Ripley in 1848 and bought several hundred acres of land just outside the city limits. (Courtesy of Susan Partee Scott.)

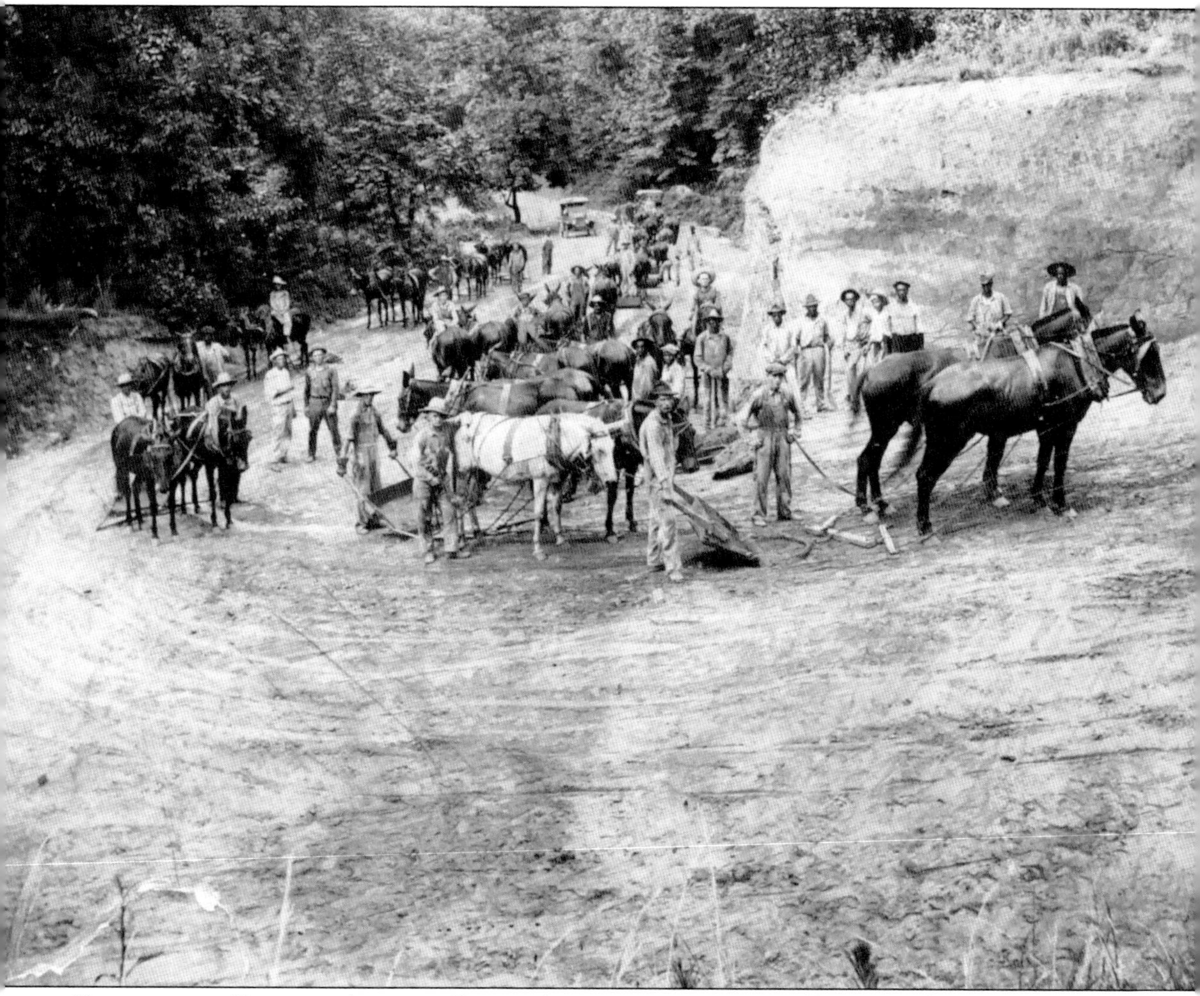

Cutting the Road to Ashport Bluff, August 1923. Teams of horses and mules are seen helping to build the road that goes to Open Lake and the Mississippi River. The road is now Highway 19 West and is the paved road that gives farmers access to thousands of acres of tillable land in the Mississippi River bottomlands.

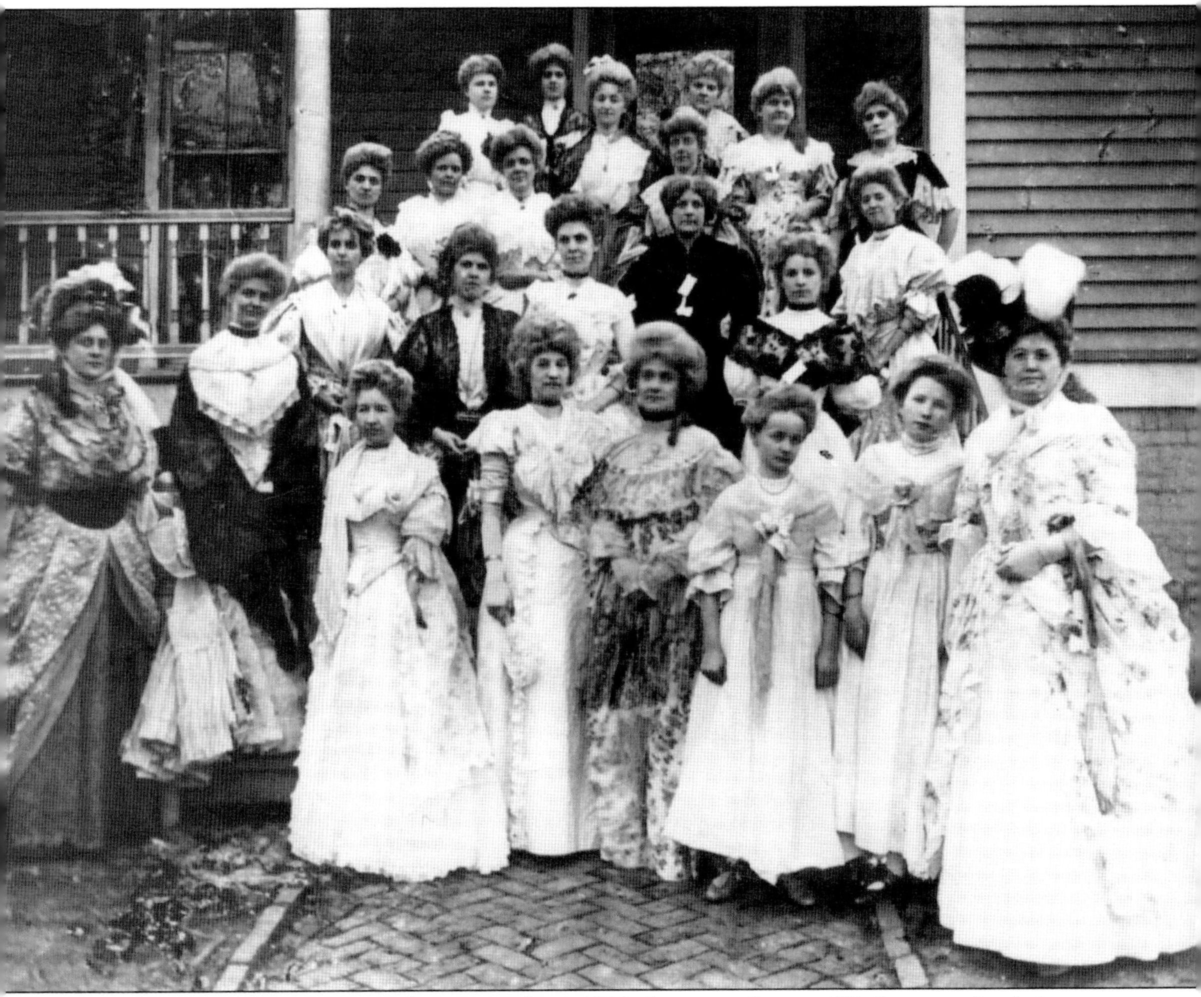

WEDNESDAY BOOK CLUB. This image from 1902 depicts a George Washington birthday party in Ripley, Tennessee. The ladies' book club was organized in 1900 and was the only social club in Ripley at that time. One of the club's major projects was to establish the Lauderdale County Library. (Courtesy of Susan Scott.)

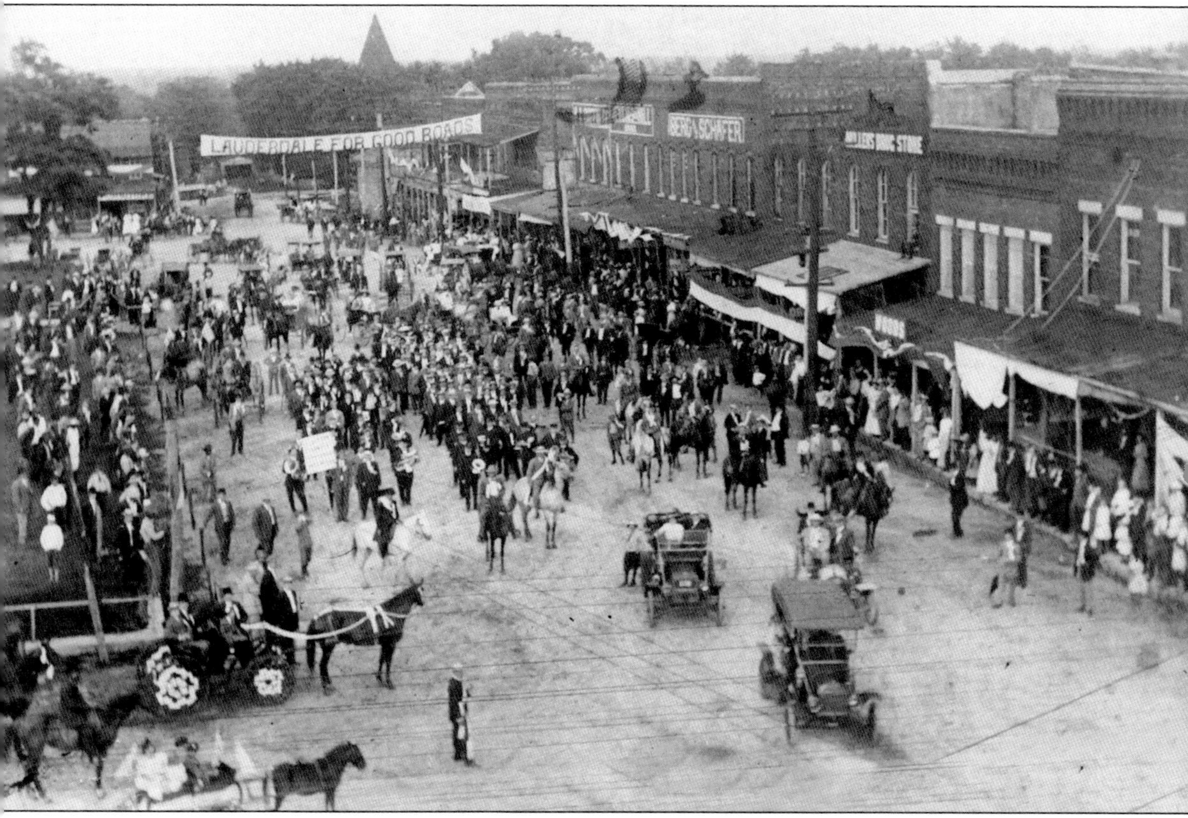

A Good Roads Rally, Ripley, June 9, 1910. A downtown parade was organized to raise funds for roads. The event was to be in Confederate Park, a mile south of Ripley; however, due to big rains, the activities were moved to the courthouse. About 2,500 people were said to have attended in spite of the weather and were fed in the courthouse and a couple of buildings near the square. The *News Scimitar* of Memphis reported that Ripley was decorated like a June bride.

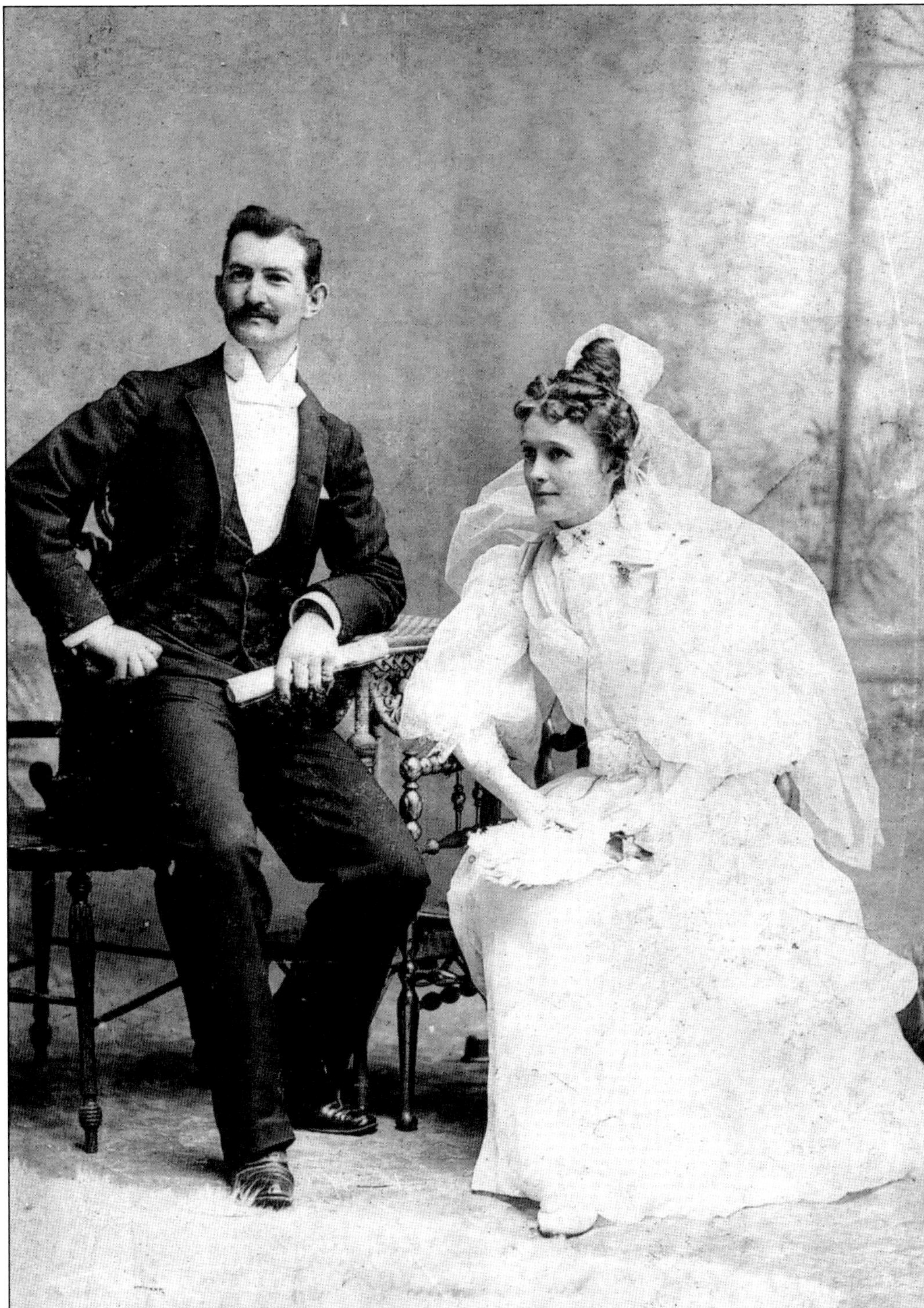

DR. J.R. CRUTCHER AND SCRAP (FLOWERS) CRUTCHER. Members of a prominent family in Henning, the Crutchers are shown on their wedding day. Note her beautiful gown and exquisite hair. (Courtesy of Emily Suggs.)

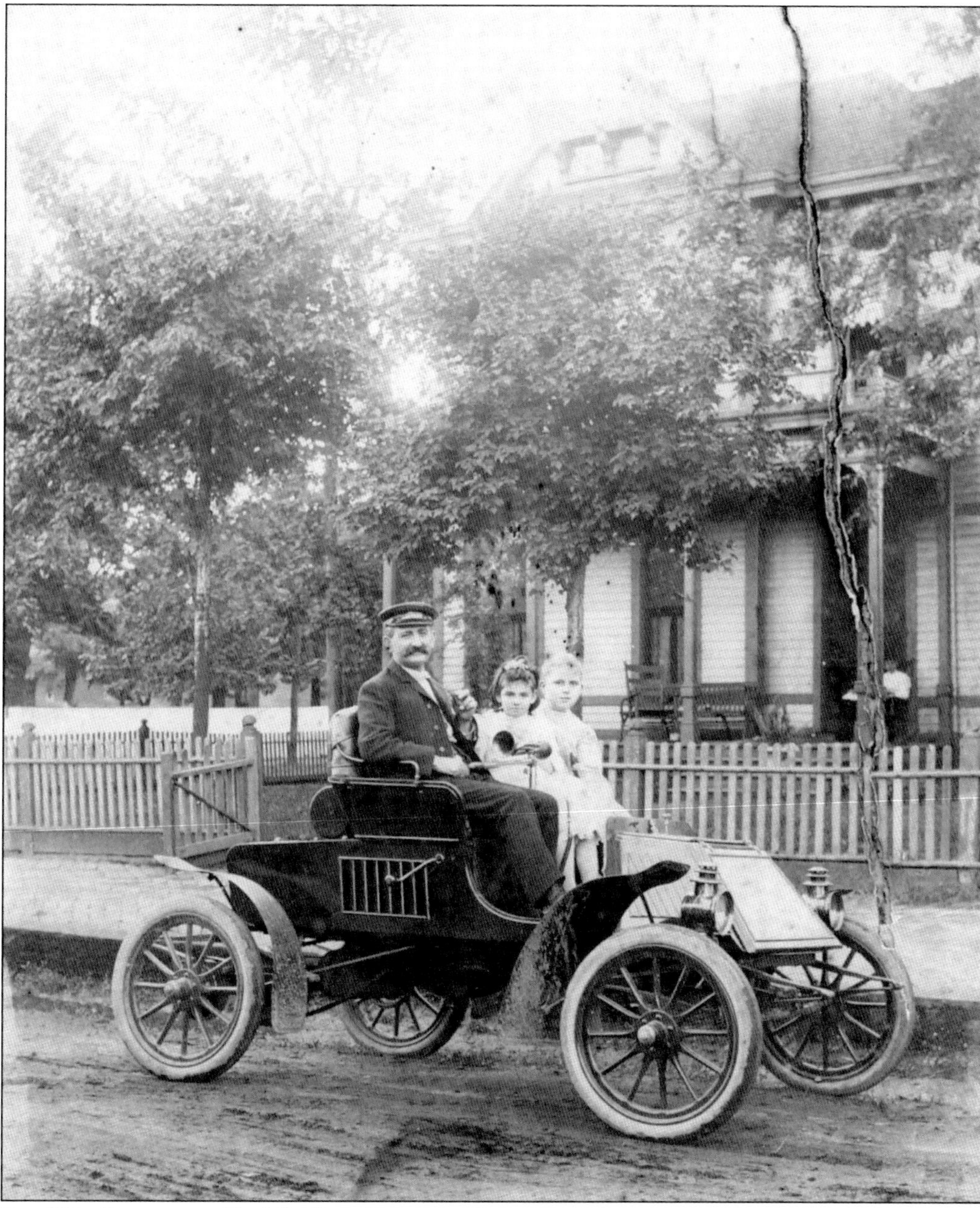

Dr. J.R. Crutcher. Dr. J.R. Crutcher tours the streets of Henning, Tennessee, with two small children. Dr. Crutcher practiced medicine in Henning and the Durhamville and Orysa communities. (Courtesy of Emily Suggs.)

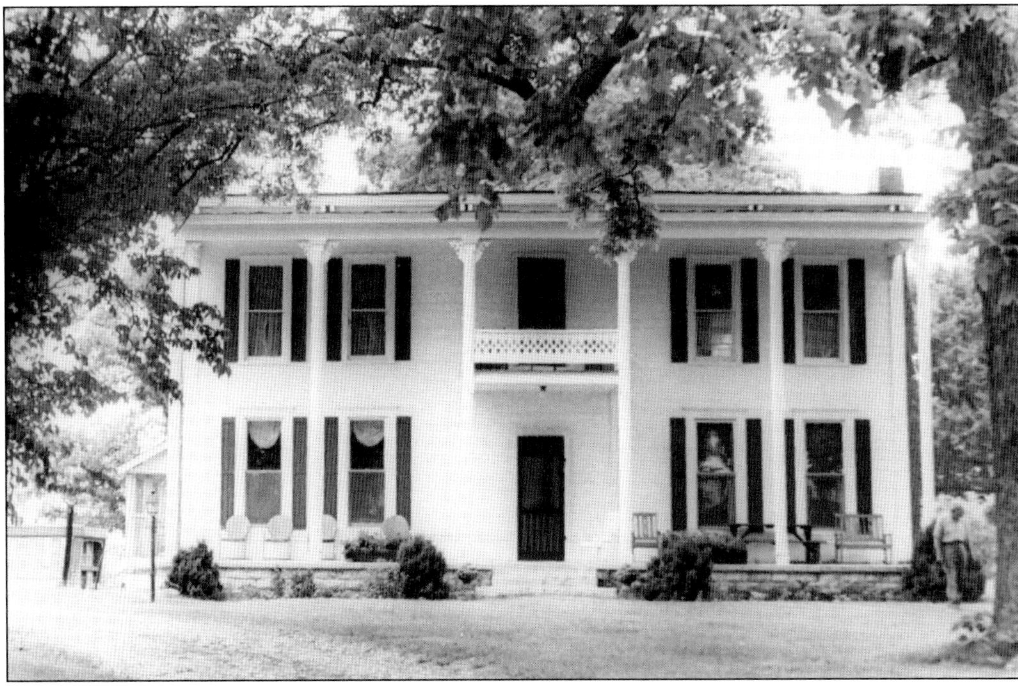

WILLIAM ALAN MOORER HOME, REBUILT IN 1870, DURHAMVILLE. The original home burned in 1865, the last year of the Civil War. William Alan Moorer rebuilt immediately using poplar trees cut on the farm. Five generations of the family lived there. The house was torn down in 2005. (Courtesy of Elizabeth Parker.)

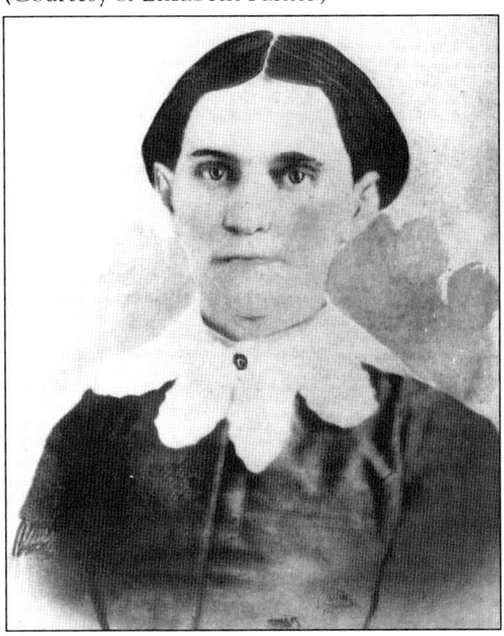

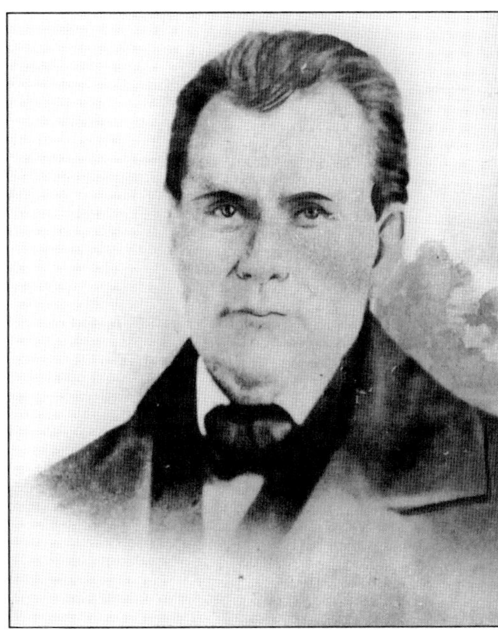

HARRIETTE BOONE (JENKINS) MOORER AND WILLIAM ALAN MOORER. Harriette Boone (Jenkins) Moorer (1814–1883) and William Alan Moorer (1807–1878) had six children. William was a large landowner who came to Lauderdale County and settled at Durhamville around 1847. (Both images courtesy of Laura Culotta.)

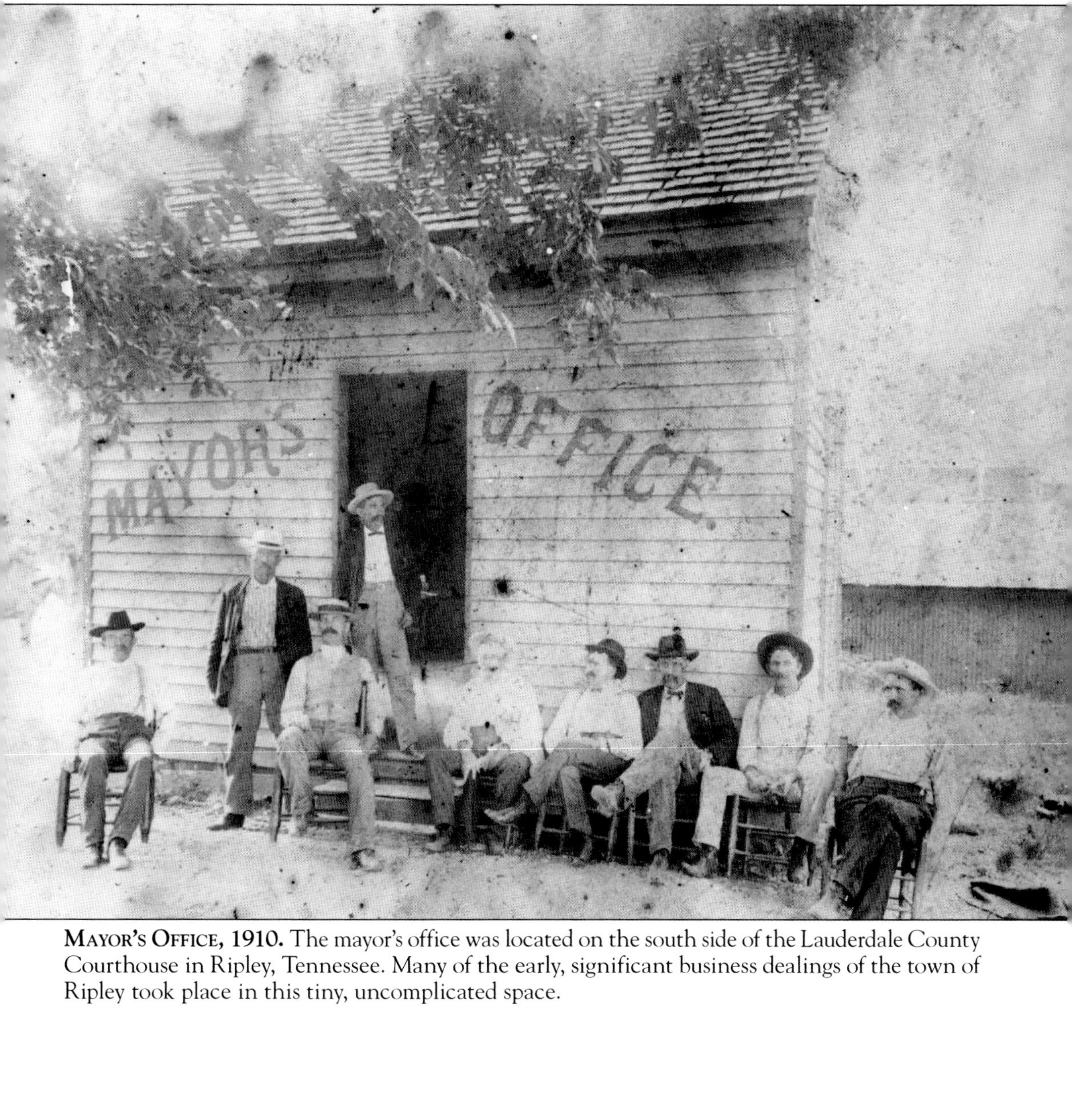

MAYOR'S OFFICE, 1910. The mayor's office was located on the south side of the Lauderdale County Courthouse in Ripley, Tennessee. Many of the early, significant business dealings of the town of Ripley took place in this tiny, uncomplicated space.

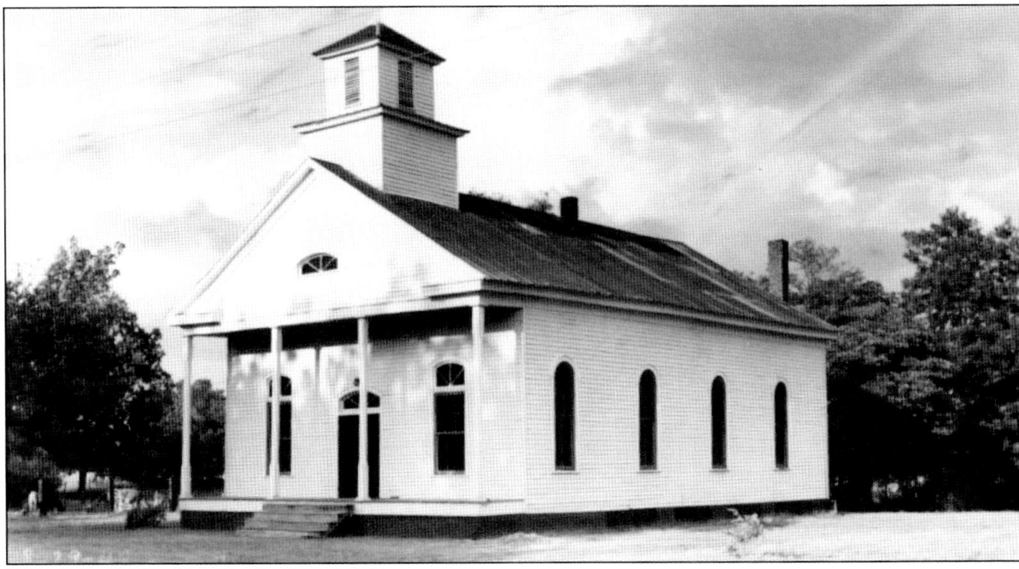

St. Paul Methodist Church, 1937. This church has been in service since 1829, making it the oldest organized church in Lauderdale County. The first church building was a small, rough, hand-hewn log cabin on or near William Turner's old frame home just southeast of Durhamville. Built by the Methodists, this church was called "Turner's Chapel." In 1847, the church was moved to Durhamville and given the name "St. Paul." The log building of 1847 was replaced by a new frame building in 1859 but was taken down and moved to become part of the building that stood until 1991. At that time, the church was struck by lightning and destroyed. As of 2004, St. Paul Methodist Church was recognized by the Memphis Annual Conference as being in service for 175 years.

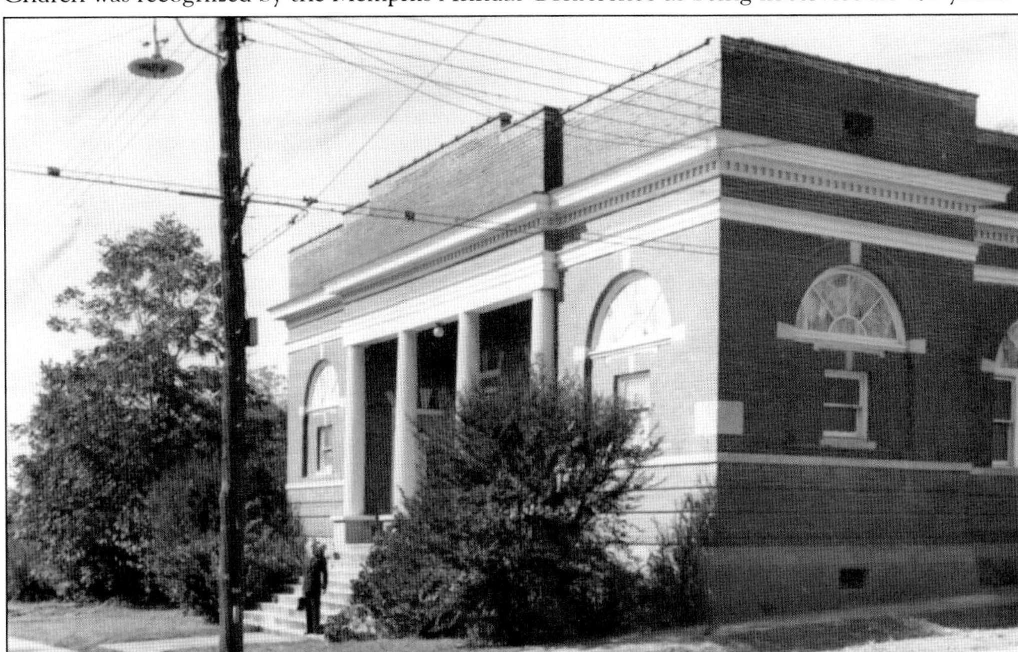

Methodist Episcopal Church South, Henning, Built in 1909. After a year of meeting with its sister church Henning United Methodist.

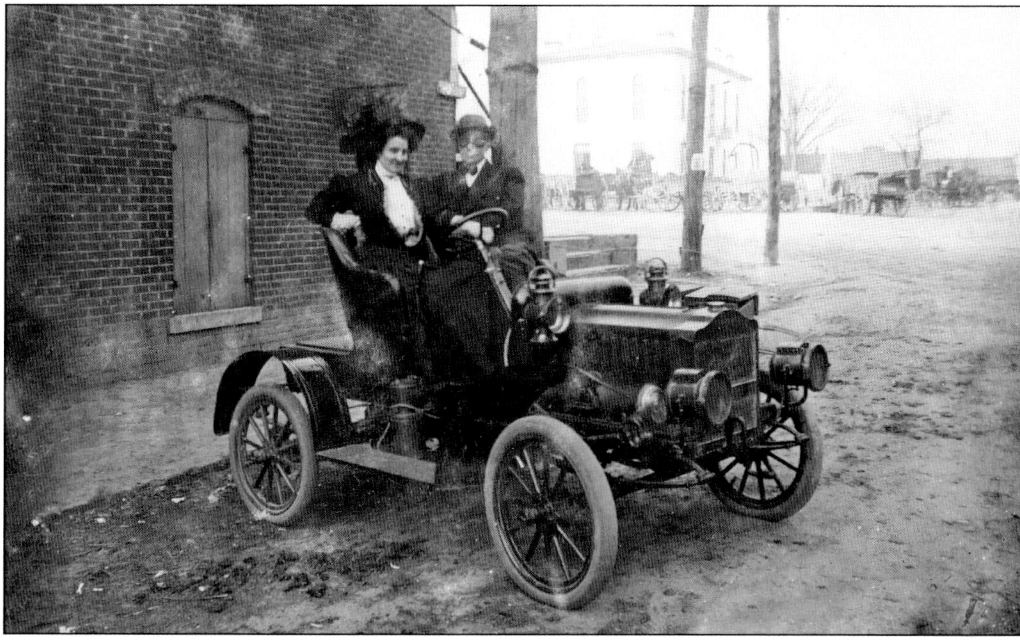

The First Car in Ripley. Dr. Gustavius A. Lusk was the first person to own a car in Ripley. Pictured in the car in 1908 are Elizabeth "Lizzie" Lusk and Solon Neighbors. The car was a 1908 cherry red Maxwell. The Lauderdale County Courthouse can be seen in the background.

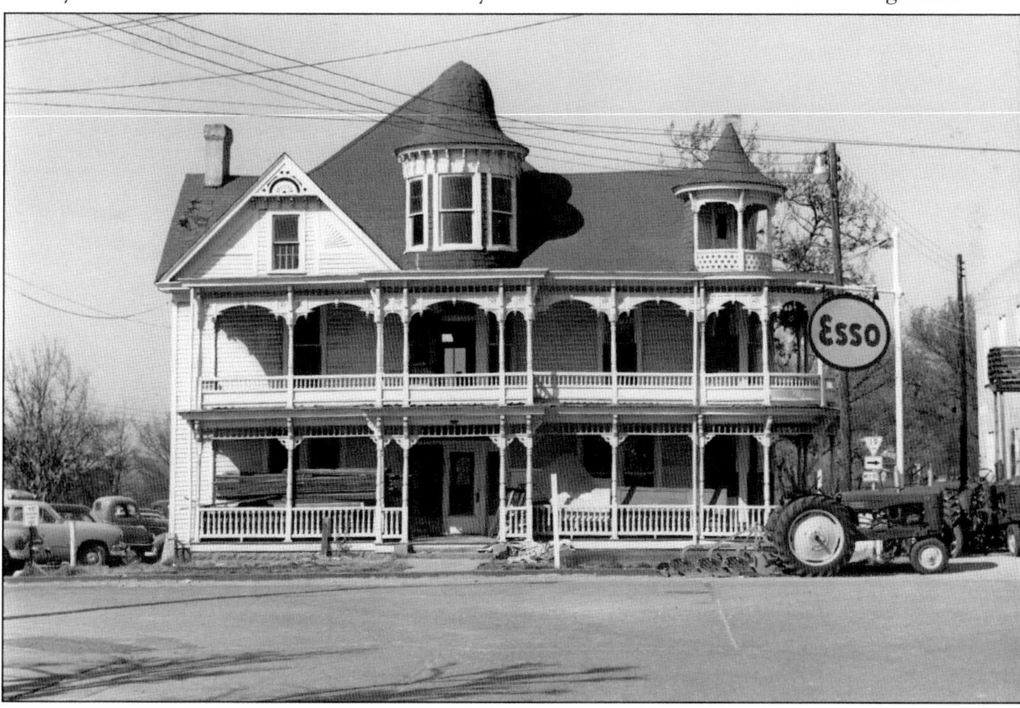

Home of Dr. Gustavius A. Lusk, c. 1860, Ripley. This home was noted for its curved glass windows and fancy frill work and belonged to Dr. G.A. Lusk, who began his practice in Ripley in 1881. Briefly in 1898, the home was used as an infirmary because it was thought that its brilliantly lit rooms and rich decorations made it ideal for the sick.

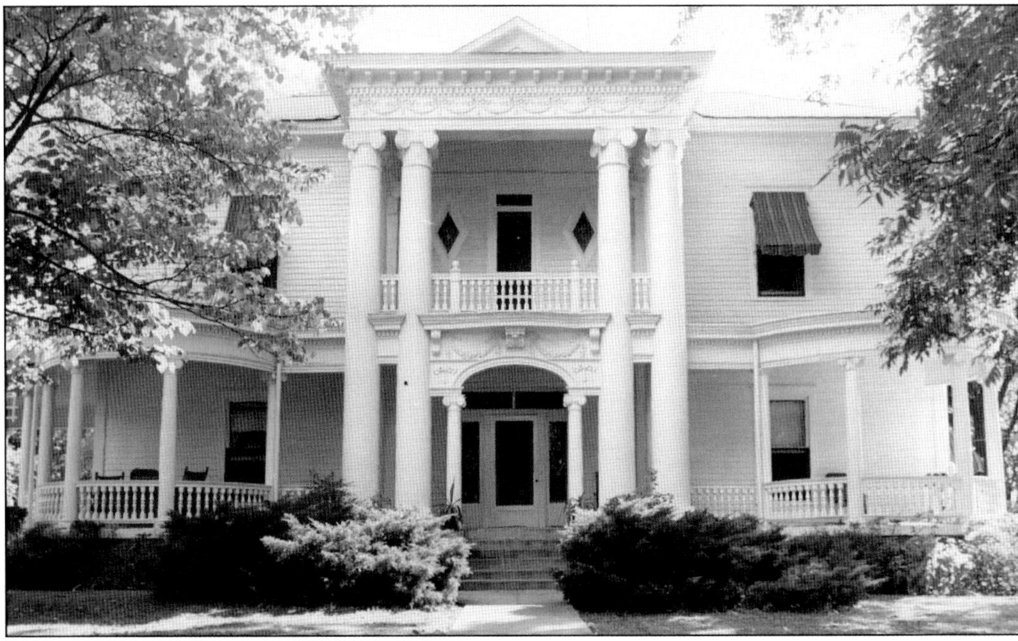

Wardlaw-Steele Mansion. Here is Dr. Jacob N. Wardlaw's home at 128 Wardlaw Circle, Ripley, Tennessee, in 1844. Dr. Wardlaw, son of Joseph Wardlaw, married Tabitha Jane Davie. After Tabitha's death, a married daughter Mrs. Thomas Steele Sr. moved in to keep house for her father. When Mr. Wardlaw died, Thomas Steele bought the property, and for three generations, the house was known as the Steele home. Mrs. Steele changed the plain columns to Corinthian, added a concrete porch, and made additions to the back. The basement rooms were no longer used. Several owners and many renovations later, the home is now owned by Ed Maynard and is in the National Register of Historic Places. (Courtesy of Lauderdale County Library.)

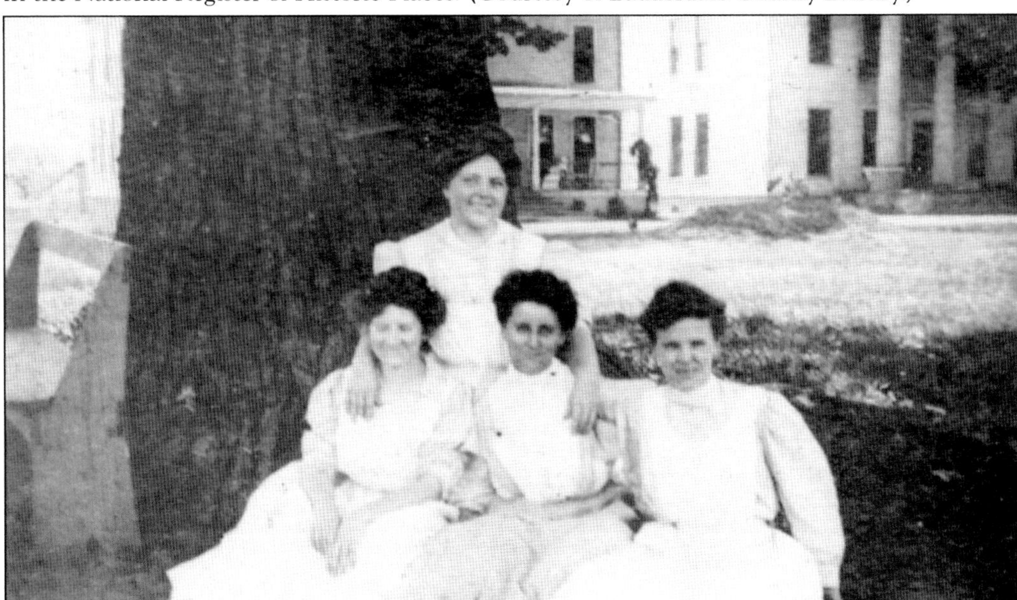

Four Young Ladies on the Wardlaw-Steele Mansion Lawn, 1890s. All four of these girls were from prominent Ripley families. (Courtesy of Susan Scott.)

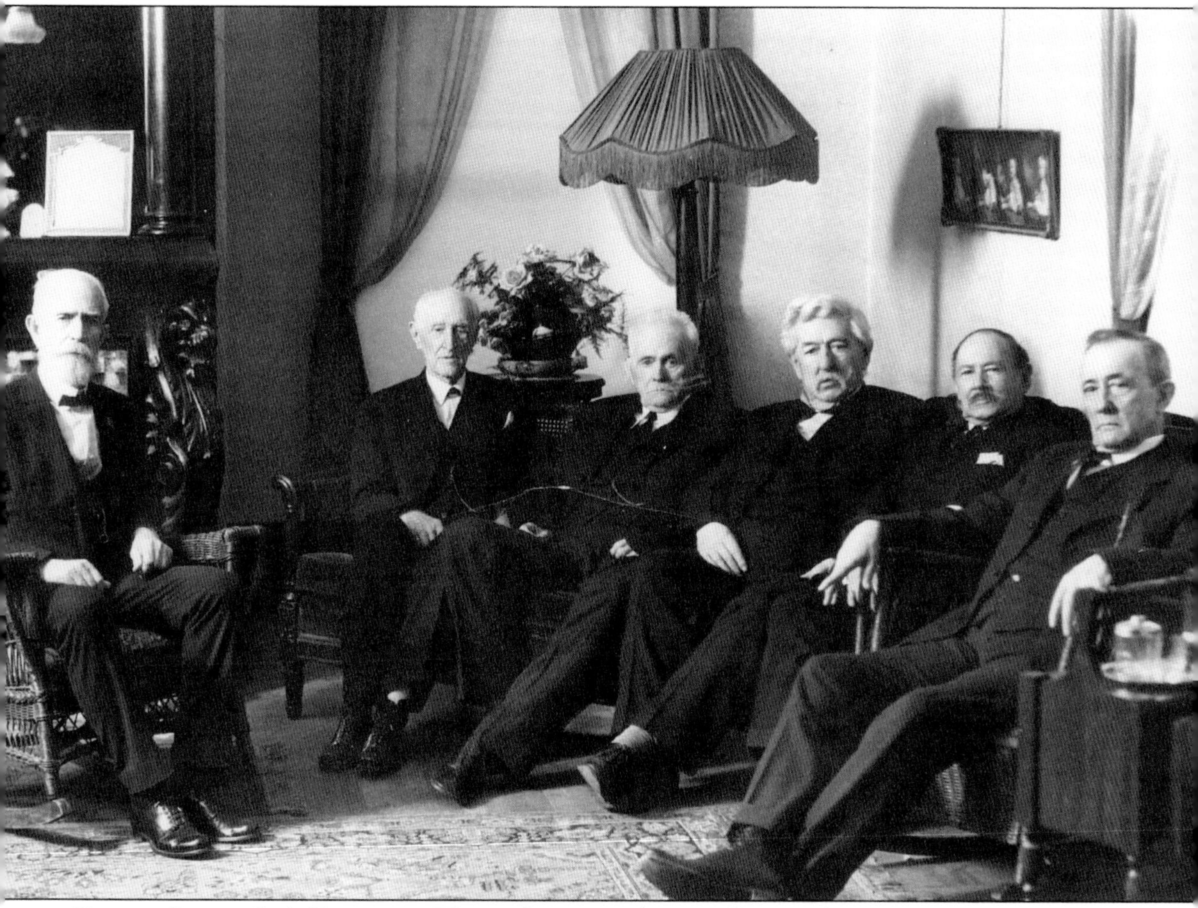

Thomas Steele Sr.'s Birthday. This gathering at the Wardlaw-Steele Mansion took place on February 12, 1931. Pictured are, from left to right, George W. Young, Rice A. Pierce, John R. Bond, Thomas Steele Sr., C.G. Bond, and E.R. Oldham. (Courtesy of Lauderdale County Library.)

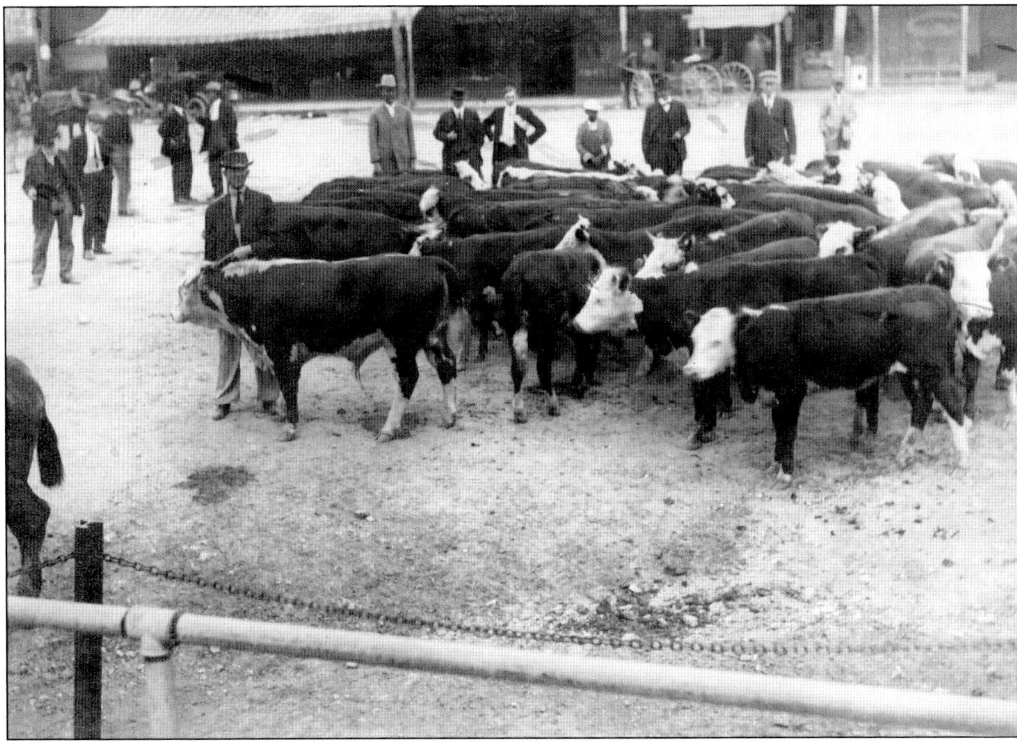

Cattle Drive. Knox Walker drove these cows through the streets of Ripley in 1912 and then walked the cows 20 miles to his plantation at Fulton. (Courtesy of Lauderdale County Library.)

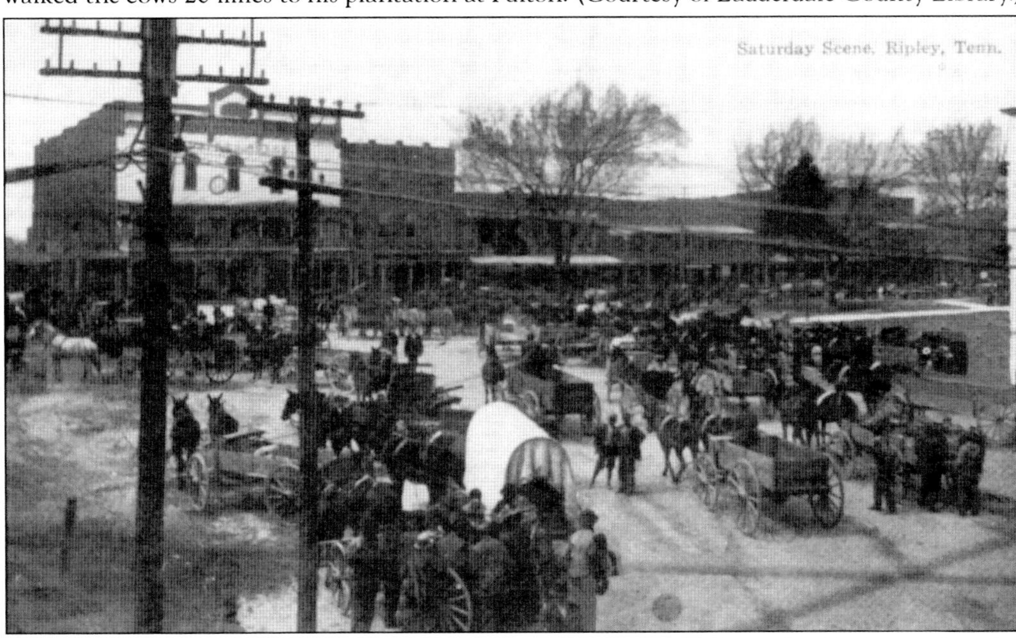

Saturday Scene in Ripley. People all over Lauderdale County would travel to Ripley on Saturday, normally dressed in their finery, to shop for groceries and household wares, visit with people, and enjoy entertainment. The Ripley Square would be humming with excitement and events until after midnight.

THE FIRST NATIONAL BANK IN RIPLEY, 1908. Pictured are, from left to right, Aubrey Tucker, John Tucker, Mr. Pritchard, and Doug Foltz. By 1920, there were eight banks in Lauderdale County, with three in Ripley, two each in Halls and Henning, and one in Gates.

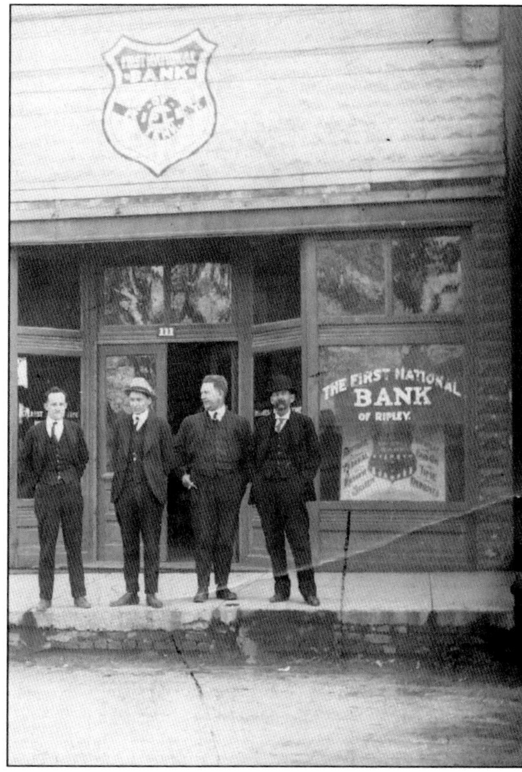

B.A. SINCLAIR HOME. The home of Ripley businessman B.A. Sinclair was located on Sinclair Circle (off Lake Drive) in Ripley, Tennessee, and extended over two blocks. It was also owned by the Baynes family.

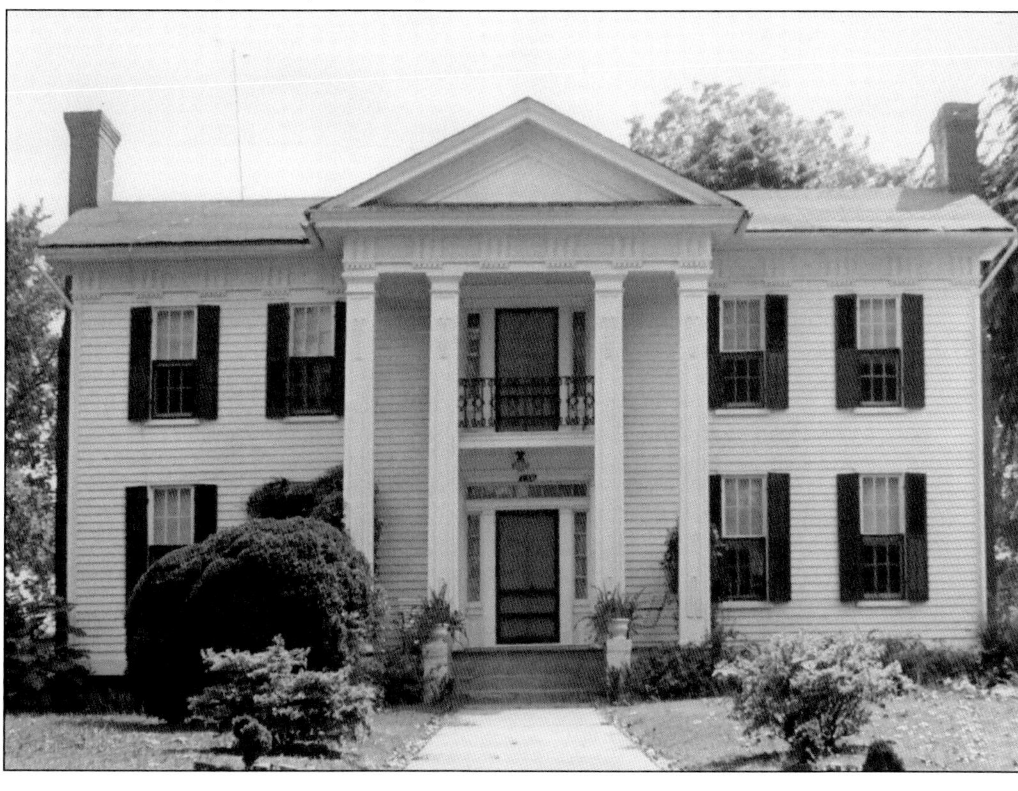

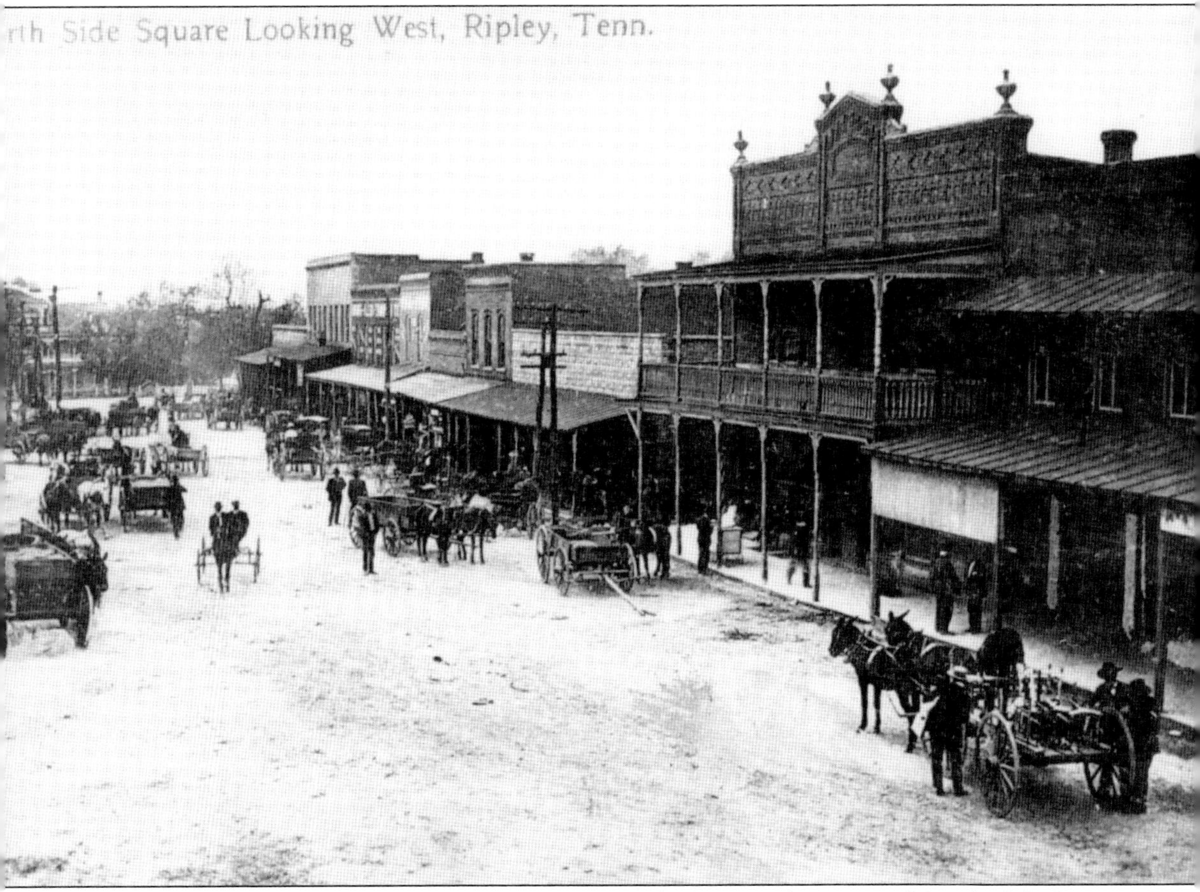

Ripley Street Scene. This north side of the square (looking west) is pictured. Lauderdale County was founded in 1836, and Ripley was chosen as the county seat, helping businesses on the town square to flourish.

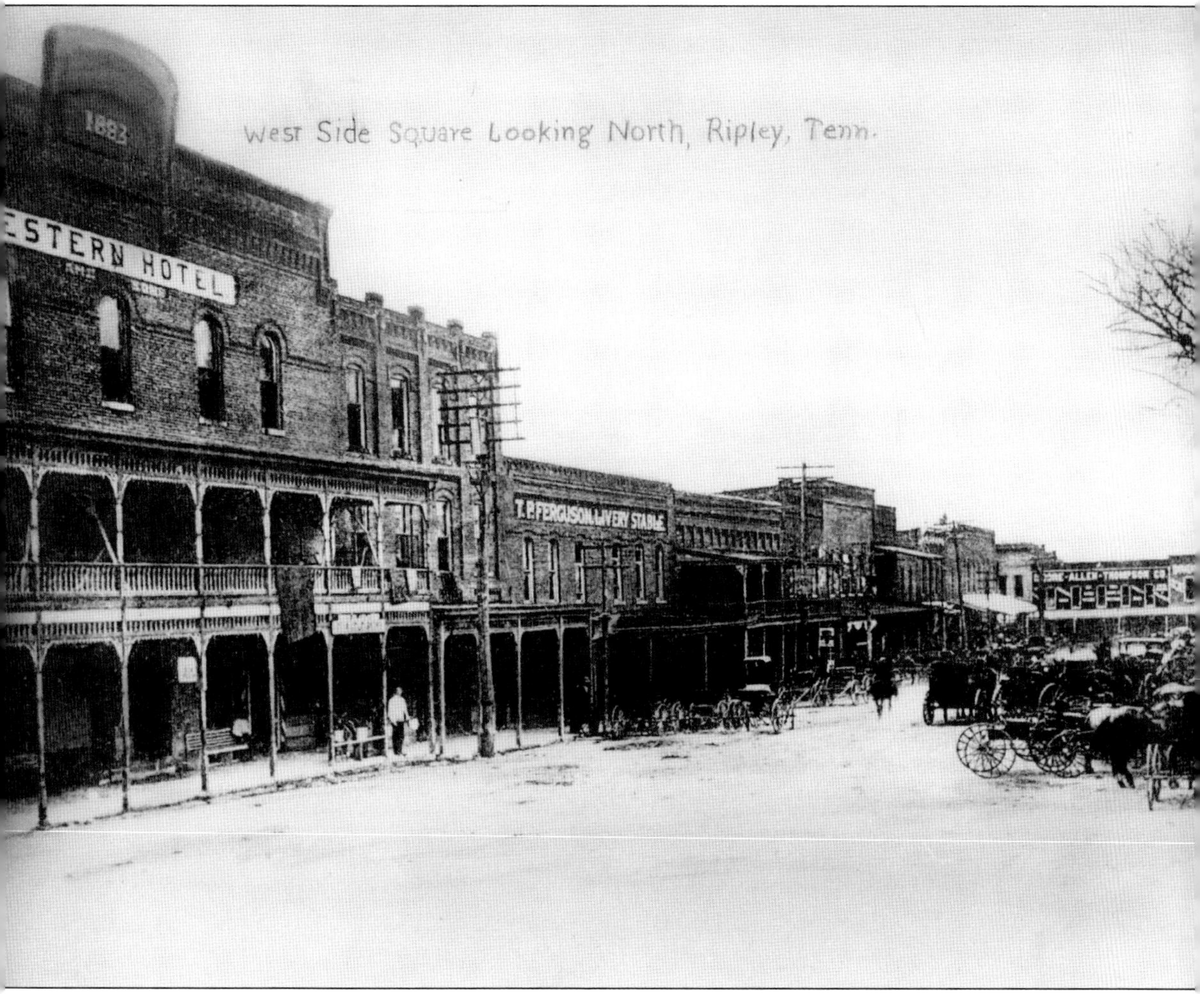

Ripley Street Scene. This photograph features the west side of the square (looking north). Businesses include the Western Hotel, built in 1883, and Ferguson's Livery Stable. The earliest known business on the west side of the square was J.N. Smith's dry goods store, which was in operation as early as 1836.

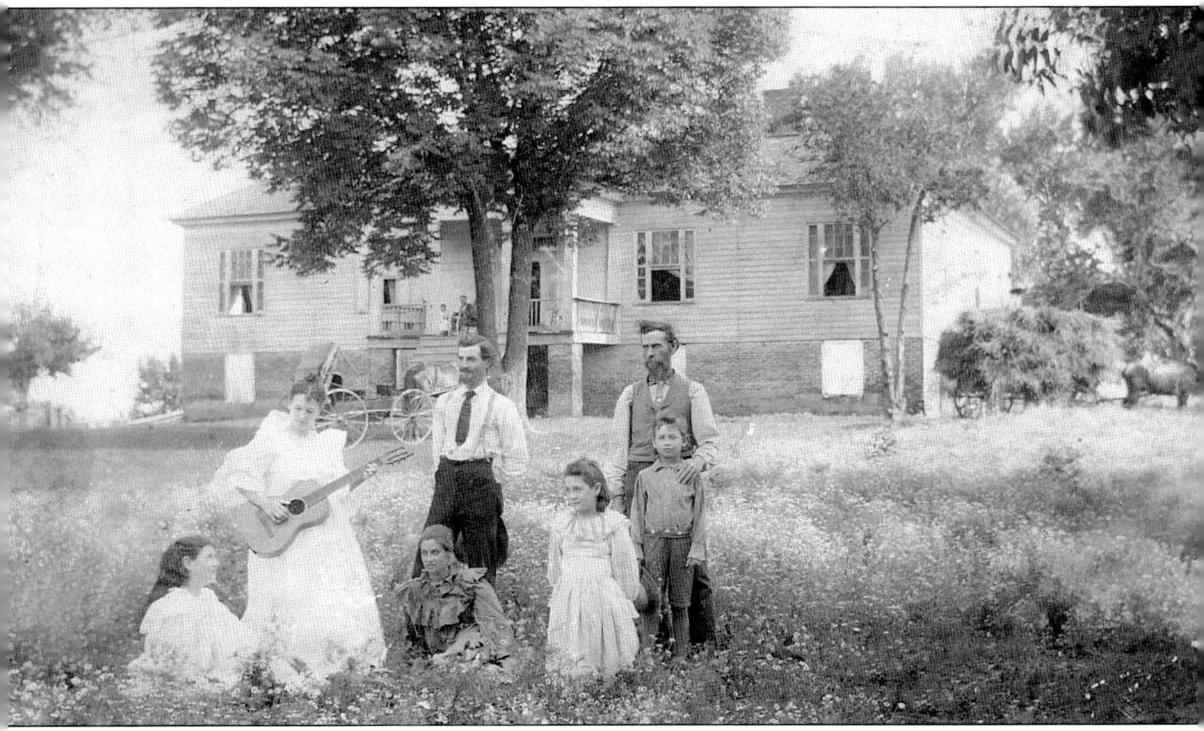

Longview, Home of the Rice Family. Longview was built in the Orysa community in 1835. It was built for one of the earliest families to the settlement, the Rices. Since there was already a town called Riceville in Tennessee, they named the community Oryza, which is Greek for rice. The spelling was later changed to Orysa. (Courtesy of Kay Green.)

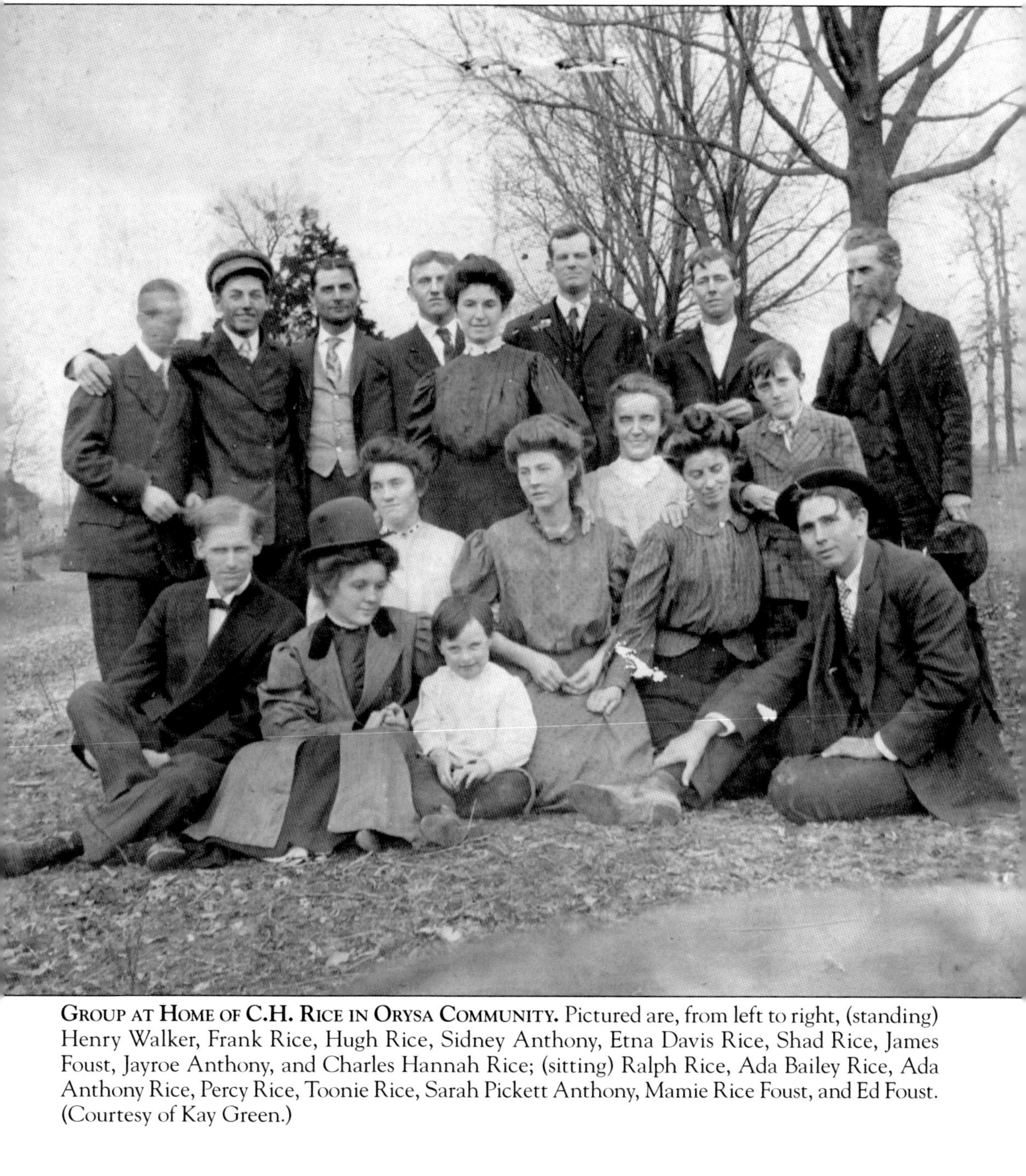

Group at Home of C.H. Rice in Orysa Community. Pictured are, from left to right, (standing) Henry Walker, Frank Rice, Hugh Rice, Sidney Anthony, Etna Davis Rice, Shad Rice, James Foust, Jayroe Anthony, and Charles Hannah Rice; (sitting) Ralph Rice, Ada Bailey Rice, Ada Anthony Rice, Percy Rice, Toonie Rice, Sarah Pickett Anthony, Mamie Rice Foust, and Ed Foust. (Courtesy of Kay Green.)

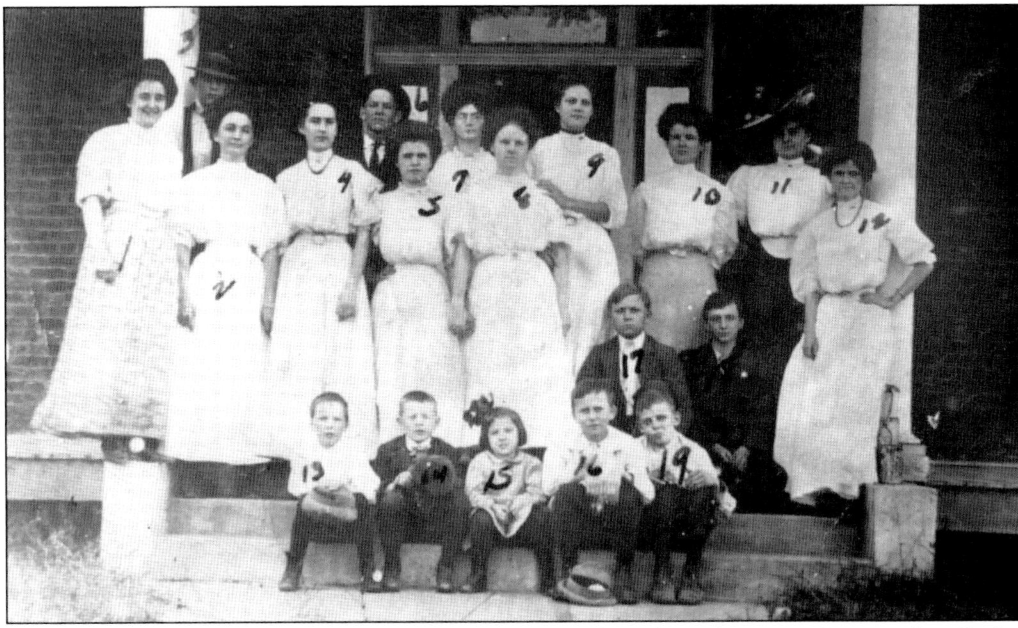

EARLY MUSIC CLASS. This music class was taught by Clarinda and Minnie Haywood in Ripley, Tennessee. Class members are, from left to right, (standing), Earlene Given, Earl Lightfoot, Annie Wells, Kathleen Given, Willie Sapp, May Campbell, Emma Wells, Mary Ellen Thornley, Mary White, Clarinda Haywood (teacher), Mary Campbell, and Minnie Haywood (teacher); (sitting) J.C. Bivins, ? Faque, Ruby Faque, Gilford Read, Curtis Read, James Maclin, and J.P. Ferguson Jr.

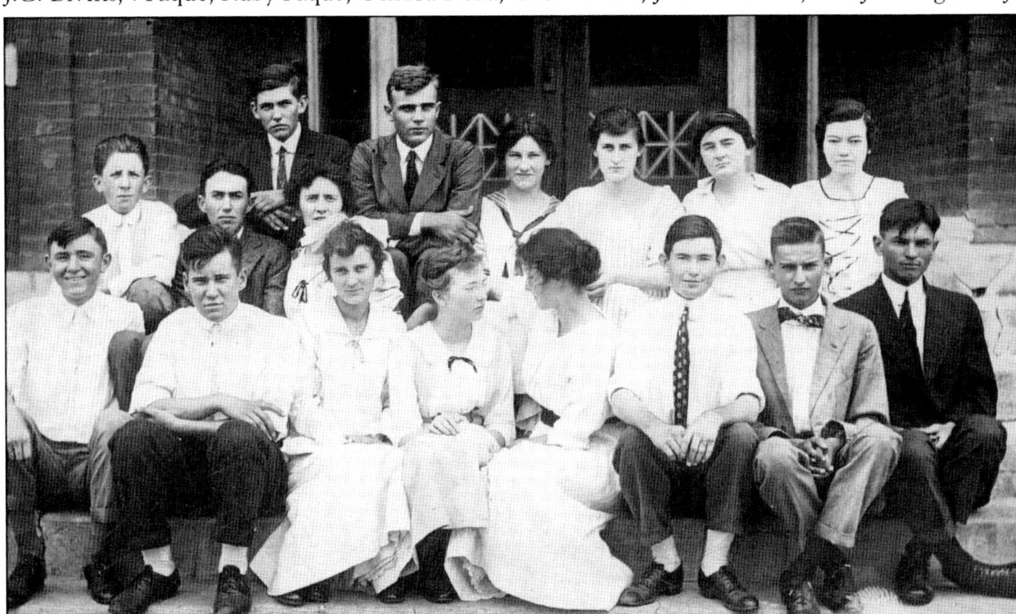

LAUDERDALE COUNTY SCHOOL GROUP, 1915. The names listed on the back of the picture are John Fields Campbell, Otis Paris, Marvin Wilson, Eddie Barbour, Mary Sue Morris, Lillian Wadsworth, Pearl Latham, George Wadsworth, Daisy Baynes, Gaston Harrison, Avery Rush, Mary McKinney, Celeste Sanford, Eugenia Read, Steve Bibb, William Alex Grimes, and Albert Thompson. (Courtesy of Lauderdale County Museum.)

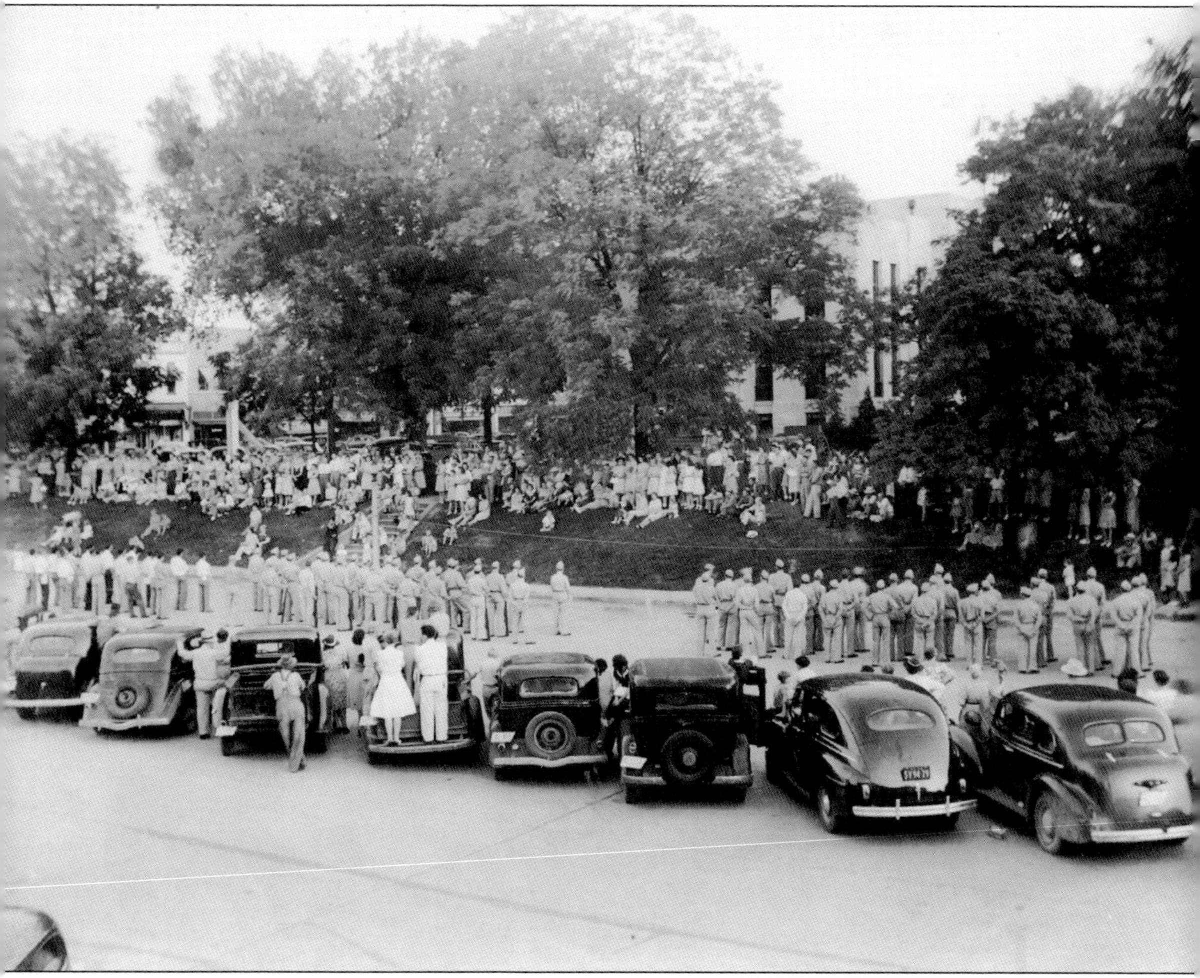

Group of Soldiers. This event on August 12, 1942, which shows the soldiers lined up and facing the Lauderdale County Courthouse, is thought to have been an effort to promote war bonds.

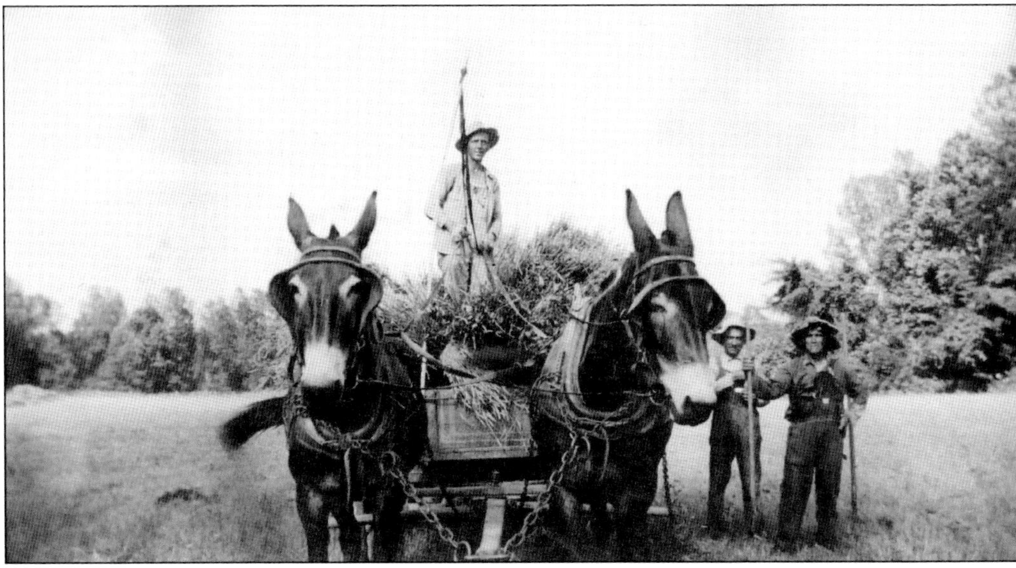

Ready for Field Work on the Chambers Farm in the Edith Community. Family members joined together and toiled from daylight to dark. (Courtesy of Joyce Henson.)

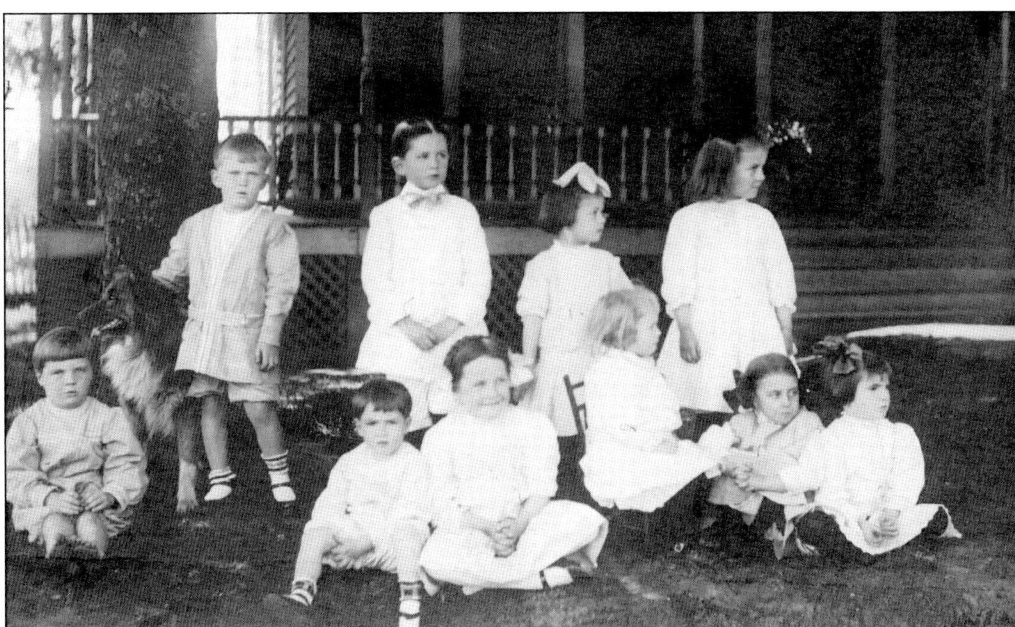

Cornelia Woods's Kindergarten Class. Pictured in Ripley in 1908 are, in no particular order, Glenn Thompson, Wilbur Luton, Virginia Rice, Molly Rhea Cobb, Goodloe Partee, Gordon Moore, Marjorie Campbell, Elizabeth Banks, Geraldine White, and Catherine Thomas.

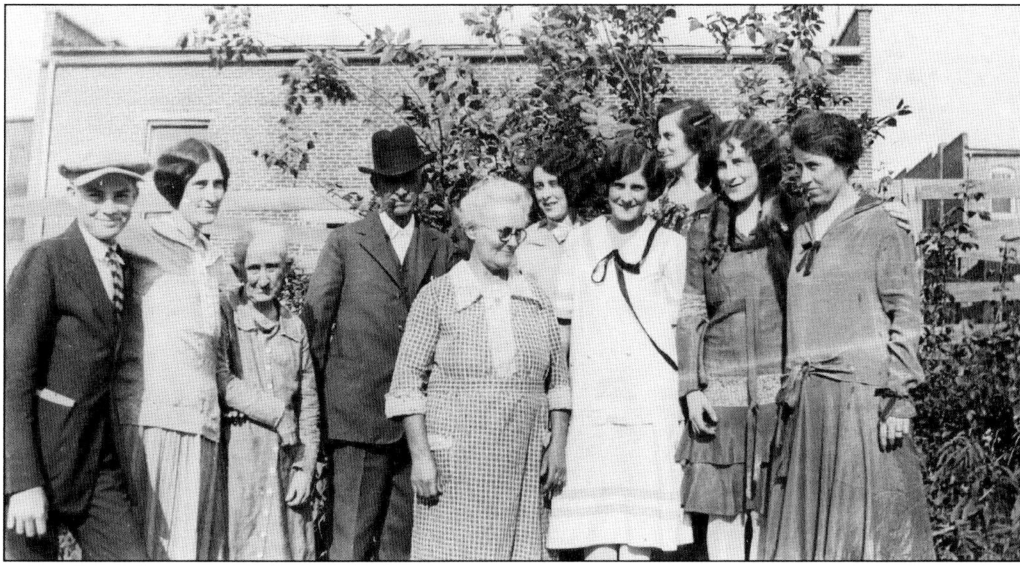

The Joseph Gwynn Morris Family. Family members pictured in 1928 in Ripley are, from left to right, Joseph Lusk "Jake" Morris, Sue Morris, Donie Thornley, Joseph Gwynn Morris, Minnie Ella Morris, Jane Morris, Josephine Morris, Ella Morris, Dorothy Morris, and Ethyl Morris.

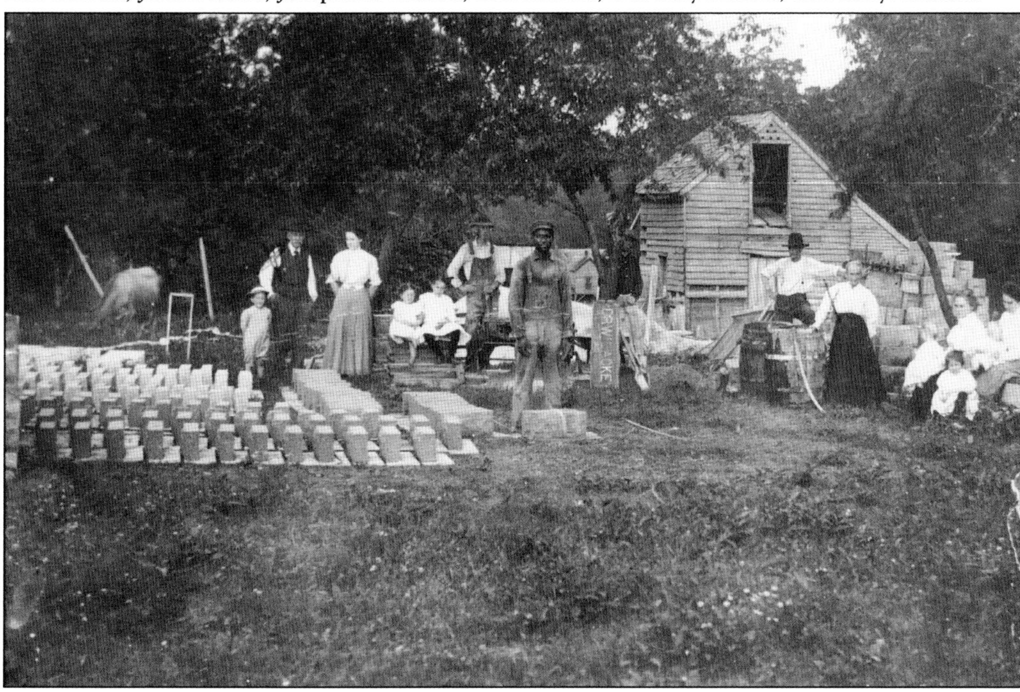

Morris Family Members and Workers Making Tombstone Markers. The family and workers are pictured on Henning Street, present-day Jefferson Street, in Ripley about 1910. Joseph Gwynn Morris was a builder, and many buildings that he built, including the old Ripley Primary School, still stand in Ripley over 100 years later. Those pictured are, from left to right, W.B. Keller, Thomas William Thornley, Ella Morris Roberson, Dorothy Morris, Jane Morris, three unidentified workers, Joseph Gwynn Morris, Donie Thornley, Minnie Ella Morris (holding infant Joseph Lusk Morris), Josephine Morris, and Ethel Morris Brown (holding infant Morris Brown Jr.).

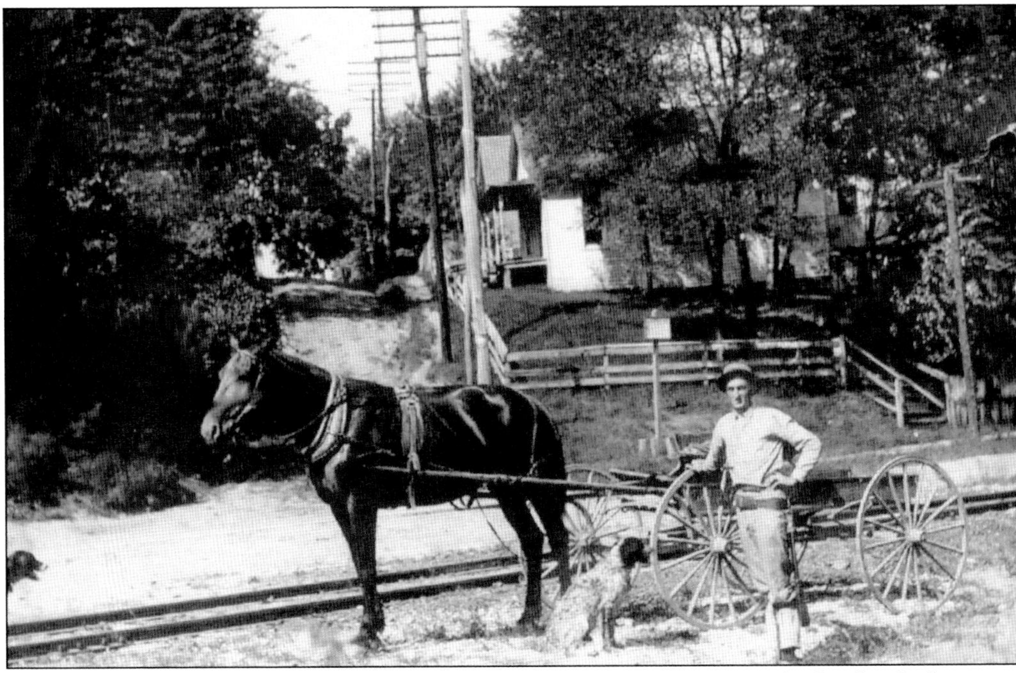

TELEPHONE LINEMAN ABE TOLBERT ON MILL STREET, RIPLEY. The Cumberland Telephone and Telegraph Company brought the telephone to Ripley in 1897. The Ripley Telephone Exchange located its offices in the Ripley Bank. There was one long distance line for Memphis, Covington, and Dyersburg. The first telephone was in Williams Lumber Shed. There were 236 phones in Ripley in 1908, 401 in 1915, 531 in 1925, 508 in 1935, 734 in 1945, and 2,214 in 1955.

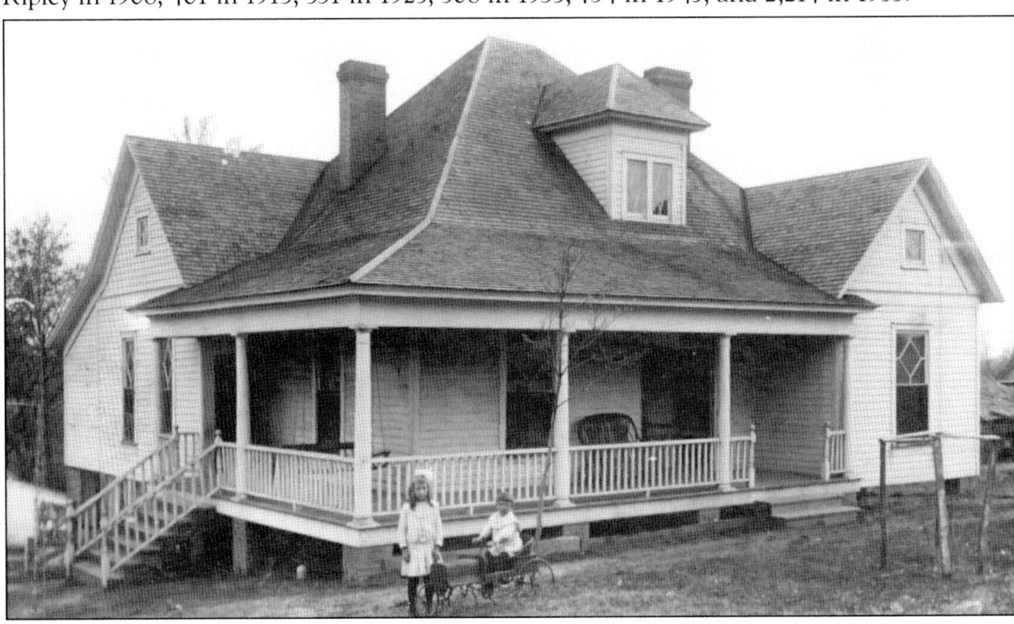

WALT HART'S HOME. Located at 150 Sinclair Circle in Ripley, Tennessee, is Walt Hart's house. The children pictured are Thelma Hart Davis and John Walter Hart. The Harts operated a dairy at the back of the property. The home and barn are still standing. (Courtesy of Martha Sue Lawrence.)

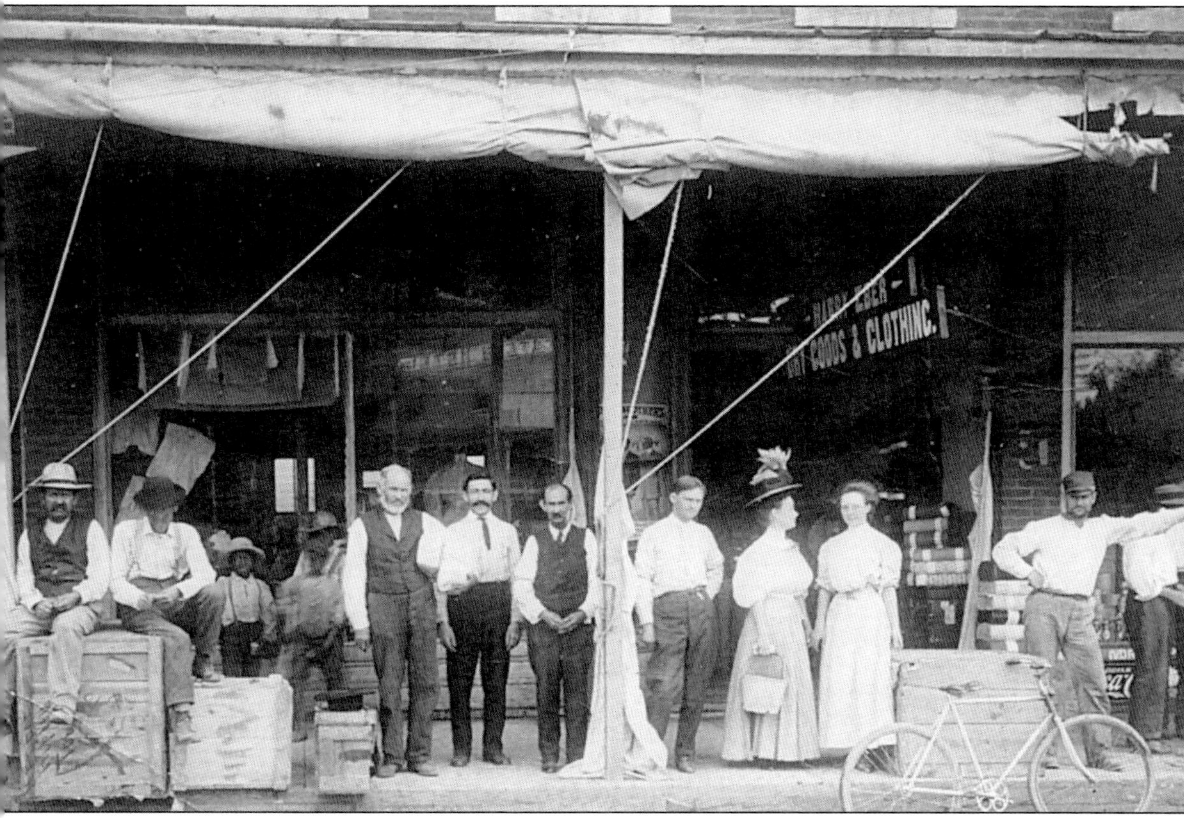

Harry Eber Dry Goods and Clothing Store in **Ripley, 1905.** The two women pictured are Irean Evans (in hat) and Mrs. Columbia Smith. Goods for sale include bolts of fabric, and signs advertise such products as Coca-Cola and Ivory Soap. (Courtesy of Marion Morris.)

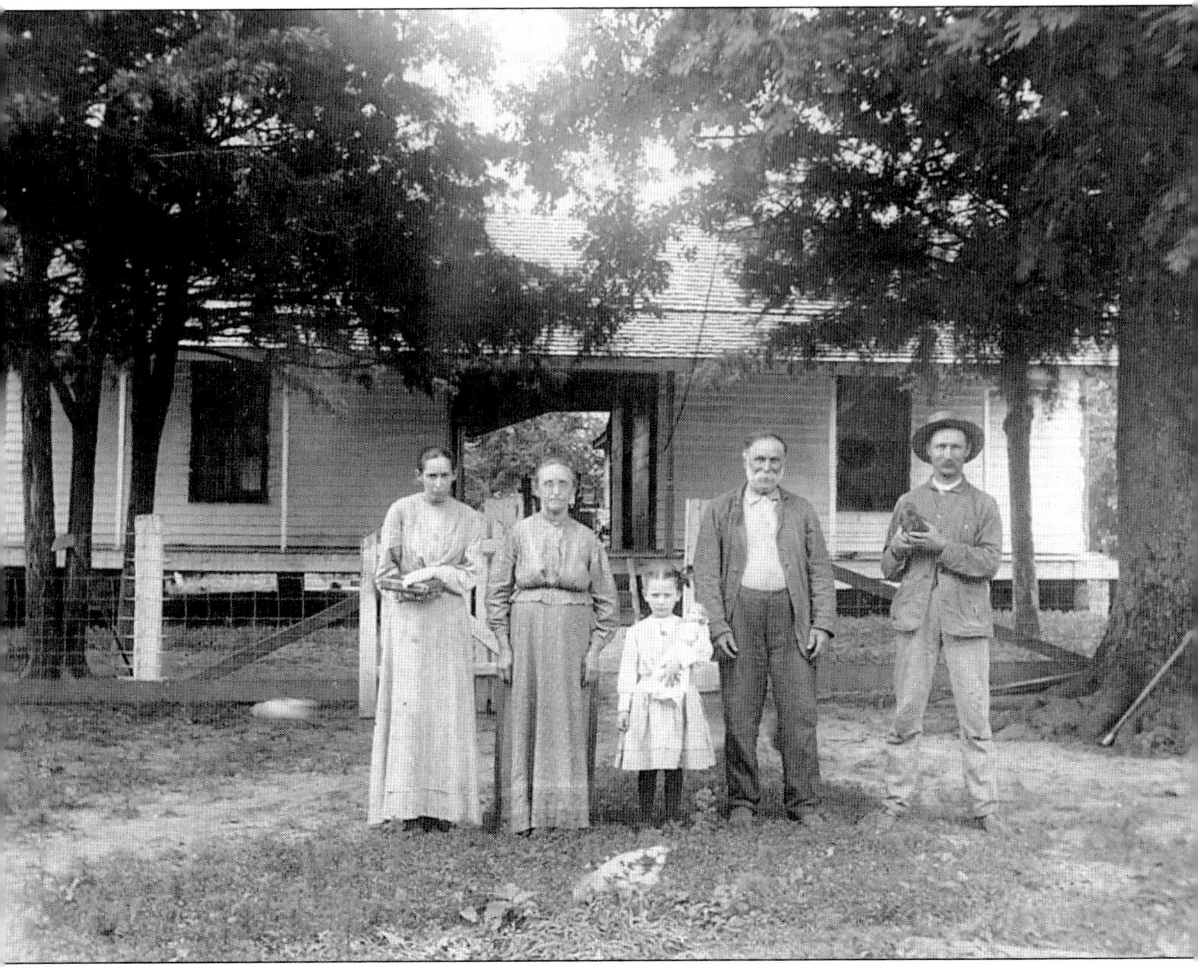

The George Thomas Hargett Family. The Hargett family lived on the Chisholm Lake Road and was a typical farming family. Pictured from left to right are Nancy Hargett (with her bible), Mrs. Hargett, Pearl Grady (with doll), George Thomas Hargett, and Dave Hargett (with a chicken). (Courtesy of Evelyn Stewart.)

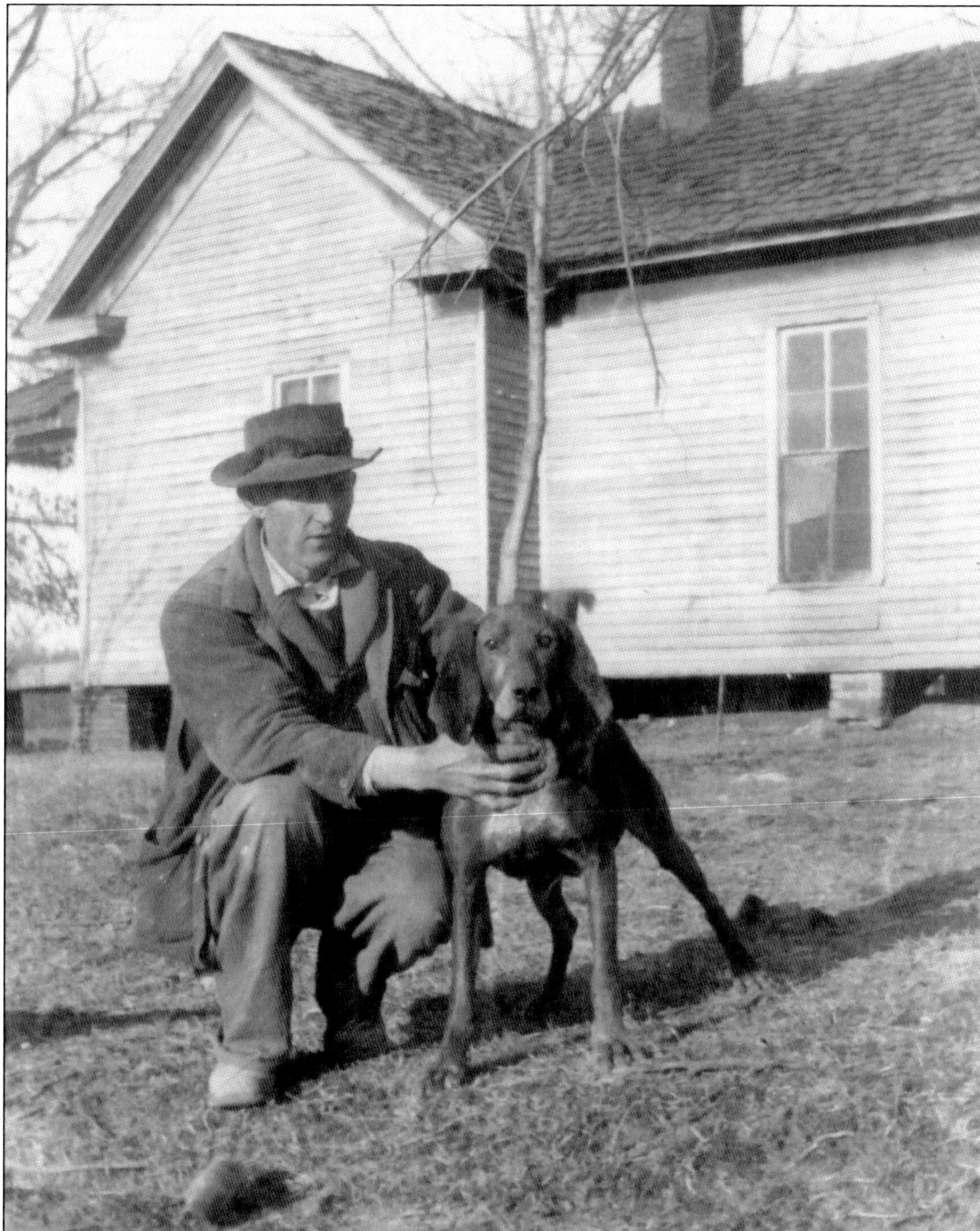

CHARLIE T. SNEED. Charlie is pictured with his prized hunting dog in the Conner community. As a local musician, Charlie T. Sneed played at square dances on the courthouse lawn and for social events all over the county.

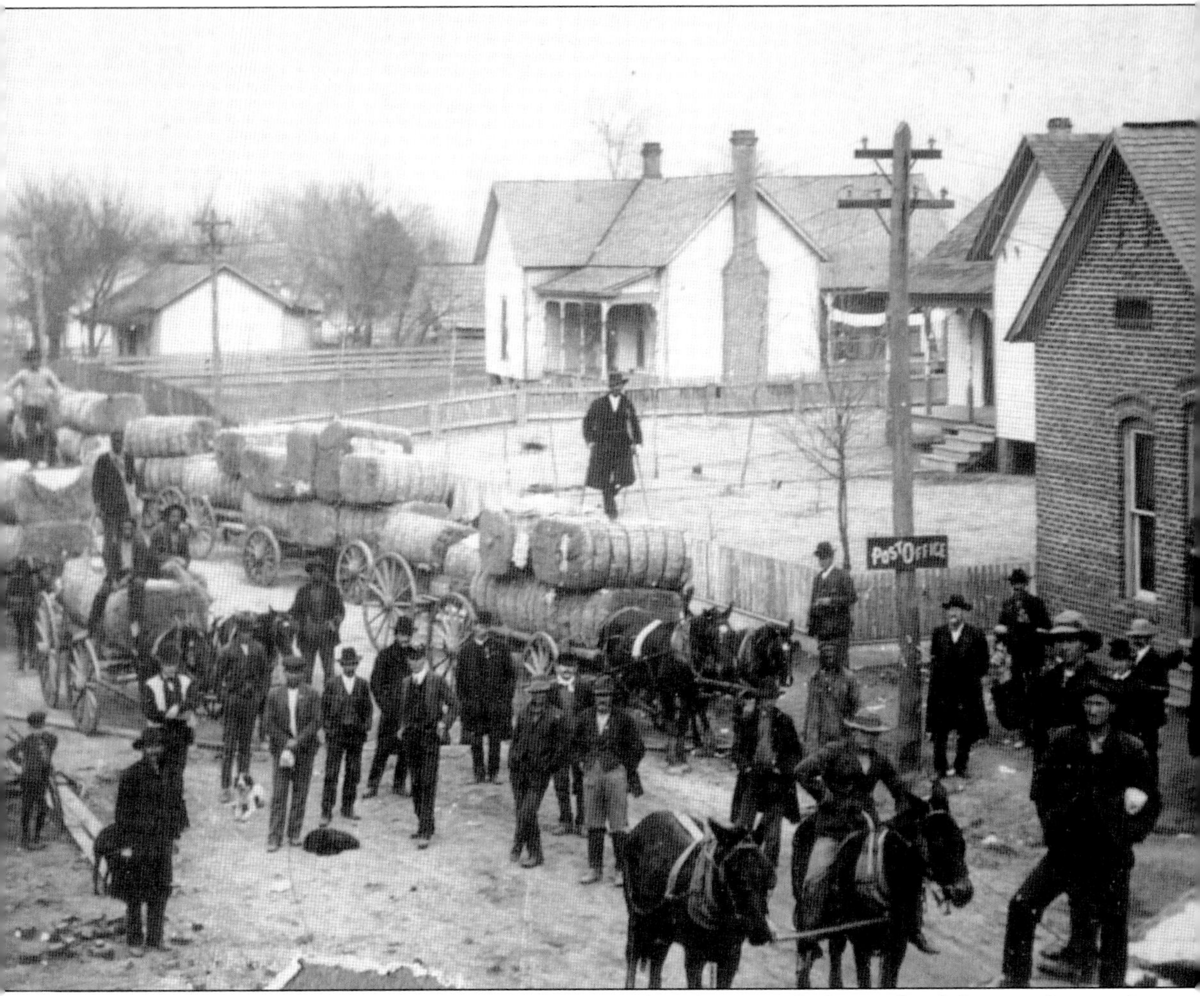

COTTON PROTEST IN HALLS, DECEMBER 1906. This photograph shows the delivery of part of the 600 bales of cotton sold in Halls on December 8, 1906. Farmers in the area had withheld the sale of their cotton that fall in protest of the low prices. This cotton brought about 9¢ to 11¢ per pound. The protest was the result of the Farmers' Union movement in the county when farmers, concerned with low prices of farm produce in general but especially with cotton, joined together in an effort to get better market information and, ultimately, to establish warehouses and gins, a bank at Ripley, and a school. (Courtesy of Bettie Davis.)

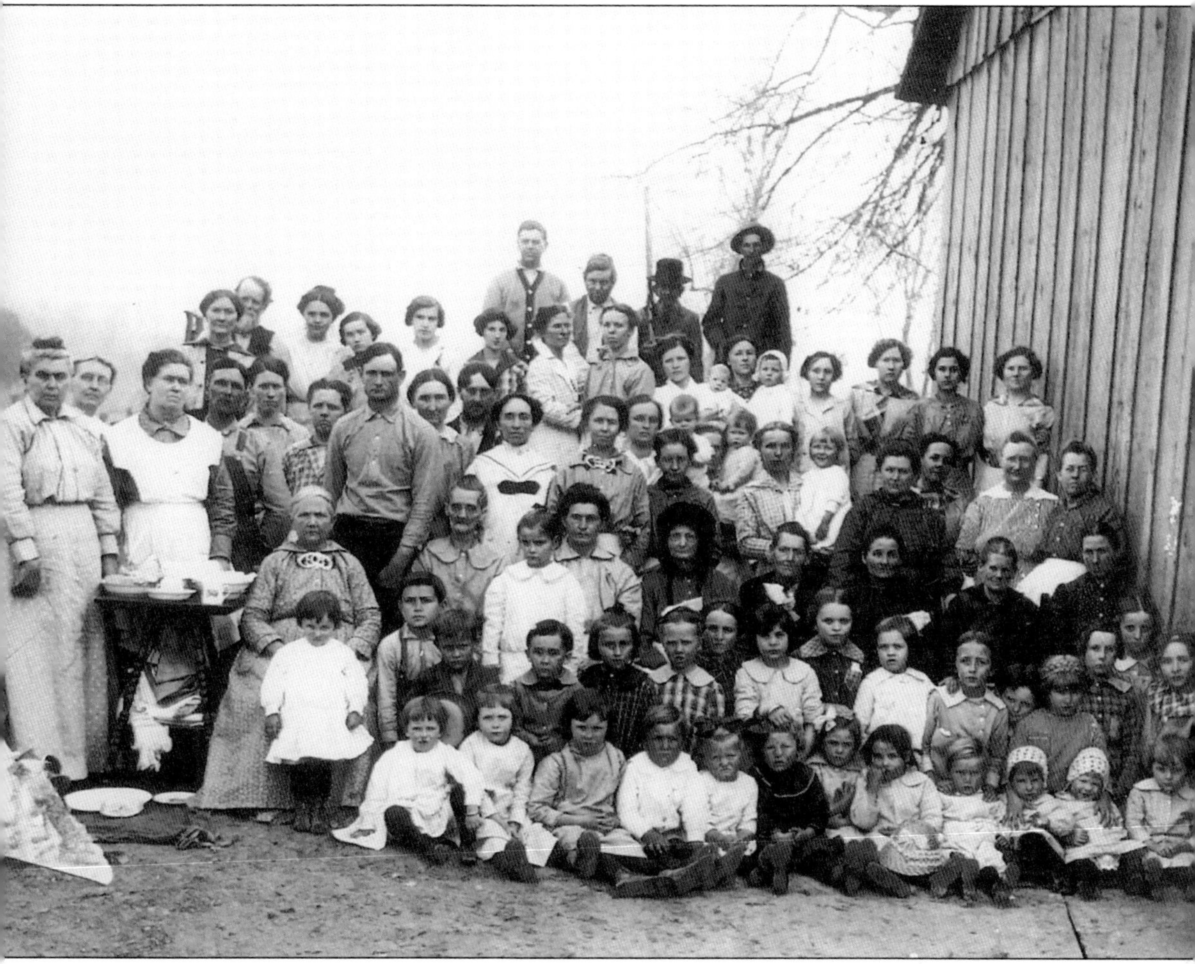

A Birthday Party Quilting at Poplar Grove, April 6, 1916. The occasion was a quilting party to honor the 64th birthday of Siszella (Williams) Brandon Palmer at the home of her daughter Mrs. Robert D. Becton. Henry Parker (back row with the rifle), a Civil War veteran who was hunting nearby, was invited to join the group. (Courtesy of Bettie Davis.)

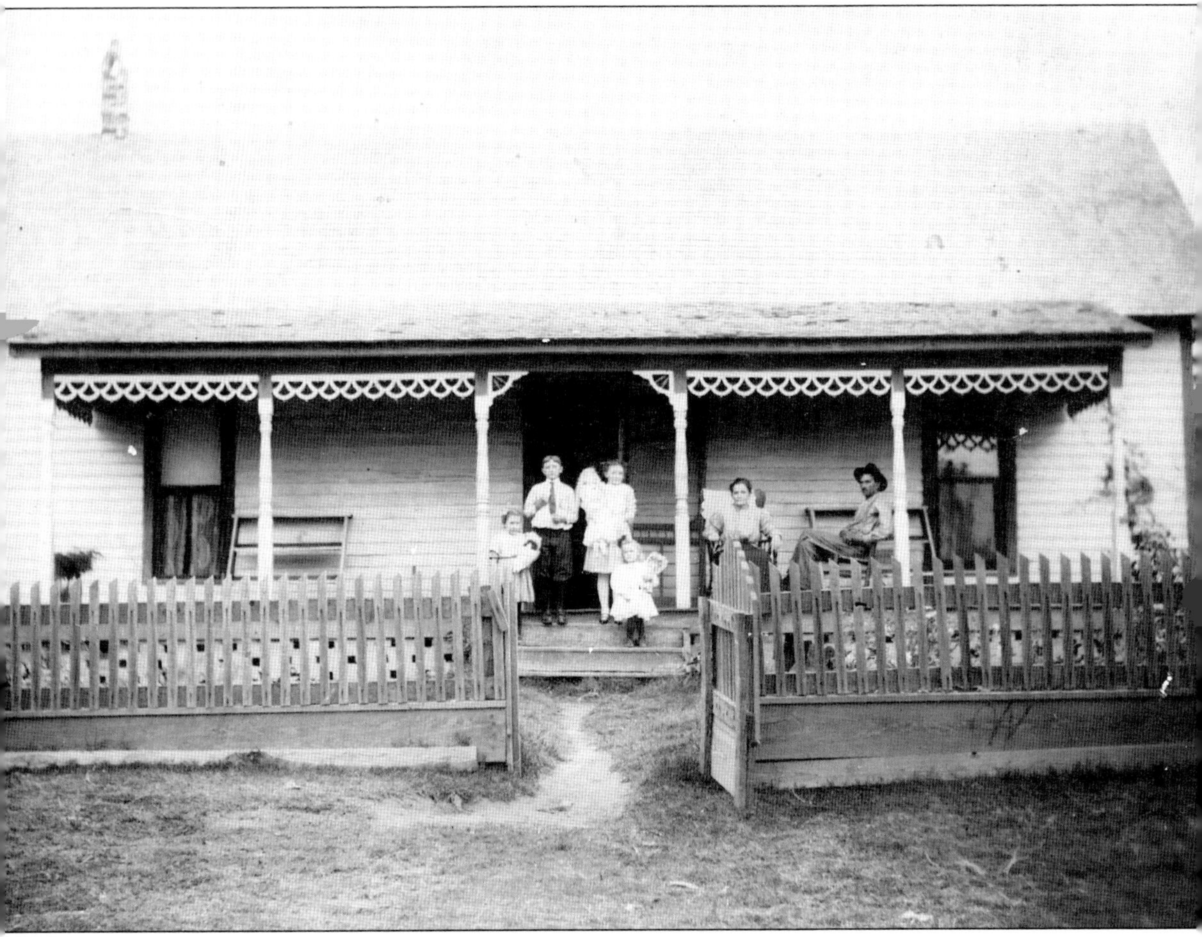

Crews Family Members on Their Porch in the Edith Community. Pictured are, from left to right, Eloise, George, Effie, Estelle, Elizabeth, and William E. Crews. (Courtesy of Joyce Henson.)

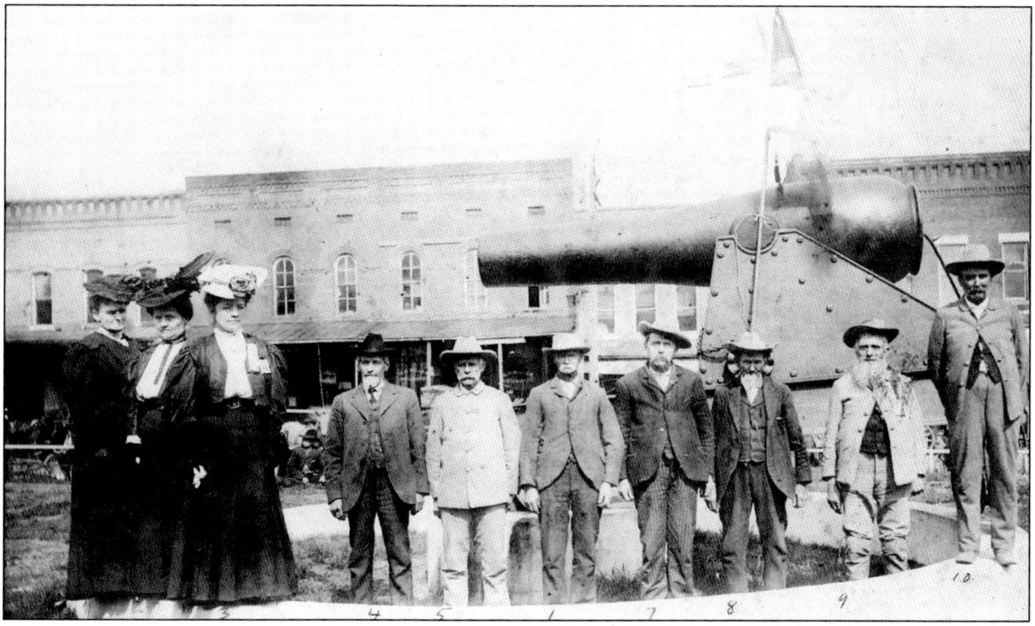

Unveiling of a Civil War Cannon in Ripley. This 1906 photograph was made at the "Old Soldiers Reunion." Women pictured are members of the United Daughters of the Confederacy, and the men are Confederate soldiers. Those known are, from left to right, Mrs. Henry Lewis, Mrs. Devinney, Mrs. Nagle, William Tucker, two unidentified people, William Ball Drake, unidentified, William Stone, and unidentified.

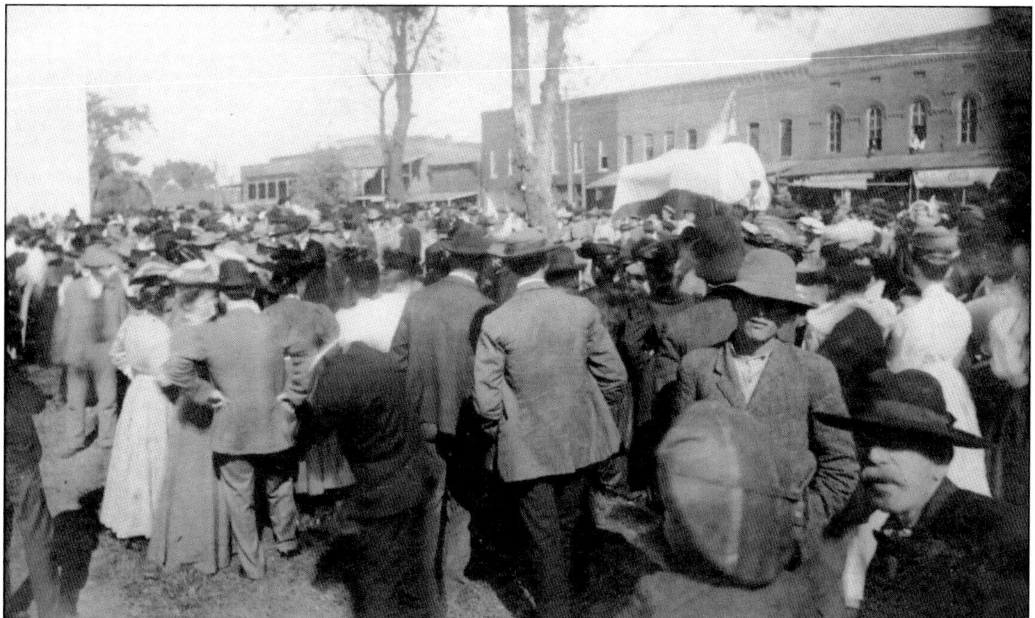

Civil War Cannon. A crowd gathers to watch the unveiling of the cannon that was brought from the battlefield at Fort Pillow and placed on the Lauderdale County Courthouse lawn in Ripley, Tennessee, in 1906. The John Sutherland Company of Confederate veterans sponsored this event.

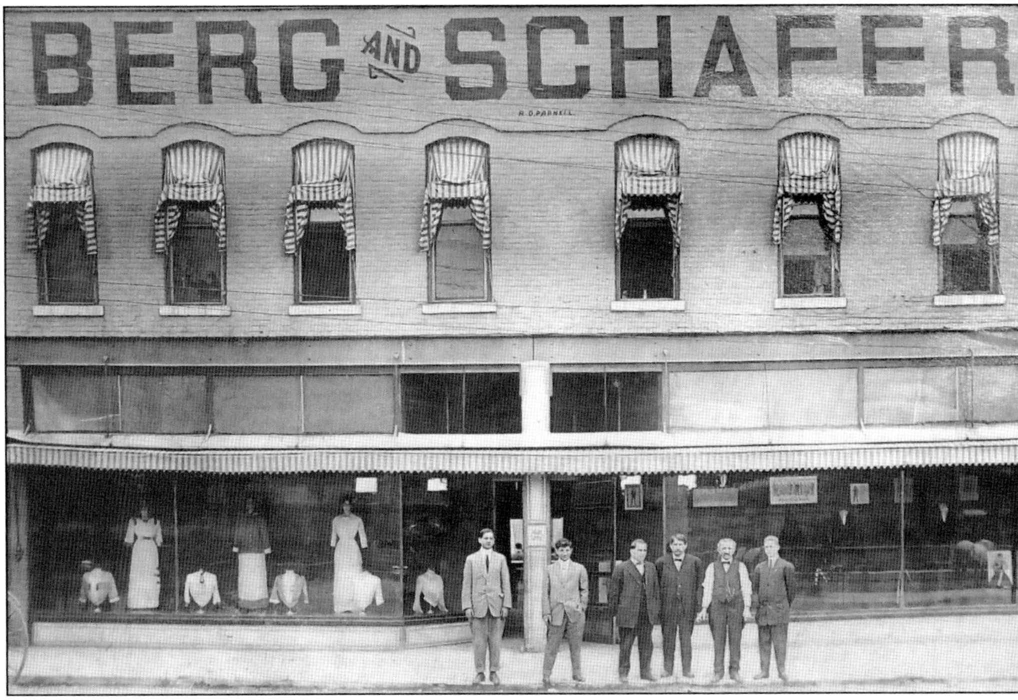

Berg and Schafer Store. The Berg and Schafer store was founded in 1879 and operated in Ripley for more than 100 years. Owner Lee Berg was naturalized as a citizen of the United States in Lauderdale County Court in 1883, Herman Schafer became a partner of Berg's, and together they built Berg and Schafer. Both men were German immigrants. The Herbie Feist family continued the business, promoted green tag sales and fabric sales, and was known for top lines of men's and ladies' clothing.

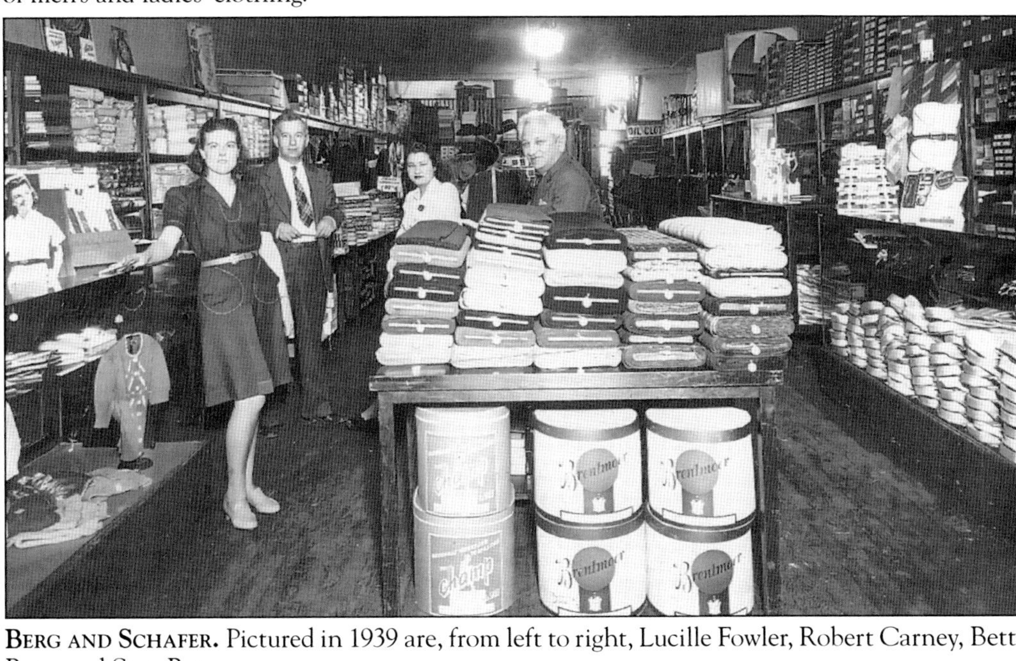

Berg and Schafer. Pictured in 1939 are, from left to right, Lucille Fowler, Robert Carney, Betty Berg, and Sam Berg.

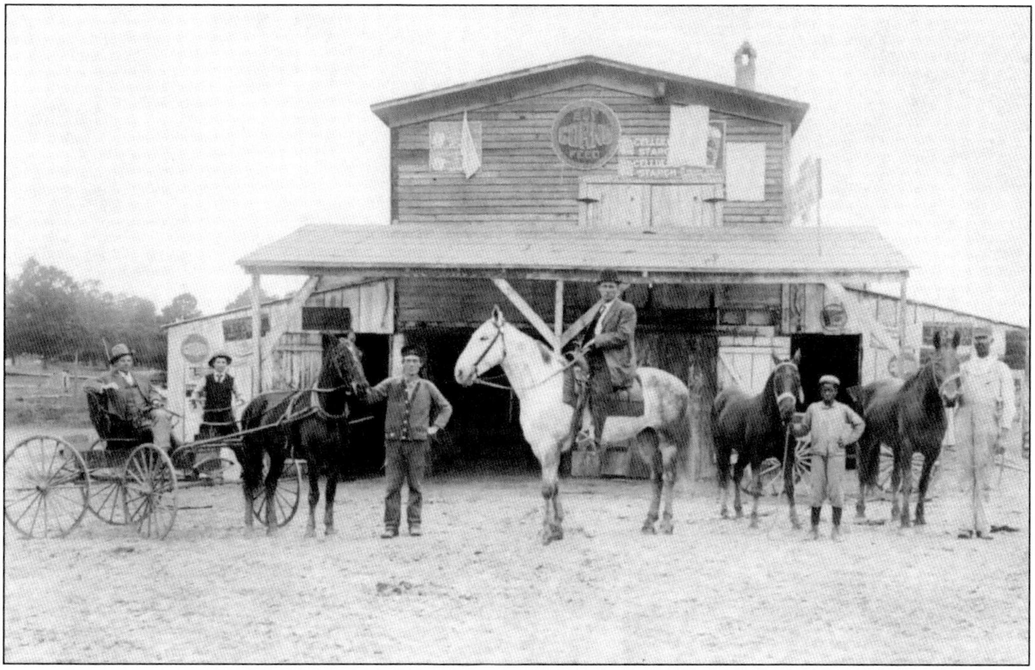

STORE IN RIPLEY. Herbert Majors on the white horse is seen at a feed and supply store in Ripley. These stores offered a place to shop, meet, gather around a wood burning potbellied stove, have some coffee, play checkers, and share news of the day. (Courtesy of Frances Fitzhugh.)

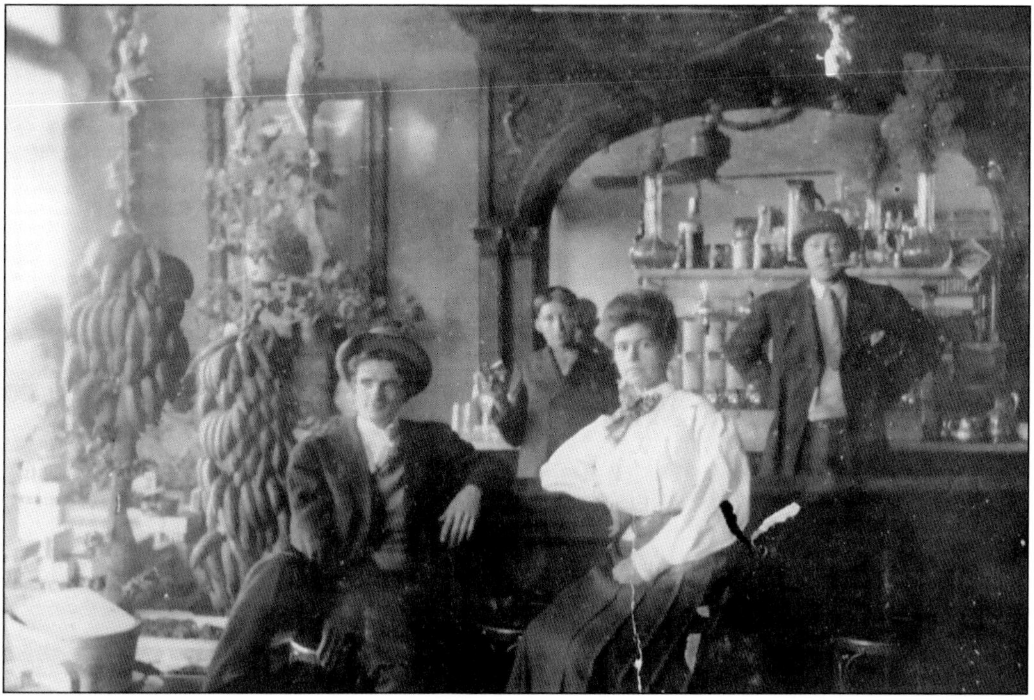

KEE BROTHERS SARSAPARILLA STAND IN RIPLEY. The sarsaparilla stand was the women's alternative to the men's saloon. Coming to town from the outlying communities, the sarsaparilla stand allowed the womenfolk a place to gather and catch up on events. (Courtesy of Terry Ford.)

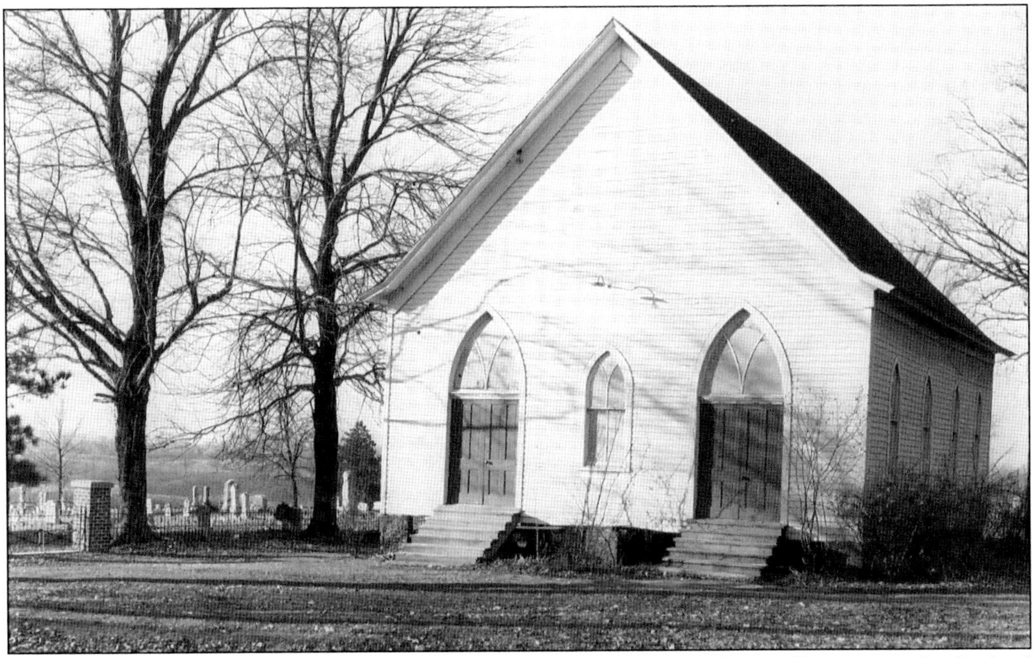

ASBURY METHODIST CHURCH, 1947. On February 23, 1854, Joseph Wardlaw gave a lot he had received as a grant from the State of Tennessee to the Methodist church at "Asberry" (Asbury). This land given by Wardlaw is the same as that now occupied by Asbury Methodist Church and Cemetery. (Courtesy of Evelyn Stewart.)

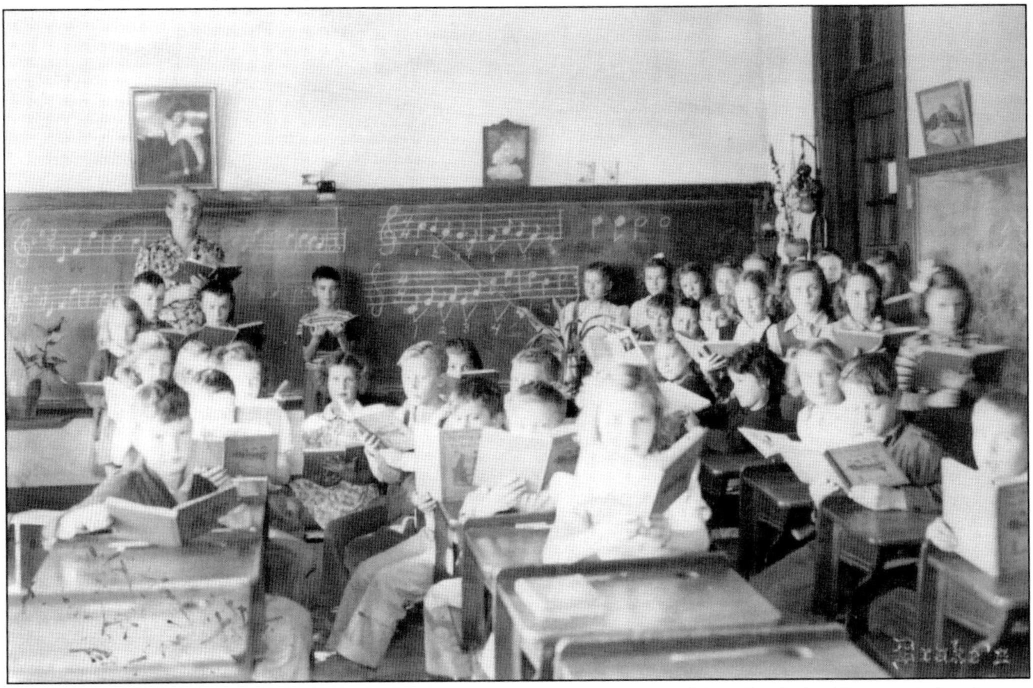

SCHOOL MUSIC CLASS. Music was always an important part of Lauderdale County's heritage. Pictured here is a music class in Ripley Grammar School in 1946. The teacher was Kathleen Given. (Courtesy of Terry Ford.)

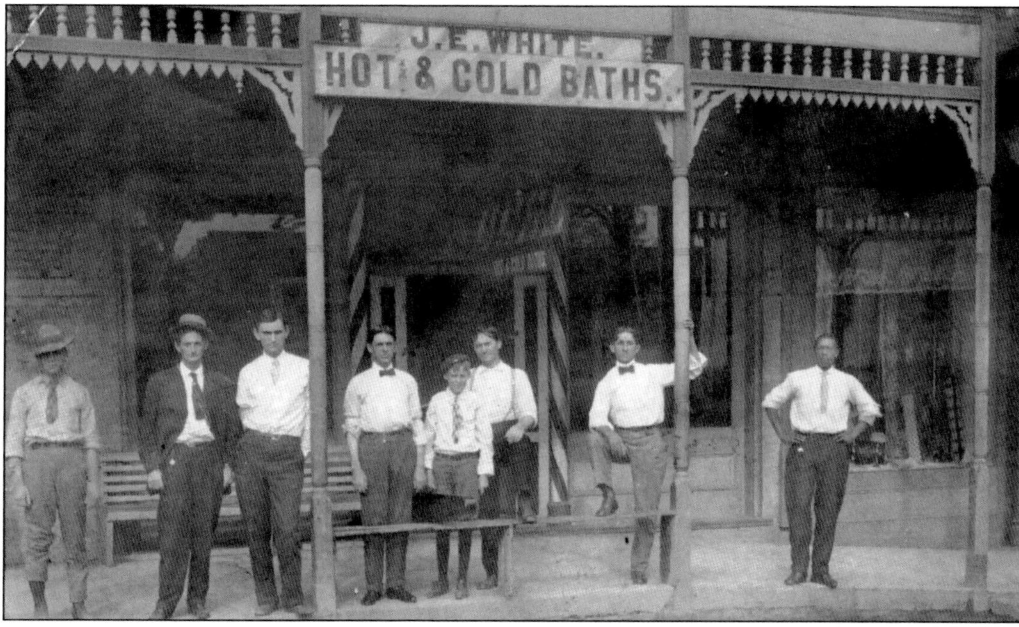

J.E. WHITE'S "HOT AND COLD BATHS." This establishment was located in downtown Ripley, Tennessee, and served the public with hot or cold baths, shaves, and haircuts. (Courtesy of Laura Culotta.)

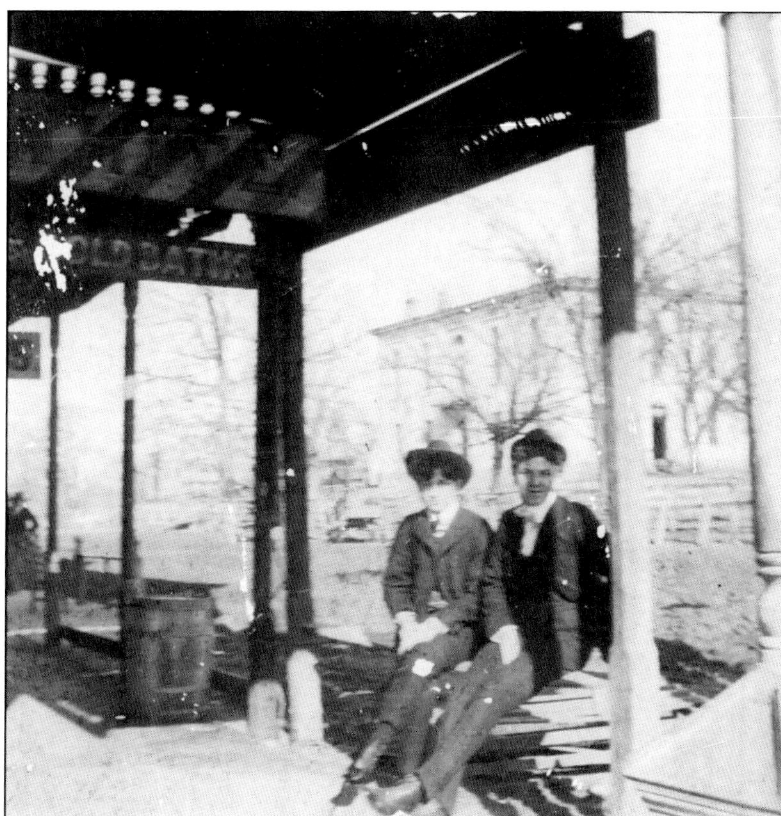

SAM BERG AND BEN CHAPMAN. In this scene, also of J.E. White's bathhouse, the Lauderdale County Courthouse can be seen in the background. Seated are Sam Berg and Ben Chapman. (Courtesy of Terry Ford.)

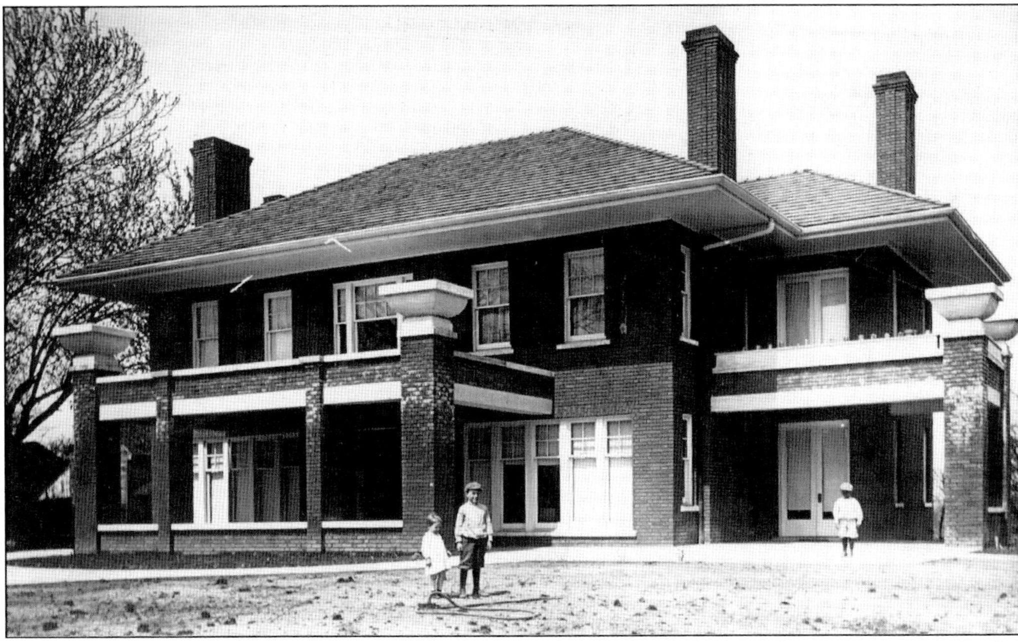

GOODLOE MALONE PARTEE HOMEPLACE. This home was located on Lafayette Street in Ripley, Tennessee. Susan (Partee) Scott and Goodloe Partee are seen playing on the lawn in 1913. The child on the right is unidentified. (Courtesy of Susan Scott.)

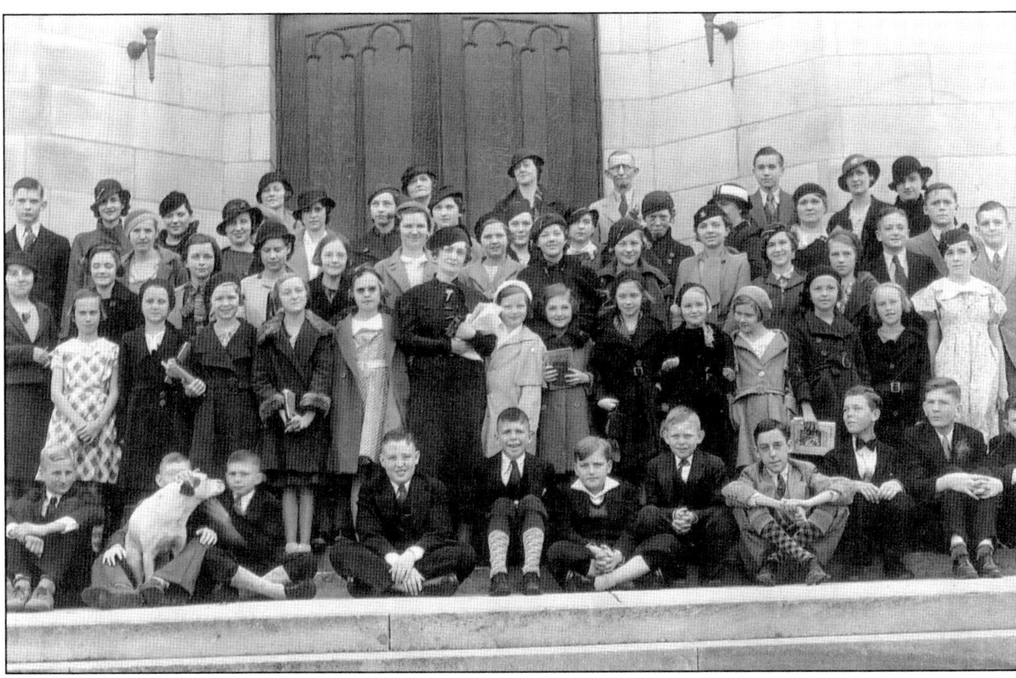

CHURCH GROUP IN RIPLEY. This group is pictured on the steps of the First United Methodist Church in Ripley. The reason for the photograph is unknown but shows various congregants of all ages. (Courtesy of Connie Duvall.)

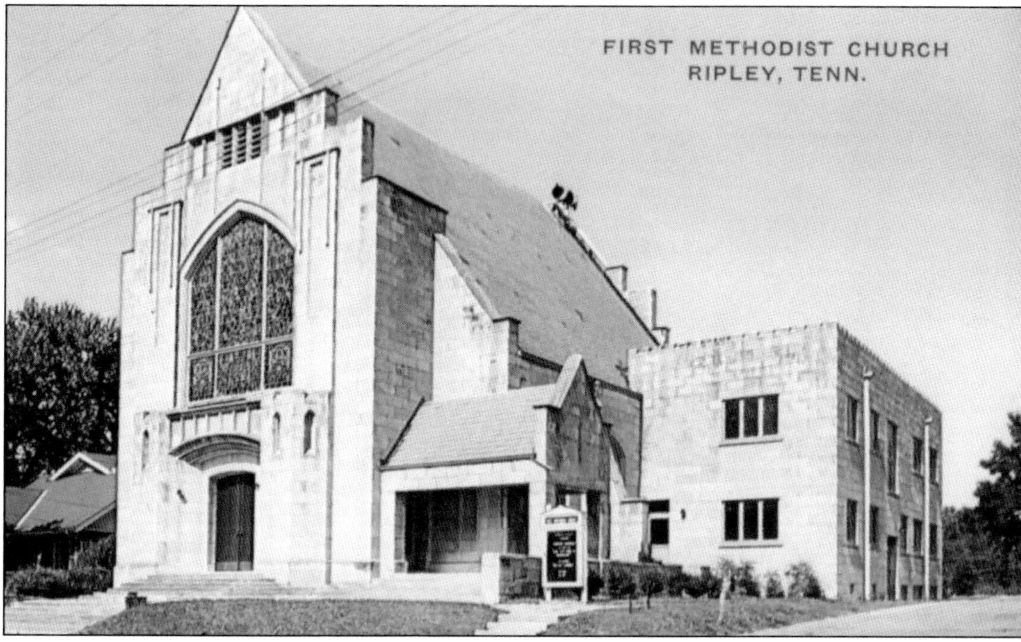

RIPLEY FIRST UNITED METHODIST CHURCH. This church was built in 1914 in Ripley, Tennessee. There have been four successive buildings at this same location, including a log cabin, a frame building in 1856, a brick building in 1886, and this Gothic stone structure. (Courtesy of Susan Scott.)

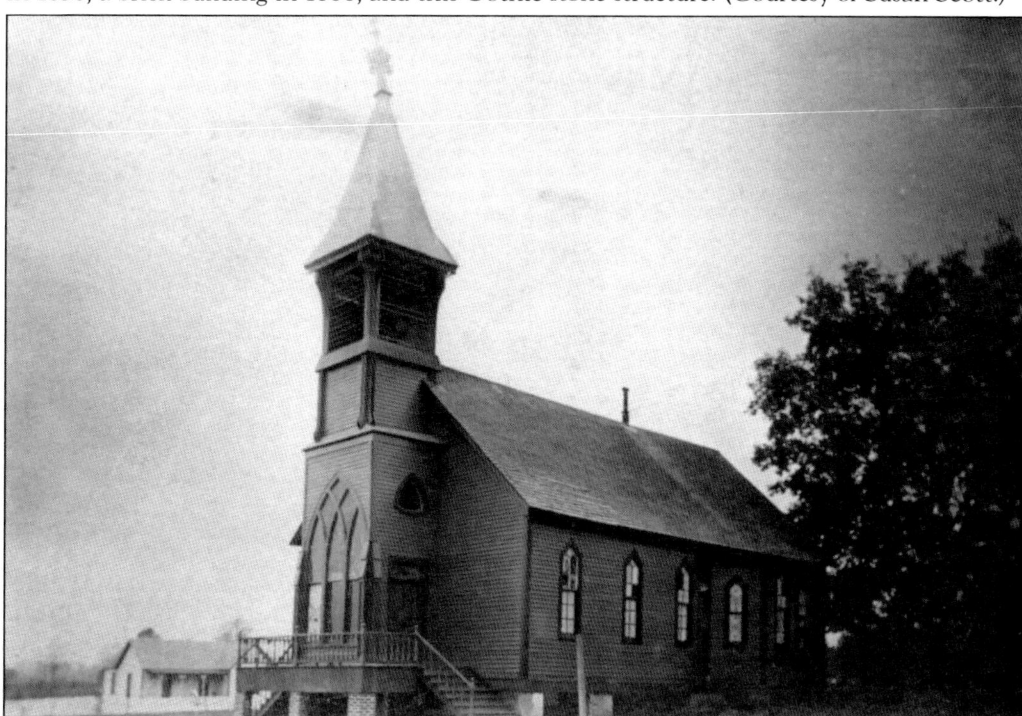

HENNING UNITED METHODIST CHURCH. The old church at Stonewall, built of logs, was moved to Henning and used for worship until this church was built in 1888. Dr. D.M. Henning had founded the town of Henning in 1873. (Courtesy of Lauderdale County Museum.)

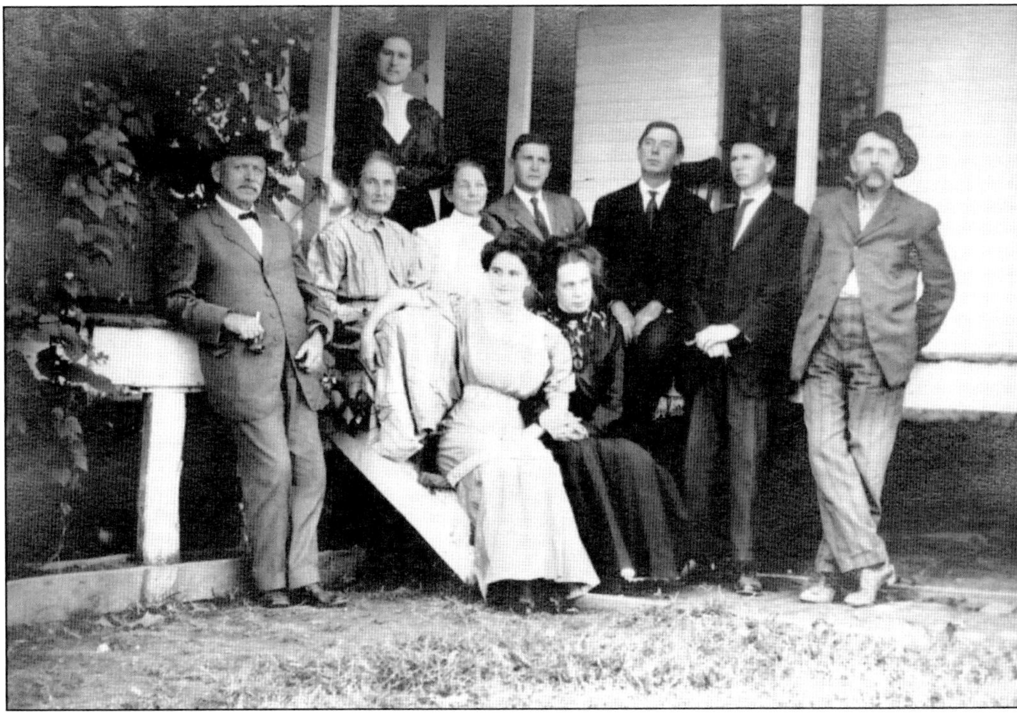

William Ball Drake Family, 1915. William is pictured on the far right. He was one of the three last surviving Civil War Veterans that lived in Lauderdale County. His grandson was noted author Robert Drake. (Courtesy of Terry Ford.)

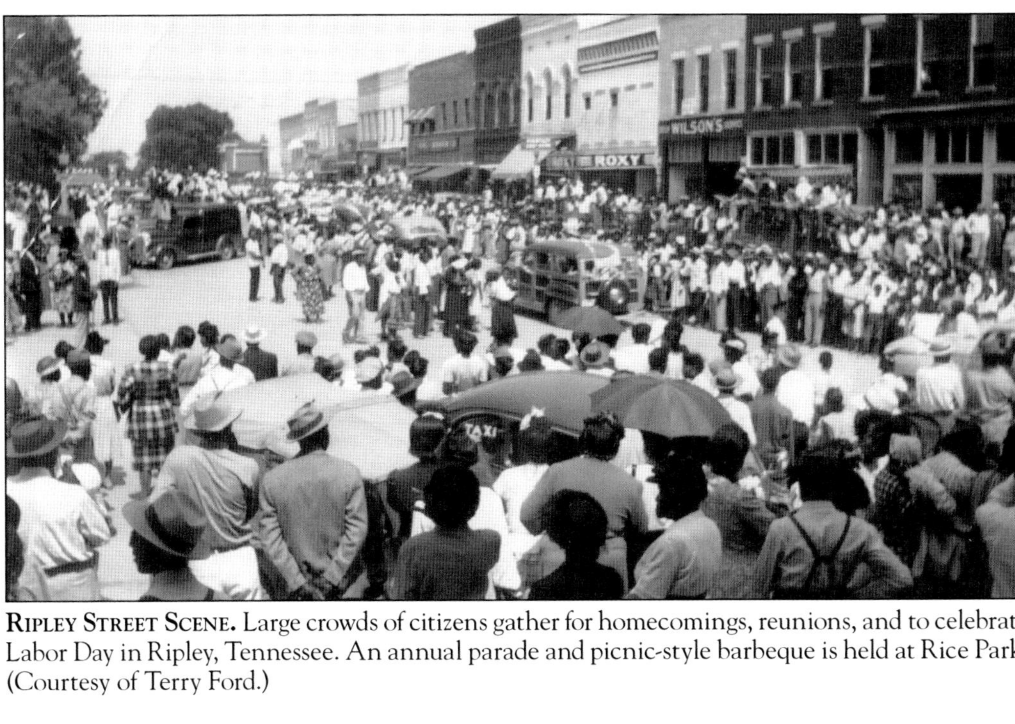

Ripley Street Scene. Large crowds of citizens gather for homecomings, reunions, and to celebrate Labor Day in Ripley, Tennessee. An annual parade and picnic-style barbeque is held at Rice Park. (Courtesy of Terry Ford.)

COURTHOUSE DRINKING FOUNTAIN. Pictured in 1912, this drinking fountain was on the Lauderdale County Courthouse lawn. This handsome fountain was erected by the John Sutherland Chapter, United Daughters of the Confederacy, to honor the Confederate soldiers of Lauderdale County. The complete cost of the fountain was $600. It was 16 feet, four inches high, and the diameter of the pool was 14 feet. A concrete sidewalk surrounded it. It had two flowing fountains on each side. Another monument that stood on the courtyard was a cannon brought from the famous Fort Pillow battle field. Both were projects of the United Daughters of the Confederacy. (Courtesy of Margie Glenn.)

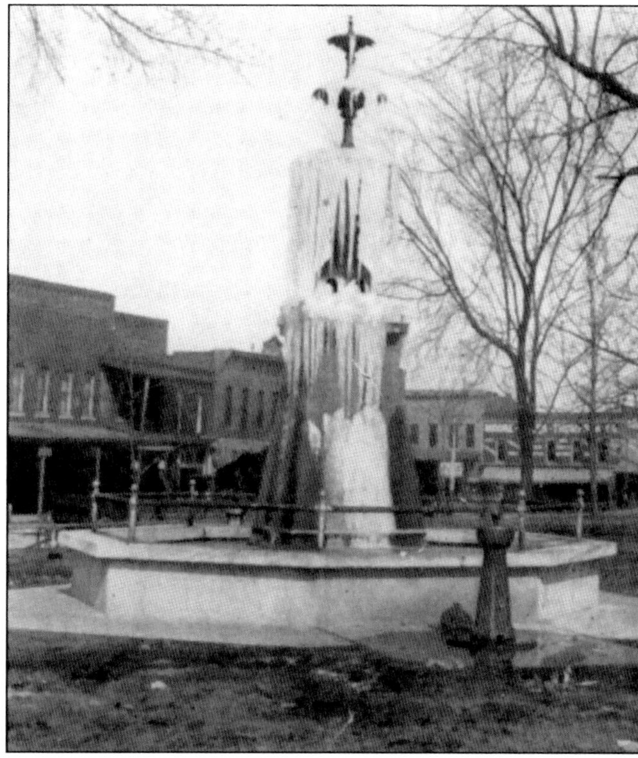

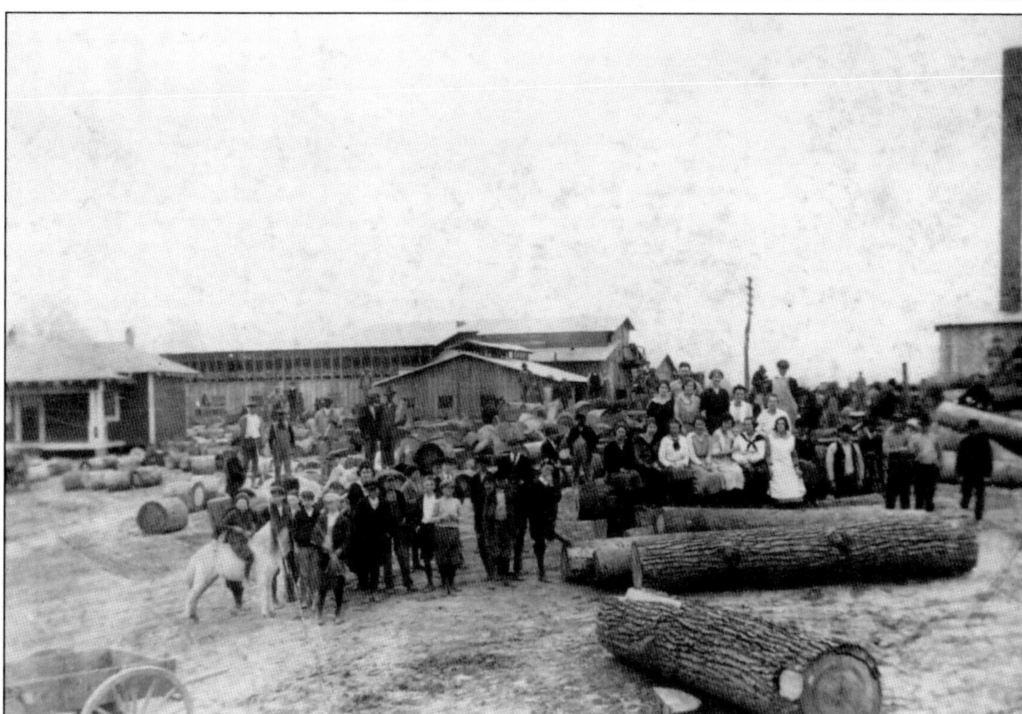

PROCESSING TIMBER IN GOLD DUST. The Gold Dust Sawmill was located near the Mississippi River in Lauderdale County. This photograph was taken around 1920. (Courtesy of Kay Bohannon.)

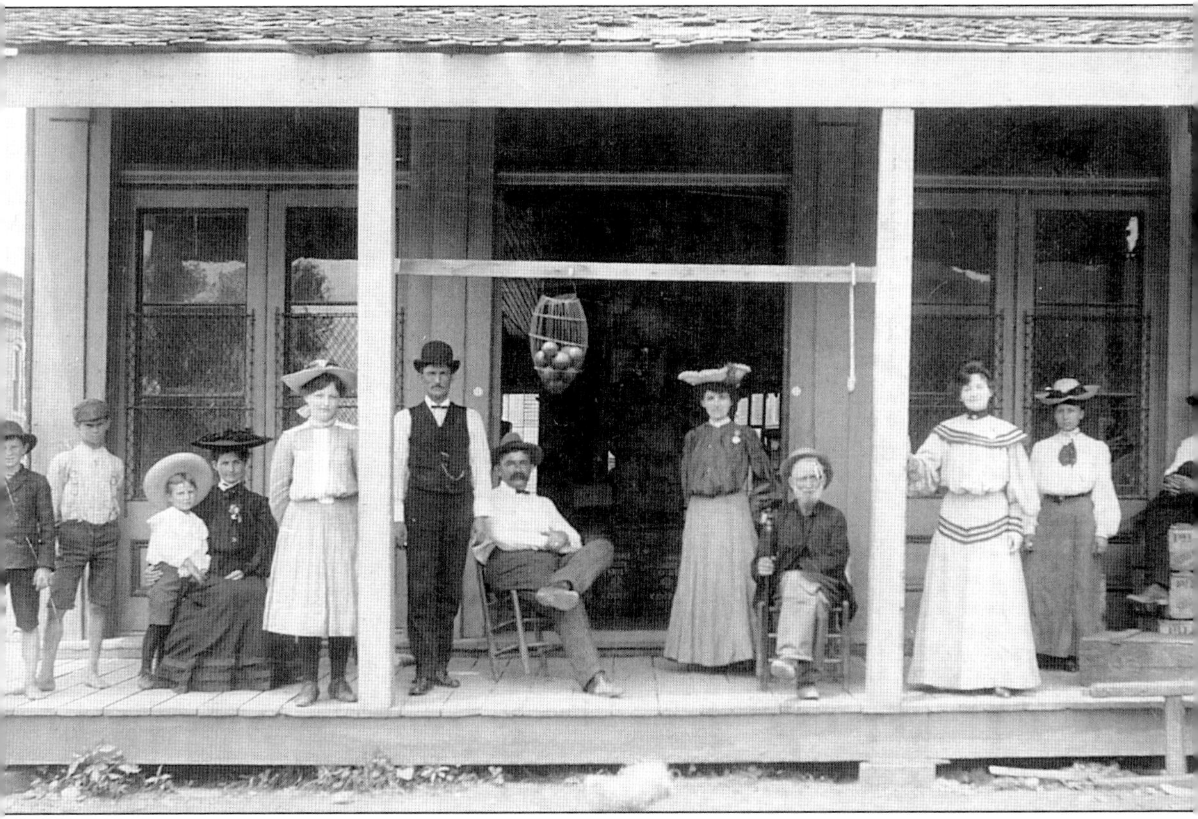

MOSE STERNBERGER'S STORE. Located in Gates, Tennessee, this store was at Second and Wardlaw Streets, facing Second Street and the railroad. Pictured in the 1890s are, from left to right, two unidentified people, Norman Sloan, Mattie Sloan, Byrd Sloan, two unidentified people, Rhea Sternberger, and Mose Sternberger (seated with cane), and three unidentified people. (Courtesy of Ken Raines.)

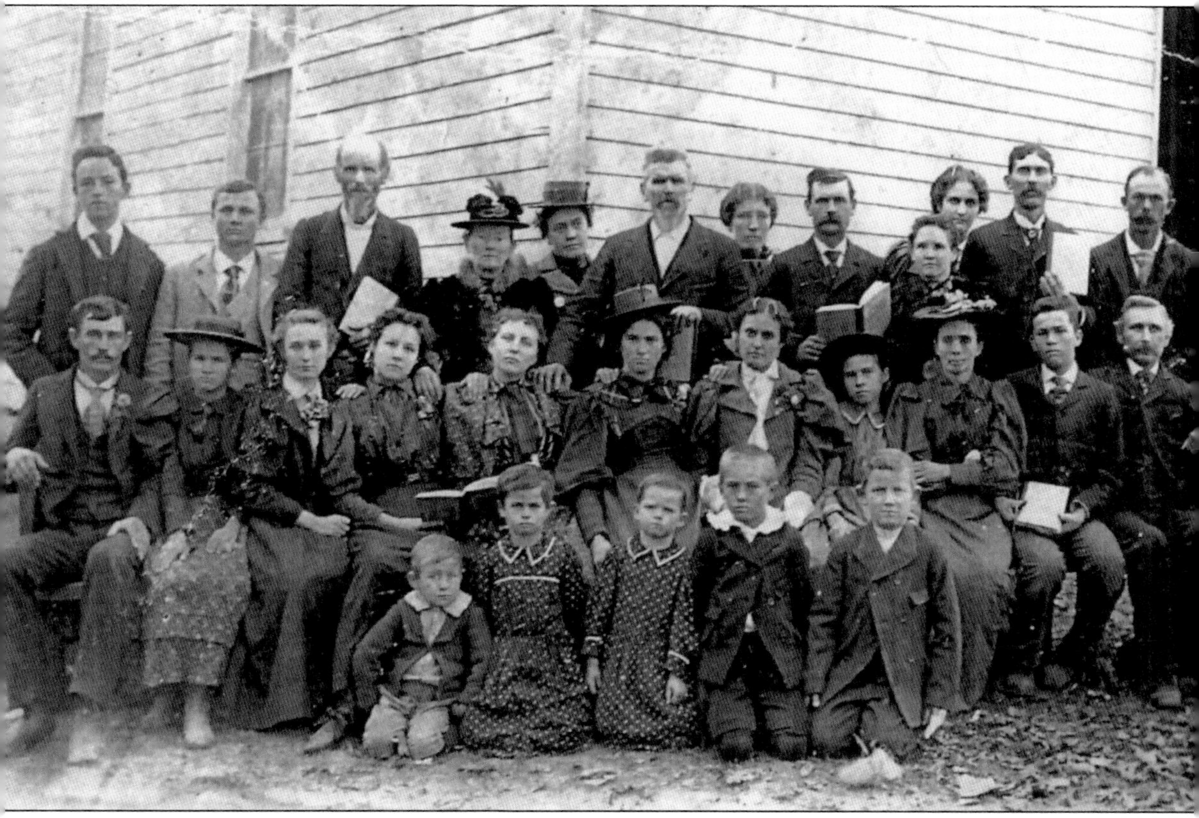

Singing School in the Arp Community, 1895. From left to right are (first row) Dupree Jenkins, Lucy Morris, Estelle Morris, John Morris, and Walter Holden; (second row) Dock Braden, Beulah Morris, Iola Greaves, Lucy Sapp, Bessie Thum, Lula Morris, Carrie Grimes, Vera Morris, Mrs. Bill Morris, Willie Morris, and Charles Thornley; (third row) Charlie Sapp, Edwin Meadows, S. Holden, Mrs. Cliff, Bessie Lewis, the Reverend Cliff, Hattie McLeod, Mr. Hardy (teacher), Bessie Thornley, Lillie Morris, Mr. Hatch, and Henry Bibb. (Courtesy of Susan Weiber.)

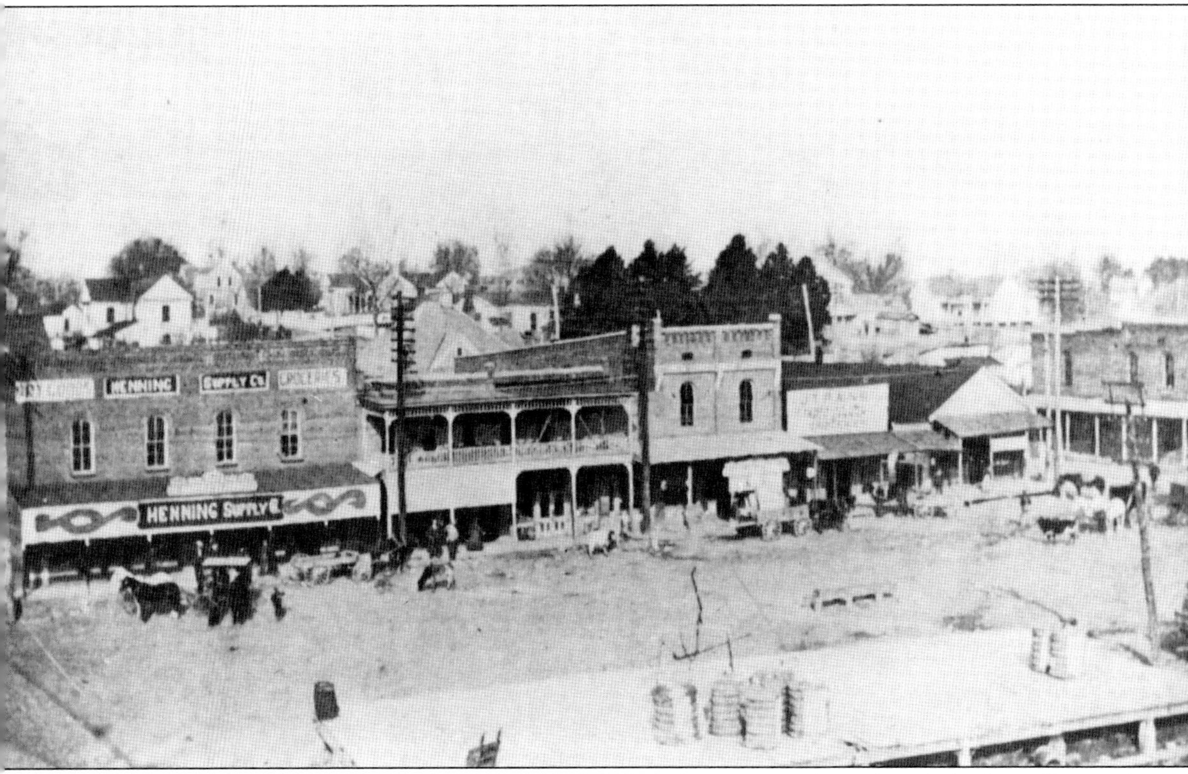

A Henning Street Scene. This scene shows bales of cotton on the railroad platform (front of picture) and the Henning Supply Company, Barnes Dry Goods, Turner's Drugstore, J.T. Rains General Store, Brandon's Grocery, and Turner's Café. In the distance are the homes of Henning.

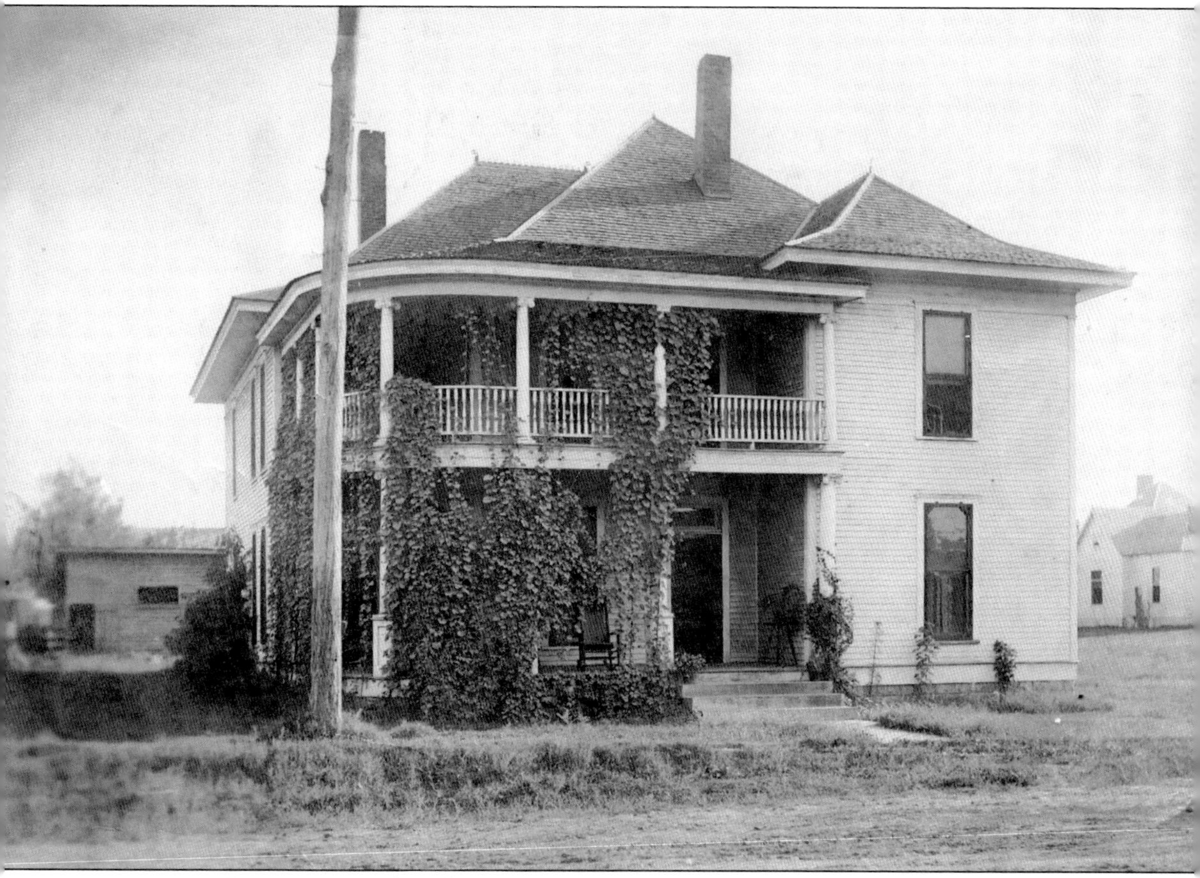

MASSINGALE HOTEL, 1911. This charming hotel was later known as the Perry Hotel. Located on Main Street in Halls, it served many regulars during the early 1900s. (Courtesy of Anna Katherine Pippin.)

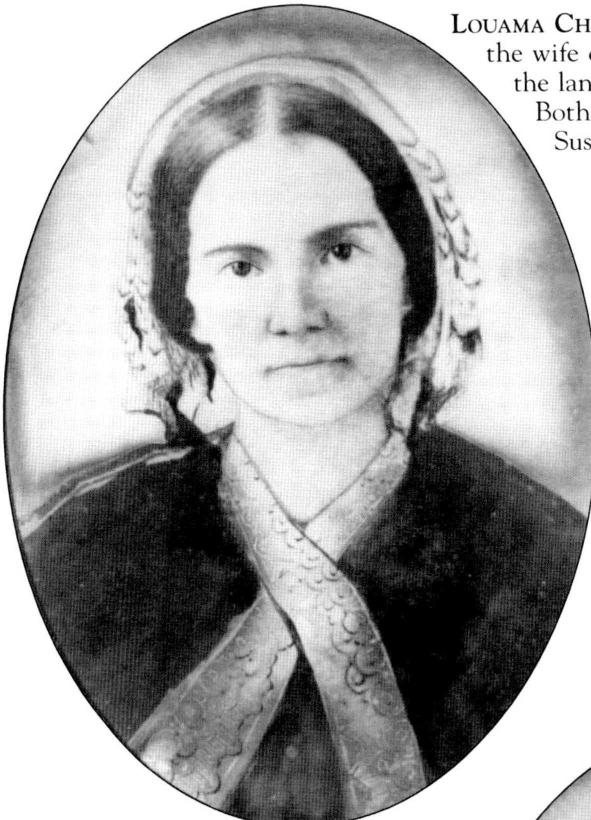

LOUAMA CHERRY PARTEE. Louama (1815–1851) was the wife of Hiram Partee. The Partees donated the land for the Old Cemetery on Lake Drive. Both of them are buried there. (Courtesy of Susan Scott.)

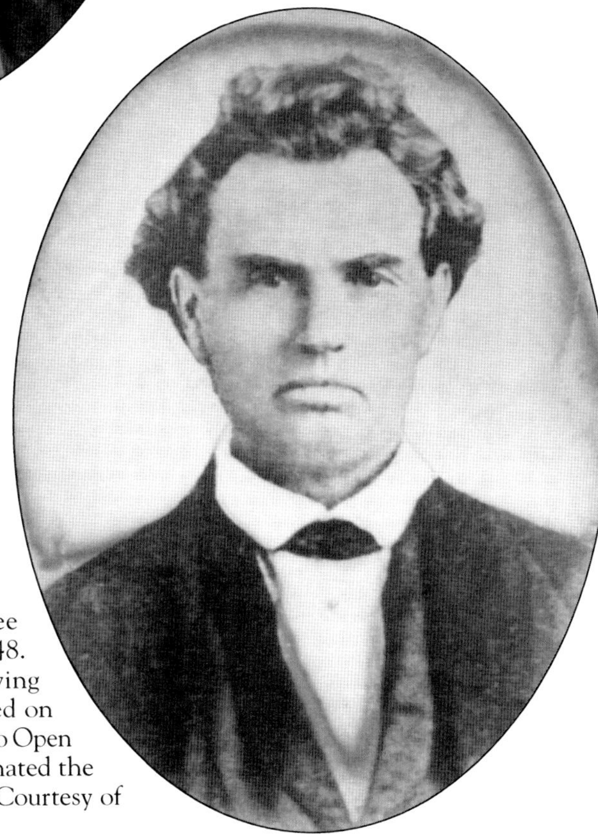

COL. HIRAM PARTEE. Colonel Partee (1799–1872) moved to Ripley in 1848. He was an extensive landowner, growing primarily cotton. His acreage extended on both sides of the road from Cane Creek to Open Lake and the Mississippi River. He donated the land for Ripley First Baptist Church. (Courtesy of Susan Scott.)

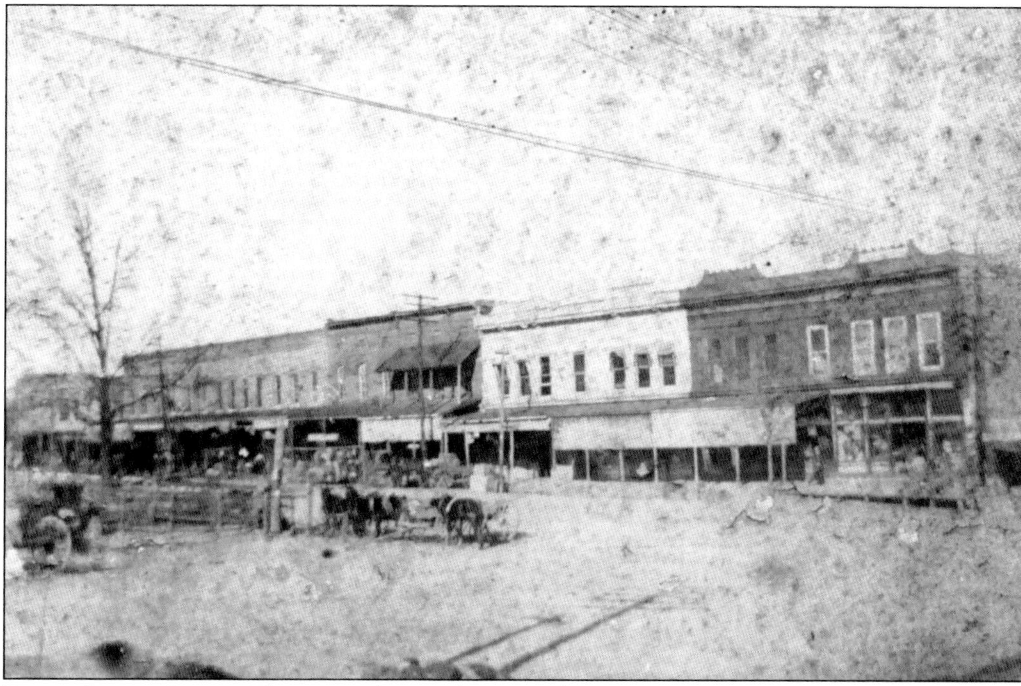

Ripley Street Scene. This scene depicts the east side of Court Square in the late 1880s. By 1830, Hart Hotel (a frame building) and Dr. James A. Lackey's office (a log cabin) were located on the east side of the square. Fifty years later in 1880, the east side was filling up with businesses.

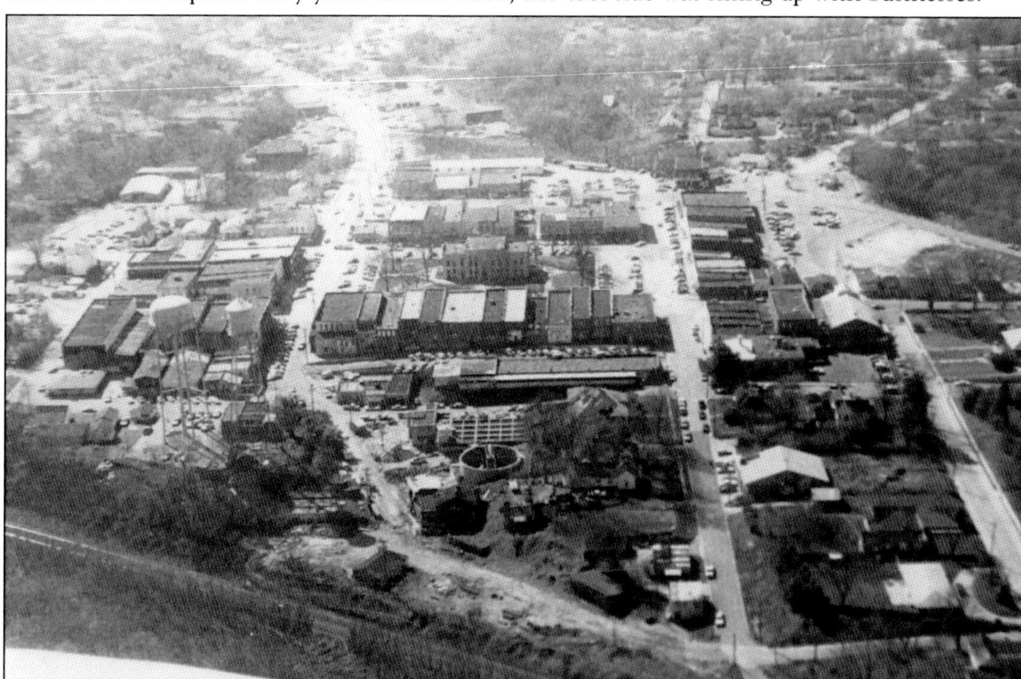

Aerial View of Ripley, 1980s. Note the Lauderdale County Courthouse in the center. (Courtesy of Terry Ford.)

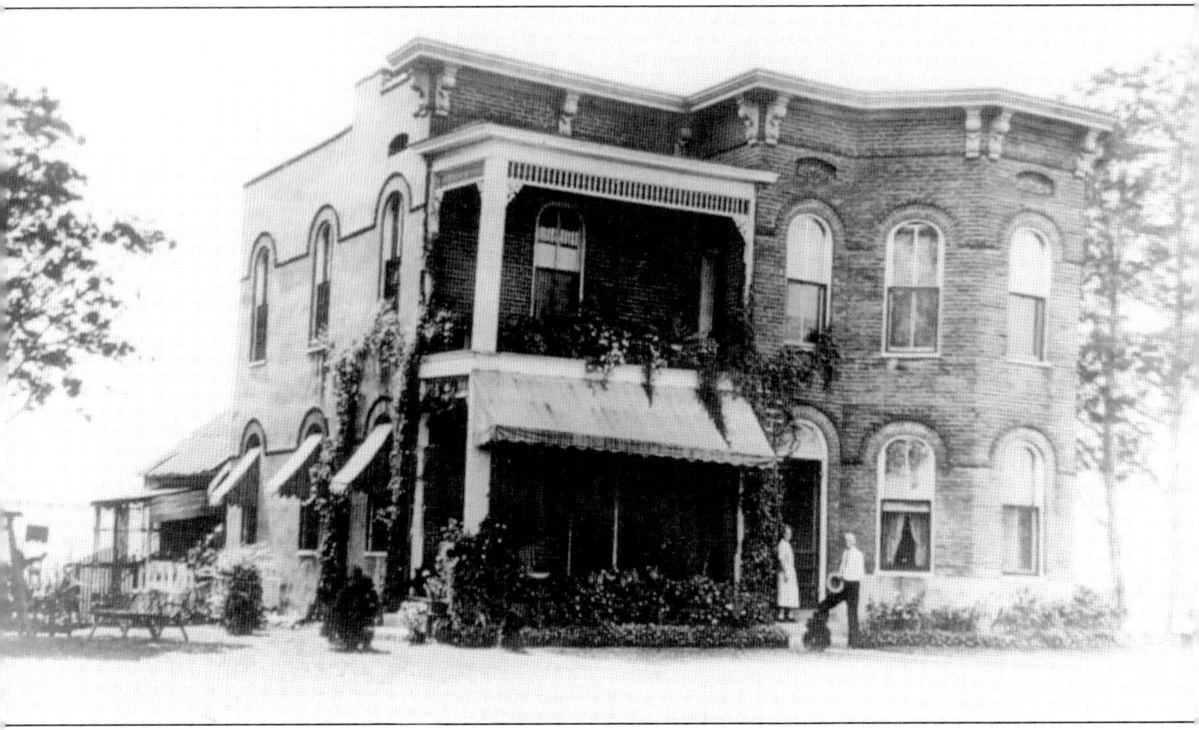

Dr. H.B. Moorer Home, 1879. Located at 105 Moorer Street in Henning, Tennessee, this Victorian-Italianate house was occupied by several generations of Moorers. The site and 30 acres of land was deeded to Dr. Henry B. Moorer by his father-in-law, Dr. D.M. Henning, the person for whom Henning was named. The Moorer house was the first solid brick house in Lauderdale County and also had the first bathroom in the county, with its lead pipes being poured and made on site. It had speaking tubes, the intercom of the 1880s. One was used to communicate to the kitchen, the other one for the boy's room upstairs. The lights on the porch were from an original Moorer carriage and were electrified. The house is still standing. (Courtesy of Emily Suggs.)

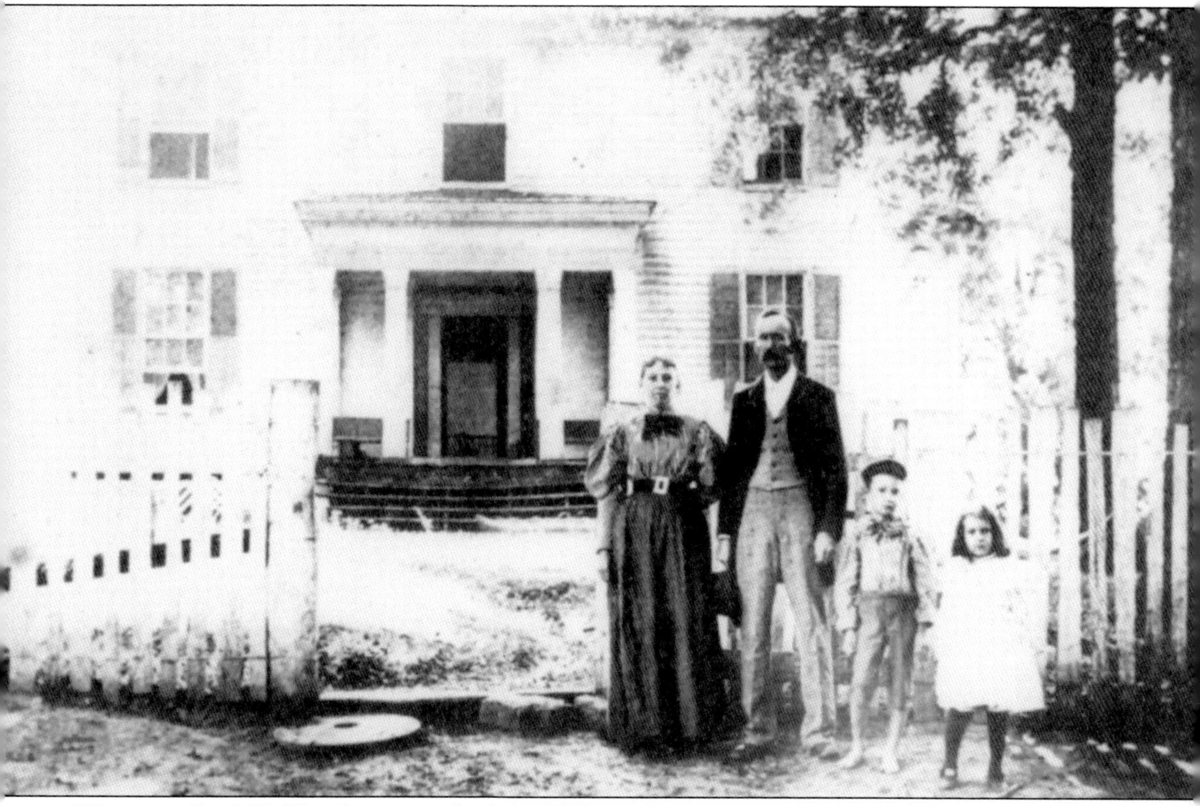

"Bellville" 1897. This home was built by William Conner in 1856. Pictured from left to right are Cornelia Conner Given, Millard Filmore Given Sr., Millard Filmore Given Jr., and Kathleen Given. (Courtesy of Terry Ford.)

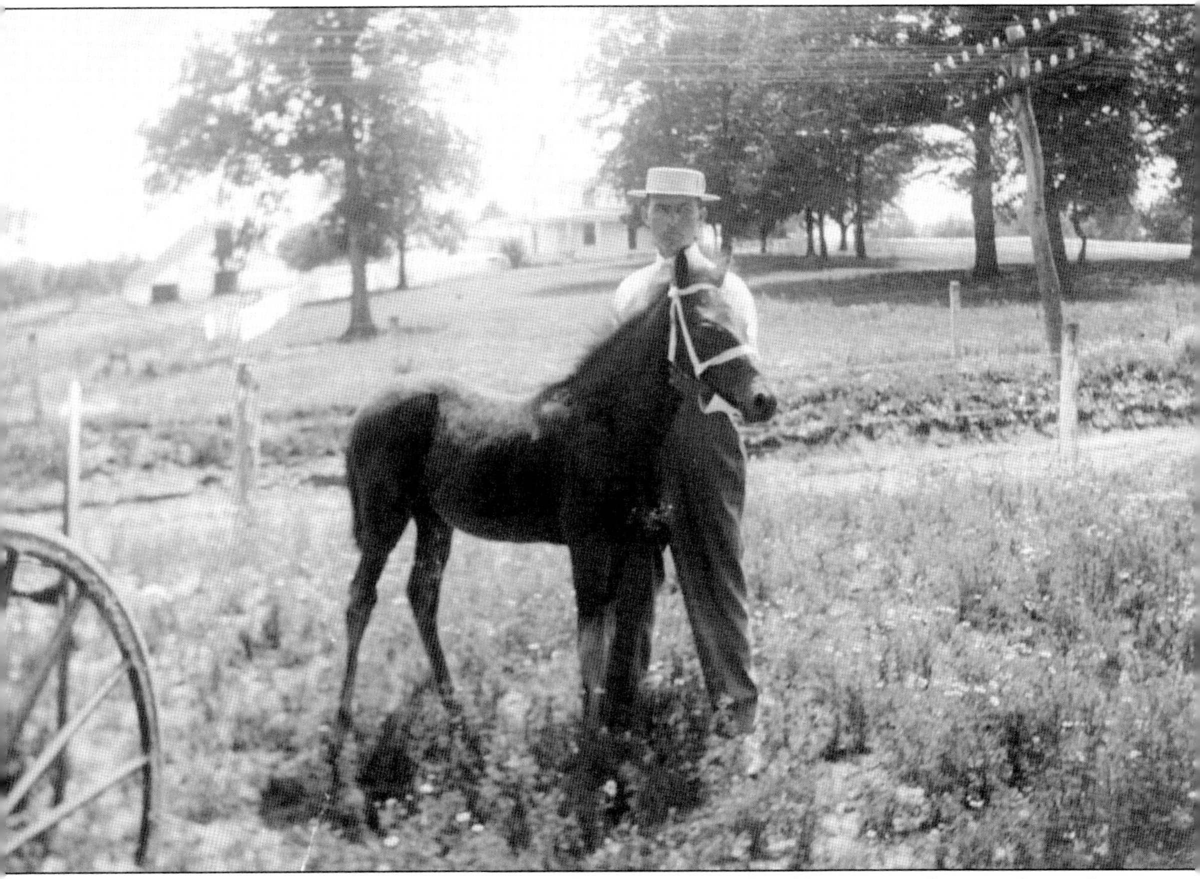

A Man and His Colt. This man reflects the simple lifestyle of living on a farm and spending the day with his colt in the rural outdoors in Ripley, Tennessee. (Courtesy of Terry Ford.)

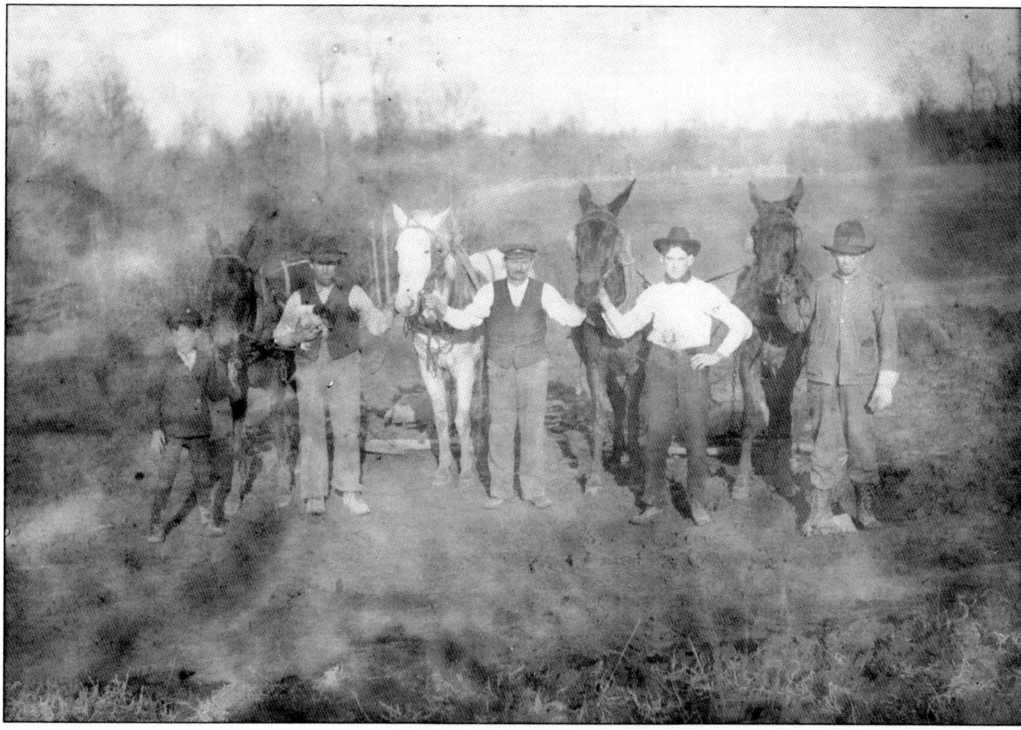

READY TO WORK IN THE FIELDS. These men ready their mules for work in Lauderdale County. Mules were used for many tasks and were often treated like family pets with first names. (Courtesy of Joyce Henson.)

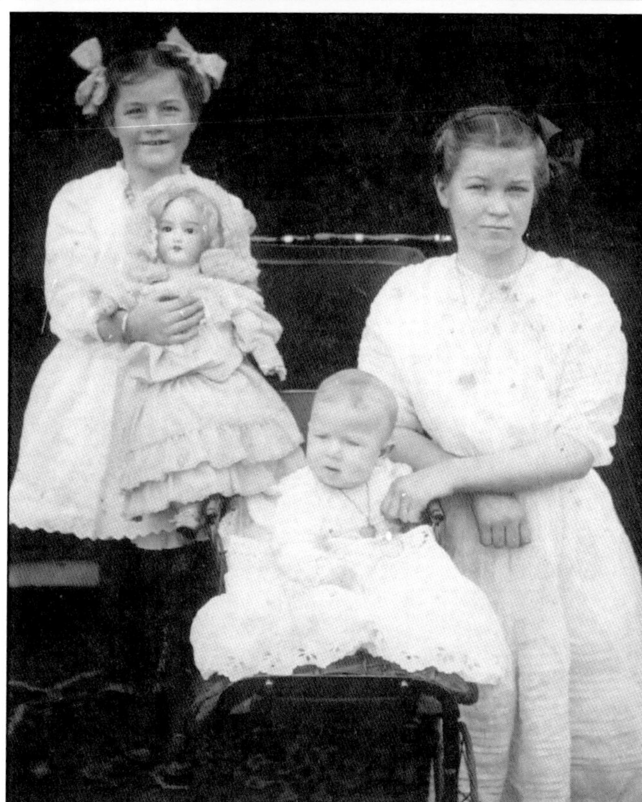

CHAMBERS CHILDREN. Pictured are, from left to right, Mattie (holding doll), Jack, and Jessie Chambers, the children of Alf and Ann Chambers. This family was from the Edith community, and descendants still live there today. (Courtesy of Joyce Henson.)

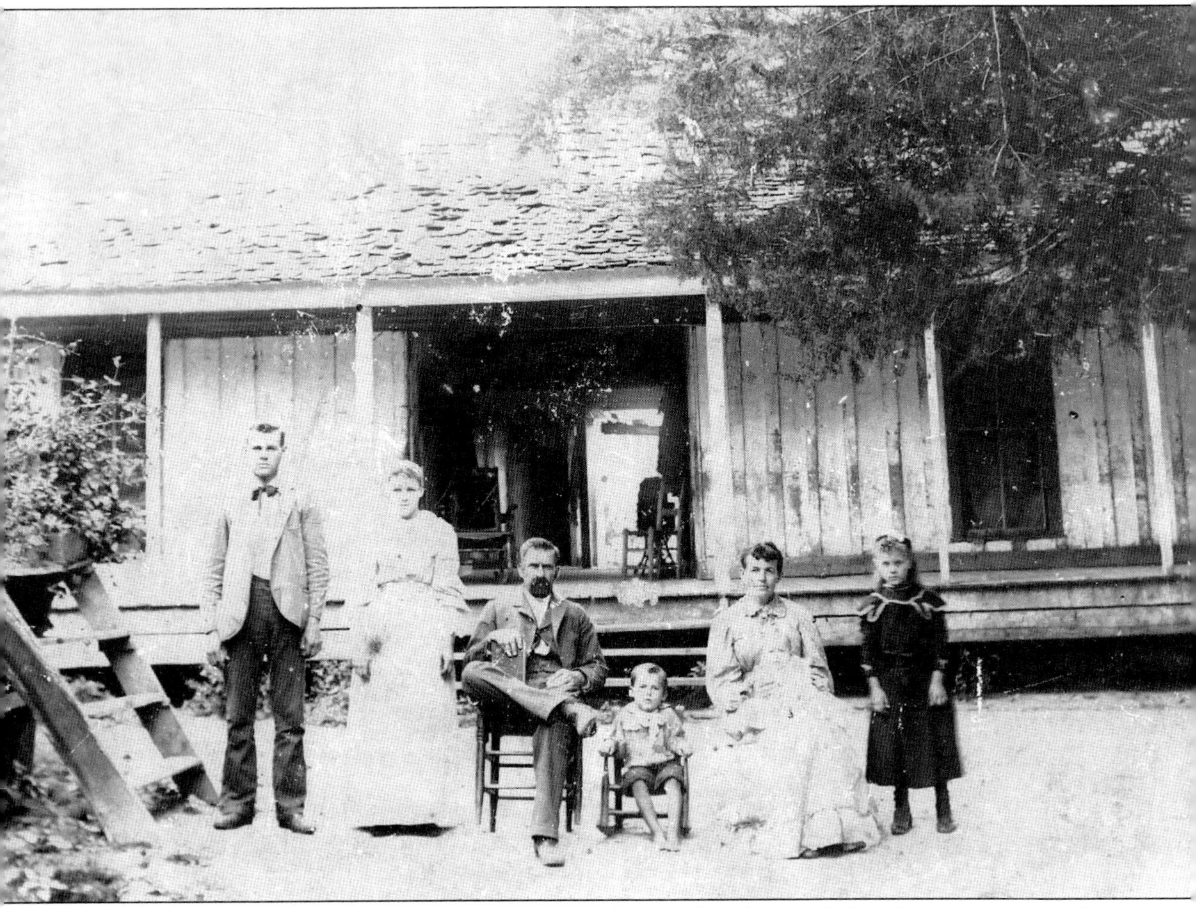

William Thomas Andrews's Family, 1892. Pictured in front of their home are, according to names on the back of the photograph, W.T. Andrews, Grandma Andrews, William Horace Andrews, and Willie, Wertie, Scott, and Wilma Andrews. (Courtesy of Joyce Henson.)

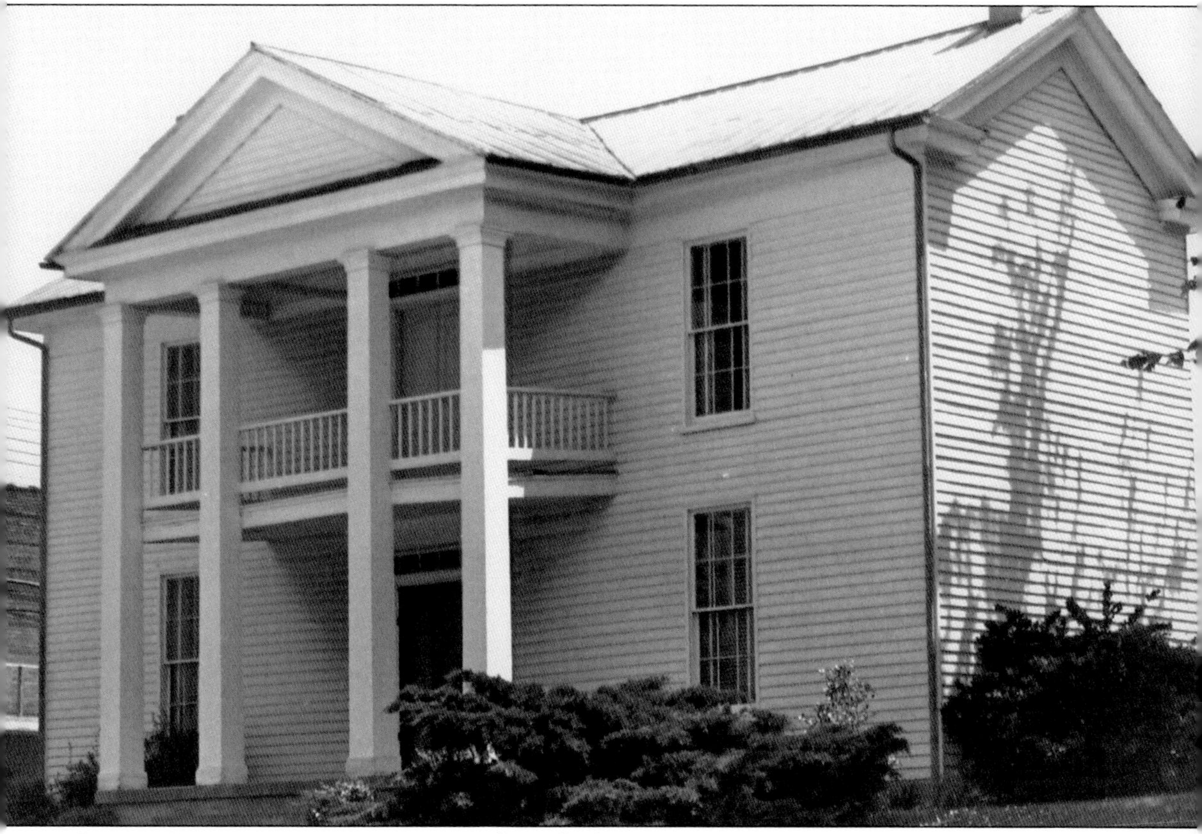

SUGAR HILL MANSION, 1842. Sugar Hill was built in 1842 at 123 South Jefferson Street in Ripley by Joseph Wardlaw. Sugar Hill was the first frame house built in Ripley. The house stood on a hill and was surrounded by numerous sugar maple trees, thus the name Sugar Hill. Sugar Hill had several owners including the Carson family and W.G.L. Rice, who donated the property in 1948 to become the first county library. It served as a library for 50 years. The Lauderdale County Chamber of Commerce moved into the facility in 1999 and began a restoration phase, which includes the Lauderdale County Museum. The home still has its original yellow poplar wood floors on the second floor. (Courtesy of Lauderdale County Museum.)

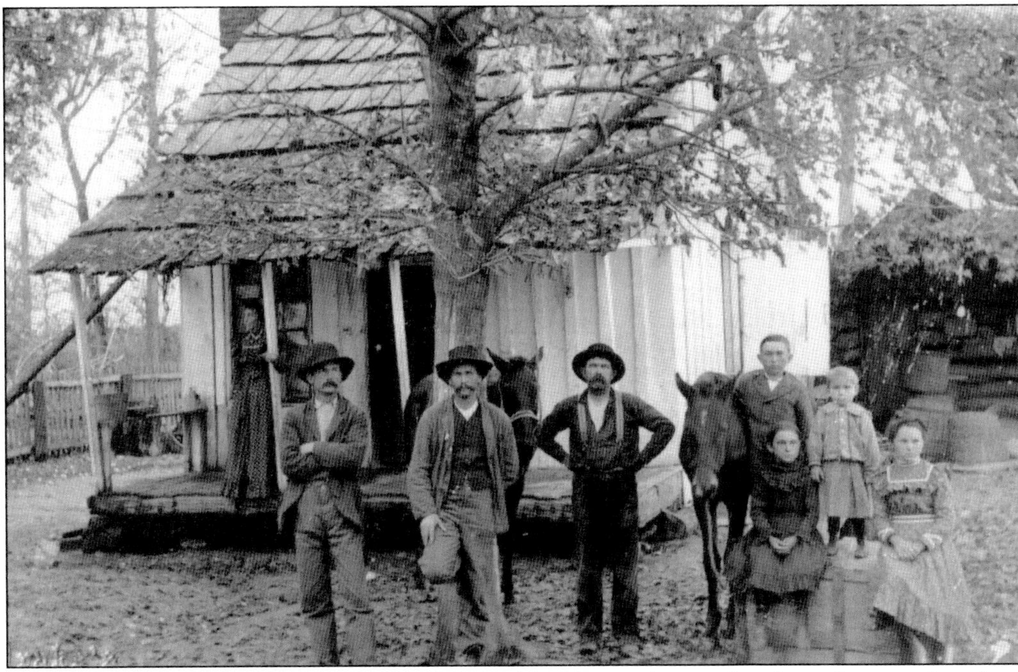

Lauderdale County Family, Arp Community. Family members gather for a photograph in front of their home in the Arp community. Arp was settled around 1830 and was called Morrisville in the early years. (Courtesy of Patsy Wood Langley.)

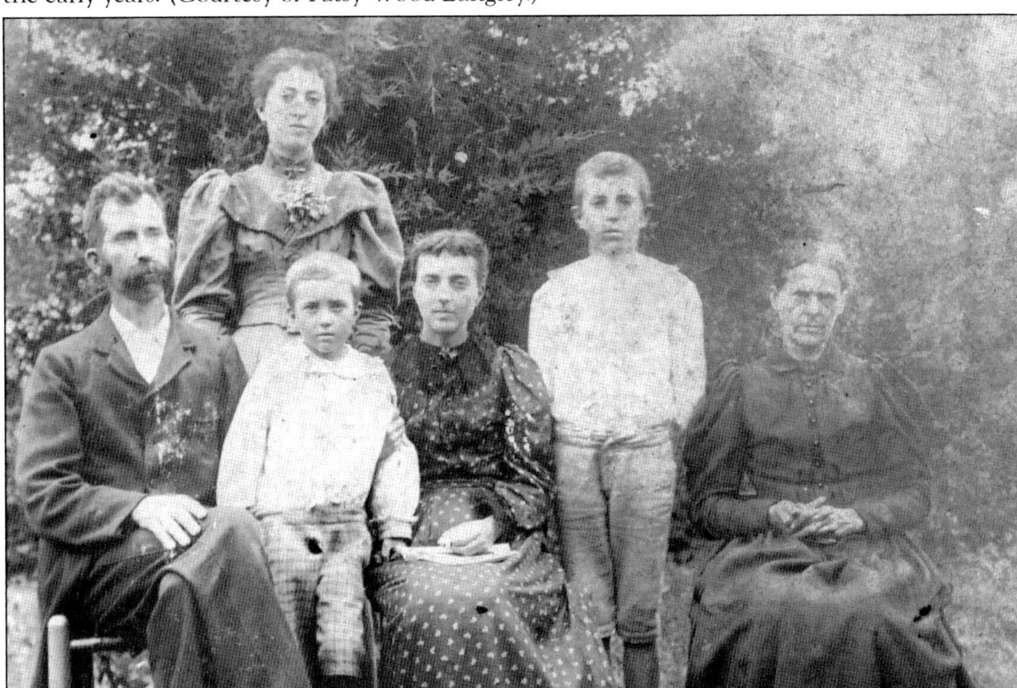

The James Allen Byler Family. Pictured from left to right are James Allen Byler, John Byler, Cynthia Tennessee Condray Byler, James Byler, Sarah Brown Condray, and Cora Irene Byler (standing). (Courtesy of Joyce Henson.)

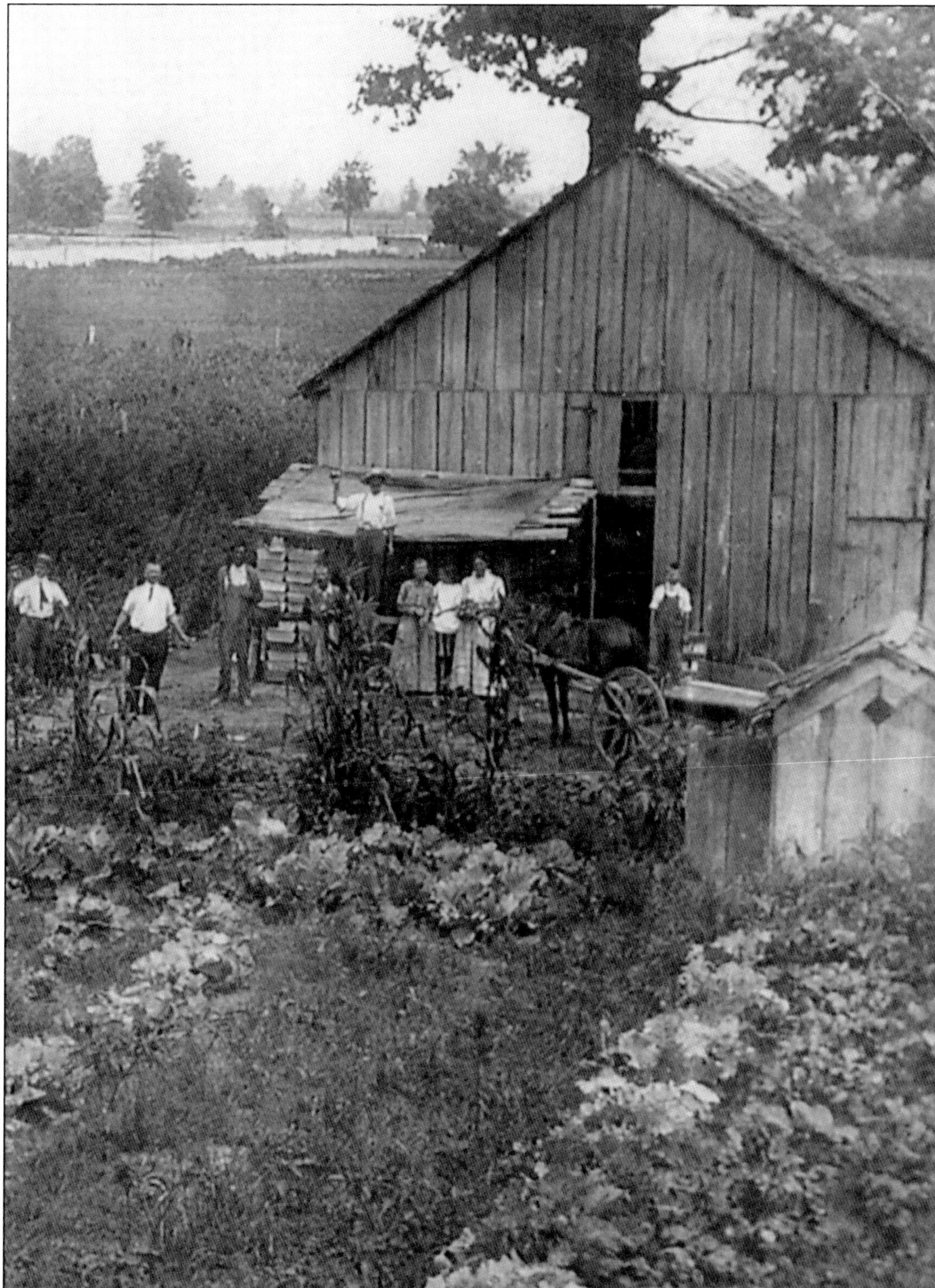

STONE FAMILY GARDEN, 1915. This garden was located on East Tigrett Street in Halls, Tennessee. The photograph shows, from left to right, Will Lynch, unidentified, Doody Stone, unidentified, Ann Davis, seven-year-old Fairries Stone, Ashlee Davis Stone, and a Coldberg (child on wagon). In the background are the railroad tracks and the town of Halls. (Courtesy of Tommy Simmons.)

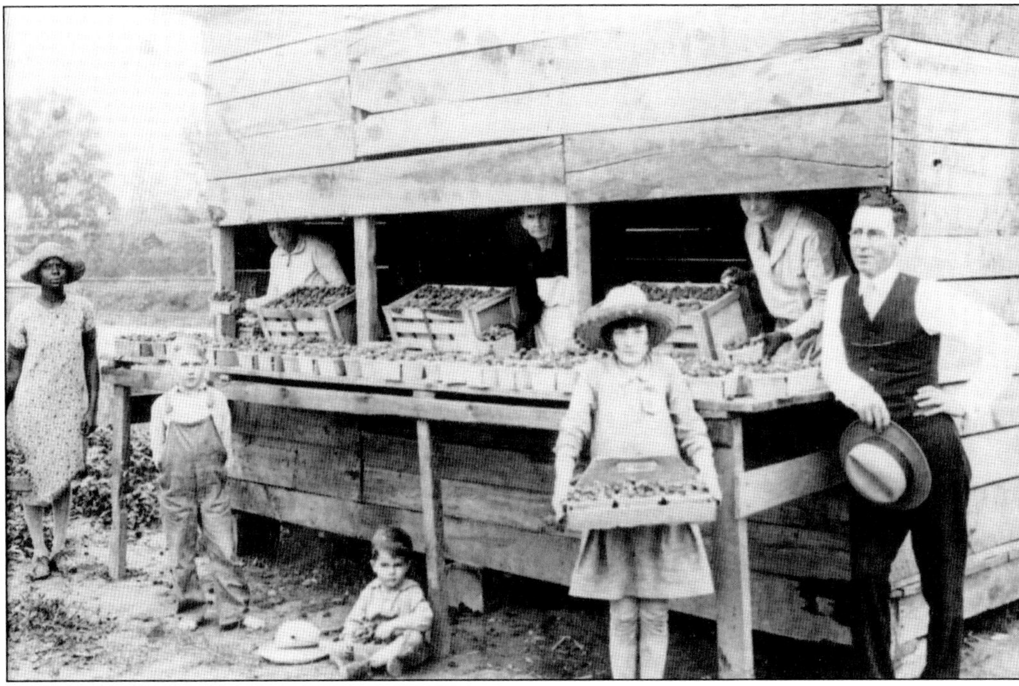

Strawberry Pack Shed. This shed was located in Gates, Tennessee. Pictured on the far right is owner L.L. McDearman. Strawberries brought a booming economy to the small communities and were shipped by carloads on the trains. (Courtesy of Bettie Davis.)

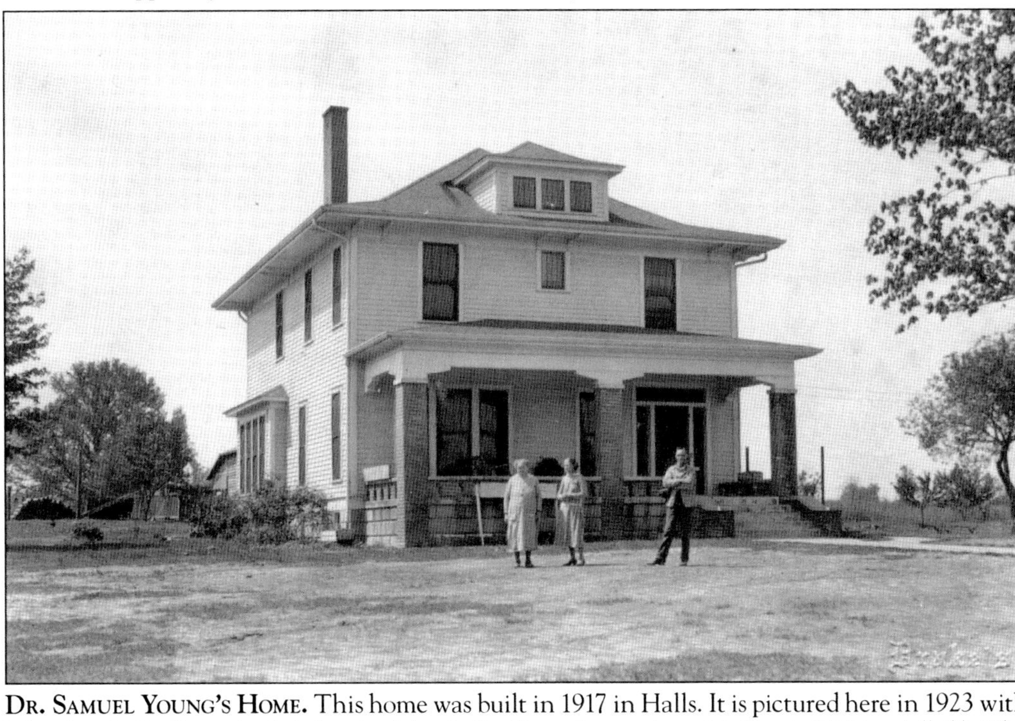

Dr. Samuel Young's Home. This home was built in 1917 in Halls. It is pictured here in 1923 with John Frank Stallings (right), Louisa Morris Stallings (center), and Johnnie Kirkland (left). The Stallings and Henderson families have owned this home. (Courtesy of Lynne Stallings Harris.)

Two

AT WORK AND PLAY

Family life revolved around hard work in early Lauderdale County. Social gatherings were secondary and took place usually at church or school. This chapter depicts the life on the Alf Chambers farm, including not only everyday events of raising crops and gardens but also the family camping at Buffalo Hole.

All communities had small schools, but larger high schools were in Ripley and Halls. Team pictures depict the pride of these students.

Not only did hunting and fishing provide food but also social time for families. Wildlife was abundant; Lauderdale County is an outdoorsman's paradise.

Citizens of Lauderdale County have worked and played hard through the years. What started as a small community with a few log structures is now a vital community with state-of-the-art community buildings, such as the justice complex, health department, and other medical facilities as well as numerous businesses. The Lauderdale County School system has evolved into a strong system, using the latest technology and providing innovative teaching methods. One of the greatest qualities of Lauderdale County is the generosity and dedication of its citizens. The county is notorious for raising funds for charitable causes and rallying behind each other when times are difficult. All of these things combine to make a great place to live, work, and play.

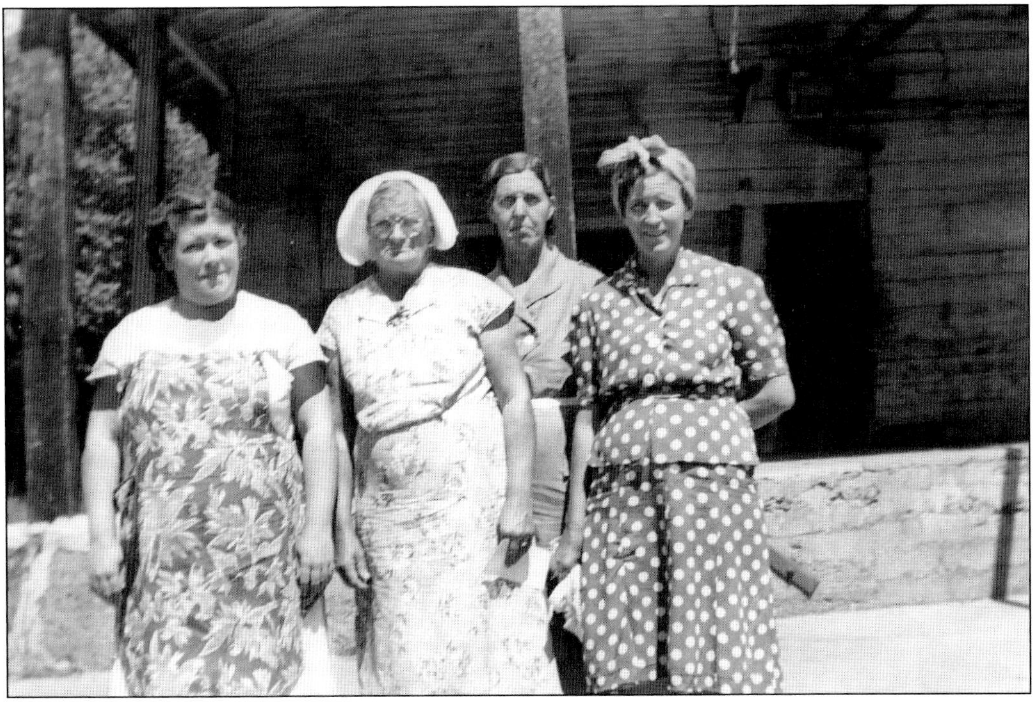

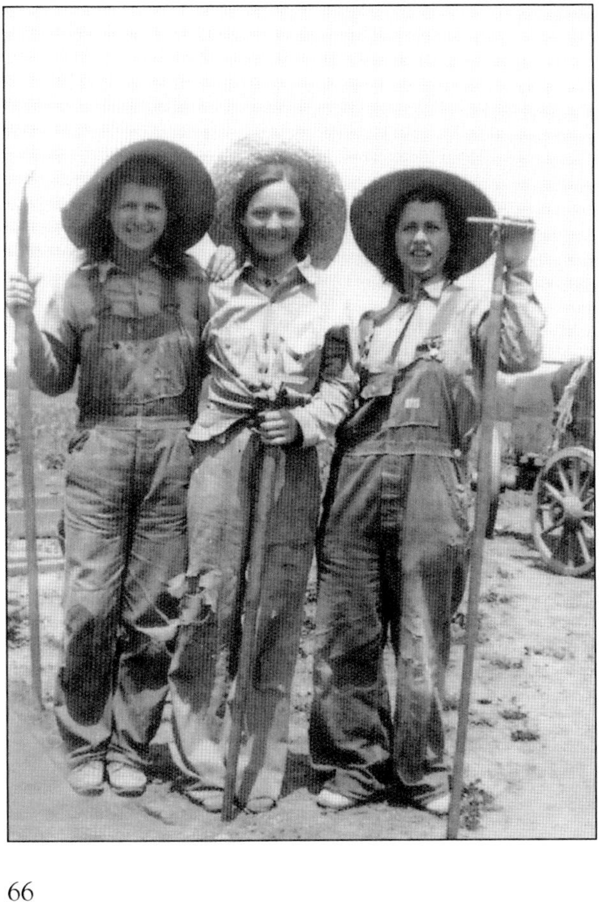

Ripley Tomato-Canning Factory Workers, 1952. Pictured cooling off on the tomato-canning factory's porch are Mrs. Herman Rhodes, Dixie Northcott, Zelma Allmon, and Kathryn Cox. Tomatoes were peeled by hand and cooked in large vats. Workers were paid for quantity output. Work was seasonal and a big boost to the county's economy. (Courtesy of Lauderdale County Museum.)

Chopping Cotton at Gold Dust. Taking a rest from cotton chopping, these three girls pose with their hoes in the field. Cotton chopping in the summer months and picking cotton by hand in the fall brought income to most county residents. Pictured are, from left to right, Ruth Yochum, Ona Chipman, and Claire Yochum. (Courtesy of Rosie Lemons.)

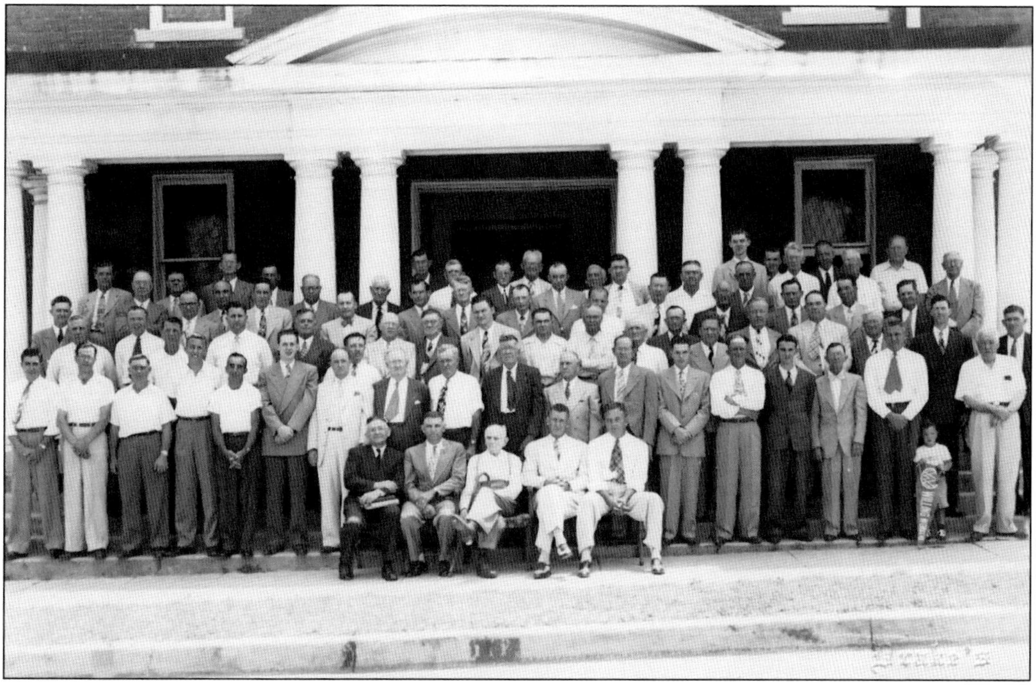

First Baptist Church Men in Ripley, 1950. The First Baptist Church was organized in 1852 by its first pastor, Rev. Joseph H. Borum. The charter members were Mrs. Read Conner, Mrs. Abner Partee, P.T. Glass, E.C. Eggleston, and Mr. and Mrs. George Eggleston.

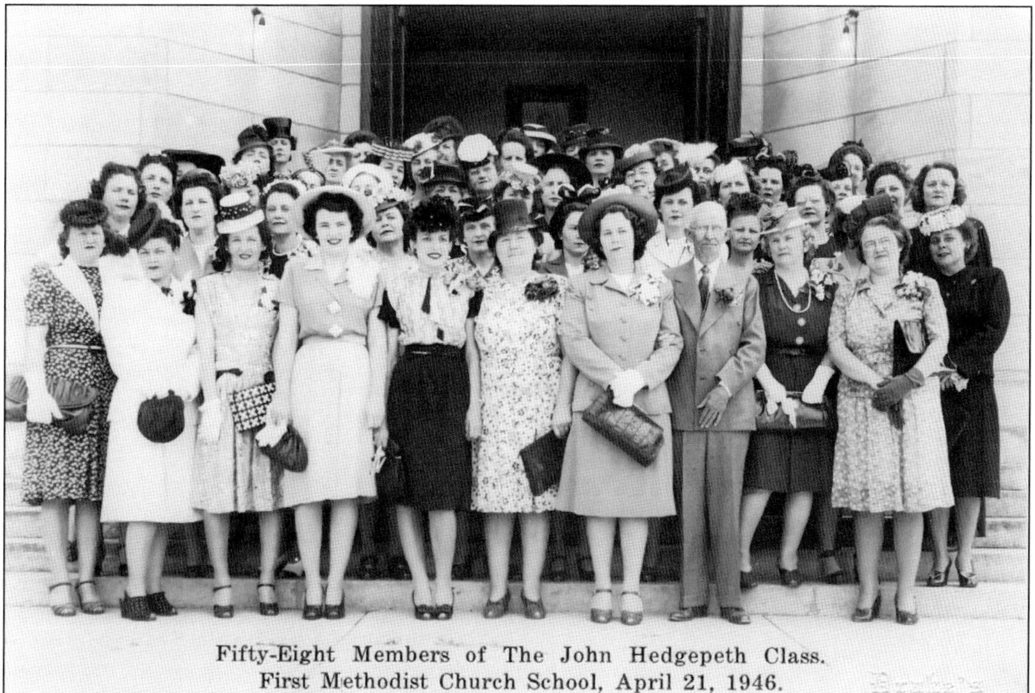

First Methodist Church Women, April 1946. The John Hedgepeth class, composed of 58 members, gathers on the steps in front of the church in Ripley, Tennessee.

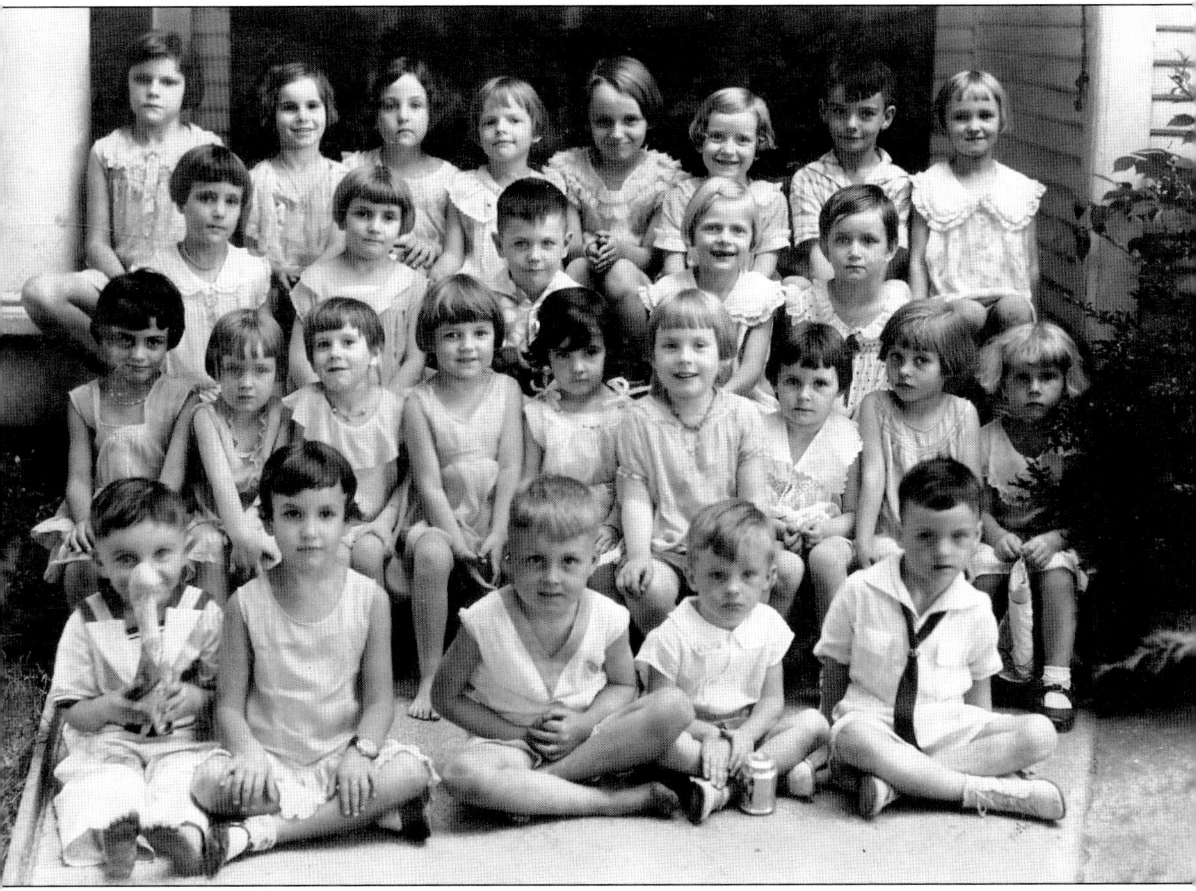

BIRTHDAY PARTY IN RIPLEY, 1930S. Pictured from left to right are (first row) Charles Wilson, Dorris Ballinger, Jack Sanford, Bill Klutts, and unidentified; (second row) Betty Martin, Martha Henderson, Billie Harlon, E'Lane Kirkpatrick, Jean Stewart, Sue Steen, Ola Jean Castellaw, Margaret Crook, and unidentified; (third row) Eugenia Green, ? Johnson, Jim Majors, Laura M. Savage, and Sara Grey McCollum; (fourth row) Elizabeth Conner, Frances Craig, Sue Dunavant, Polly Savage, Marion Stewart, Mary Lee Dailey, Jack Stewart, and Martha Archer. (Courtesy of Frances Fitzhugh.)

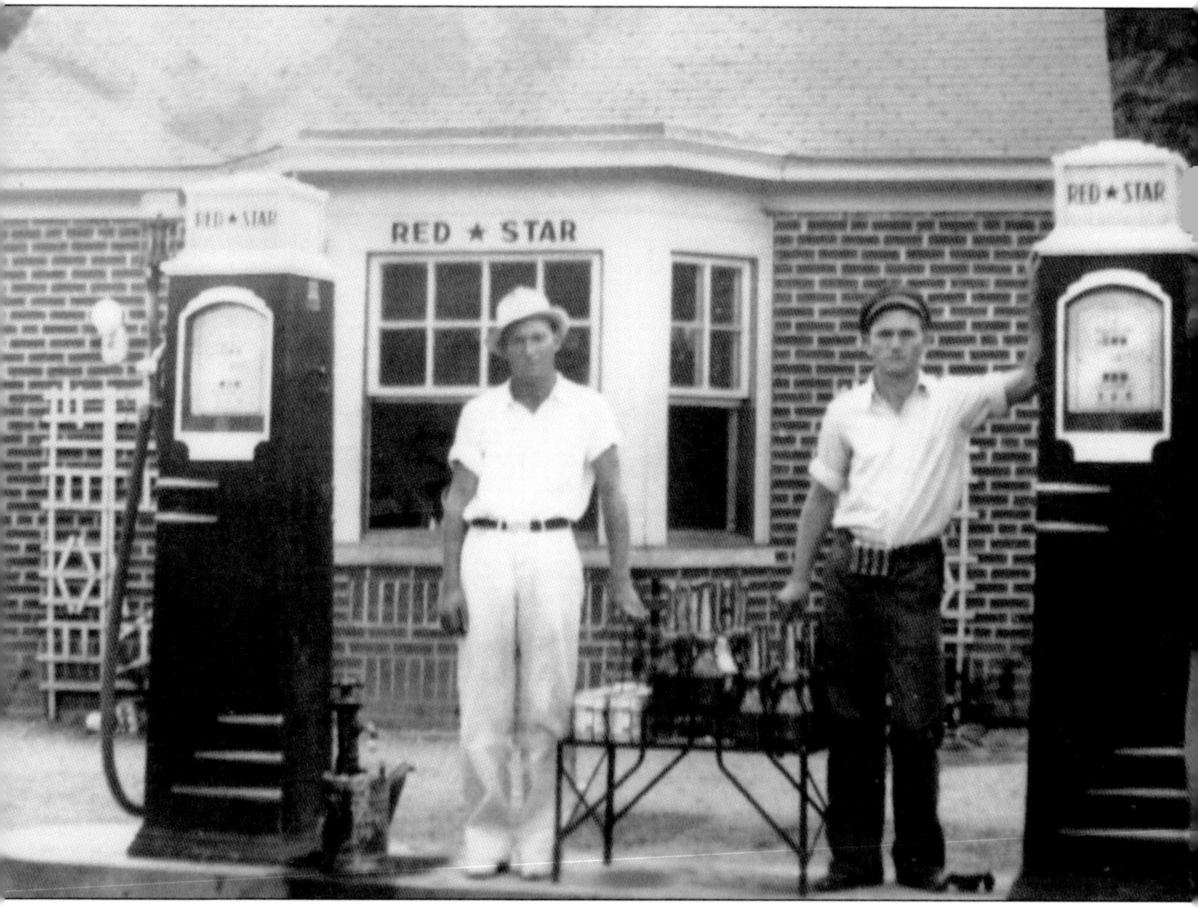

Red Star Service Station. Located in Ripley, this "full-service" gas station was a favorite in the 1940s and 1950s.

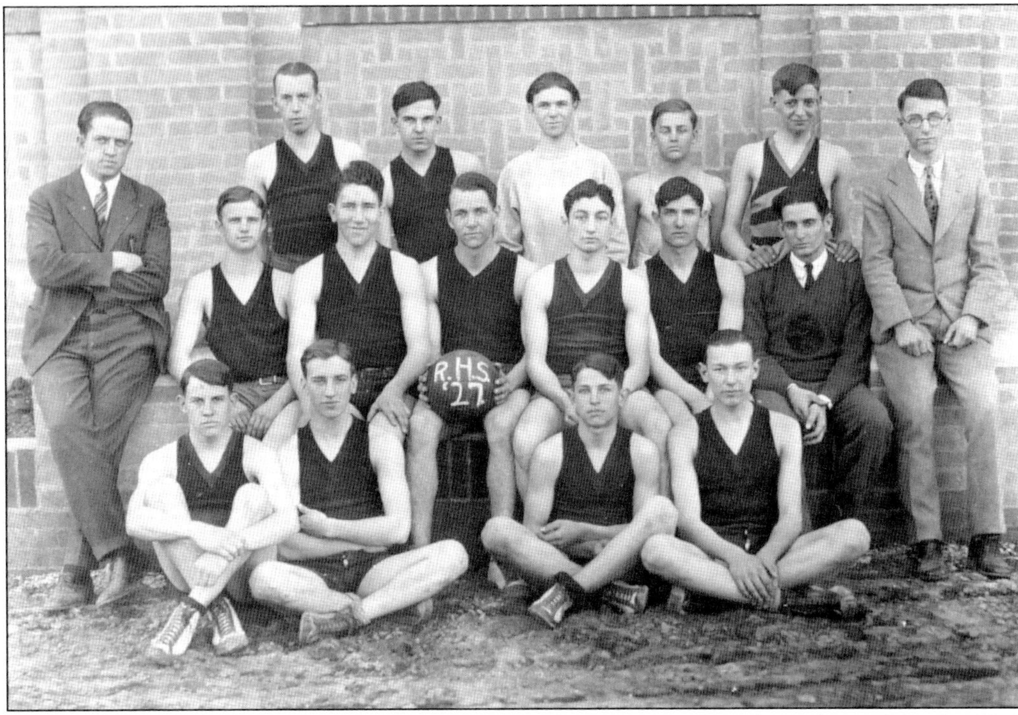

Boys' Basketball Team. This photograph depicts the team members from the 1927 Ripley High School basketball team.

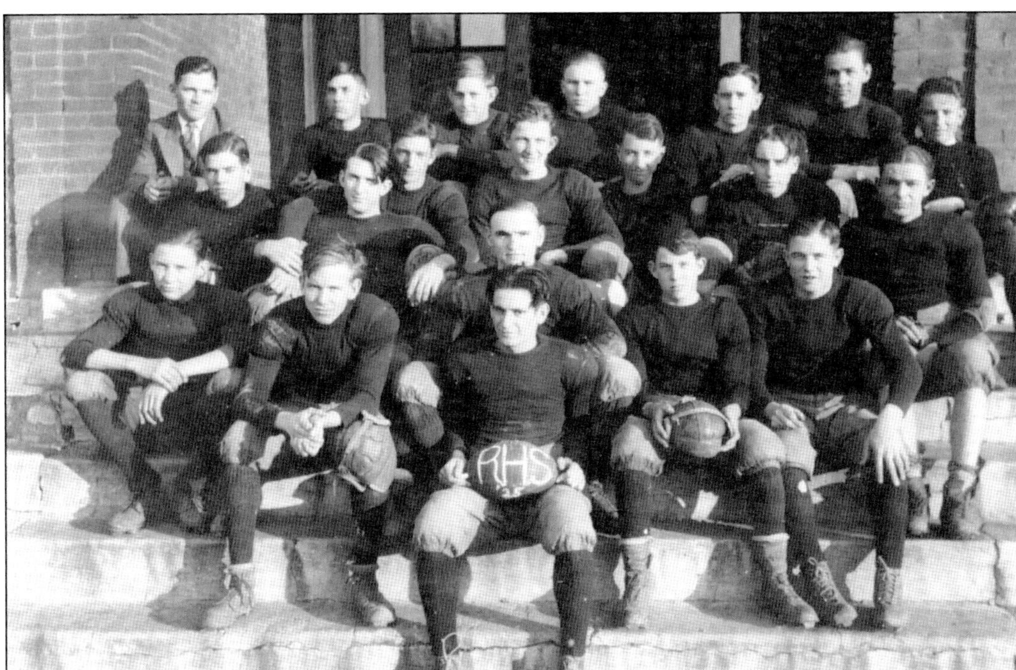

Football Team. This fine-looking group of young men represents the Ripley High School football team from 1925.

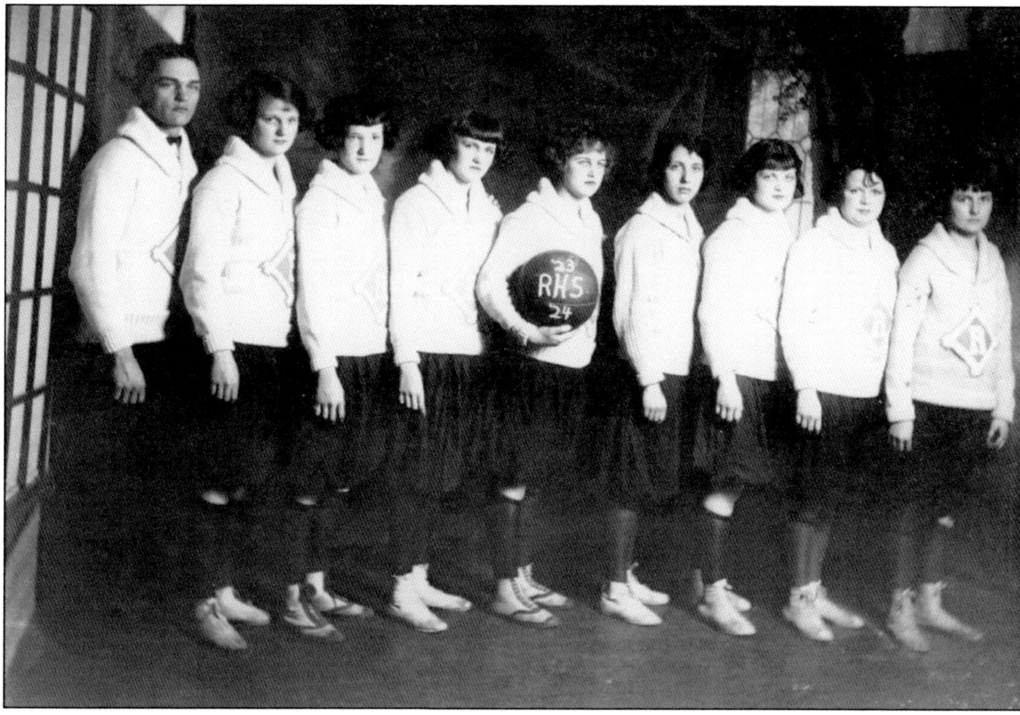

Basketball Team. Sporting their letter sweaters over their uniforms are the members of the 1924 Ripley High School basketball team.

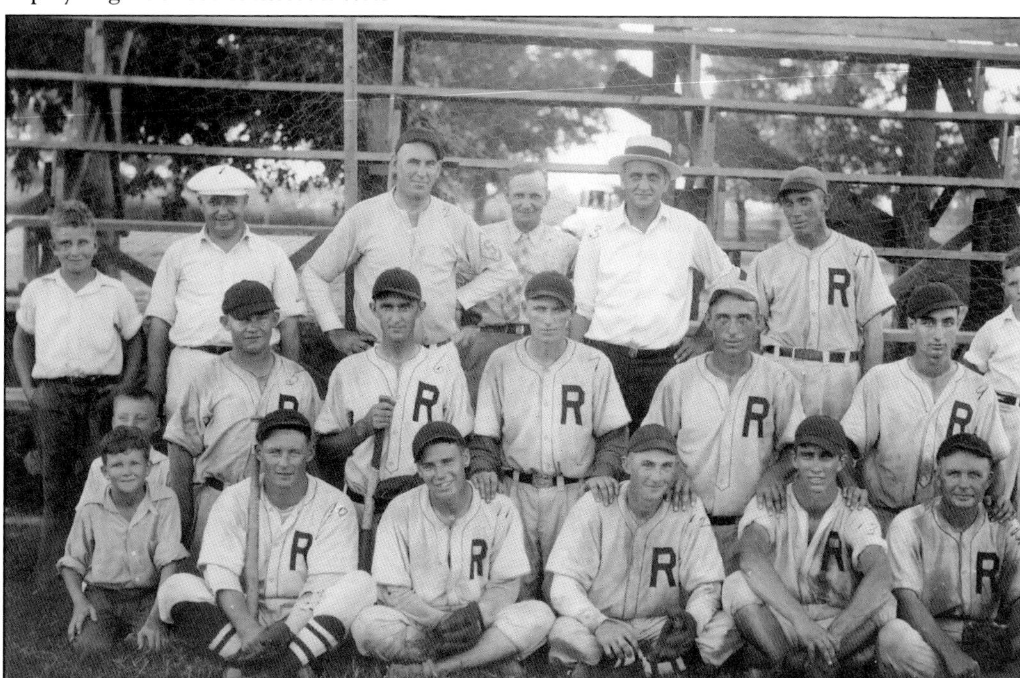

Ripley Baseball Team. Pictured with their coaches and ball boys are the members of the 1933 Ripley baseball team.

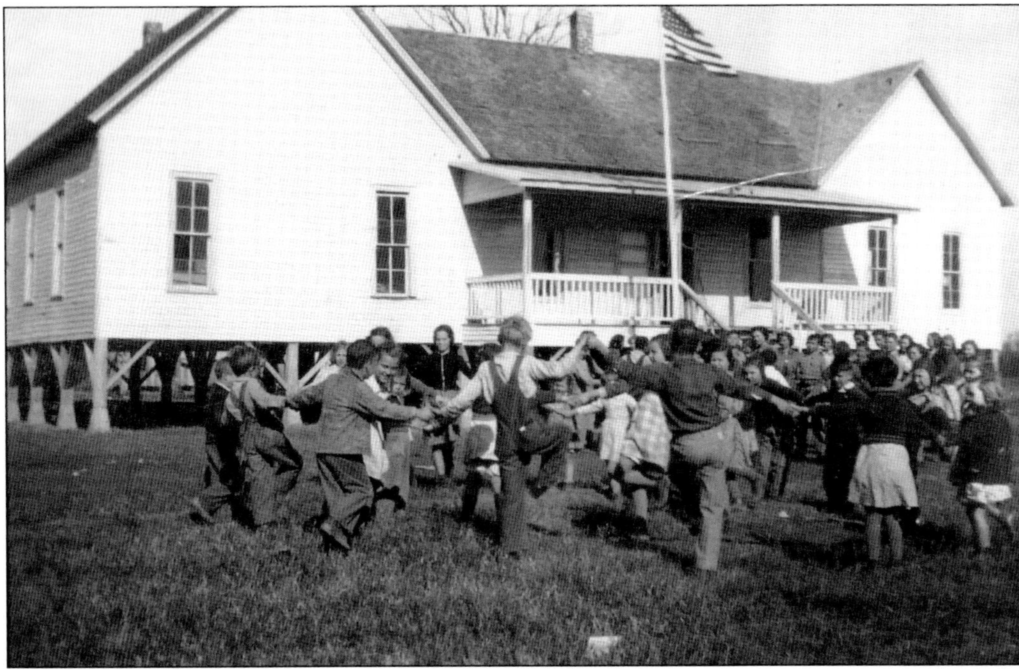

Ashport Community Schoolchildren in November 1939. Children are pictured playing a game of "Ring around the Rosey" in front of the Ashport School. (Courtesy of Rosie Lemons.)

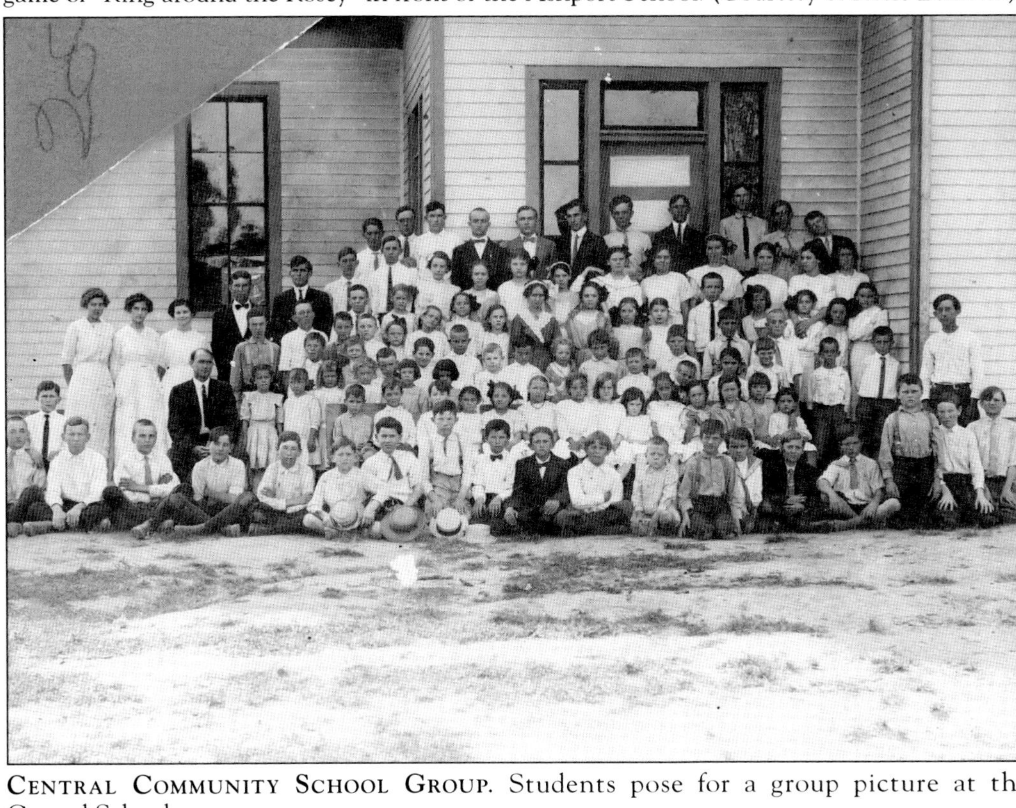

Central Community School Group. Students pose for a group picture at the Central School.

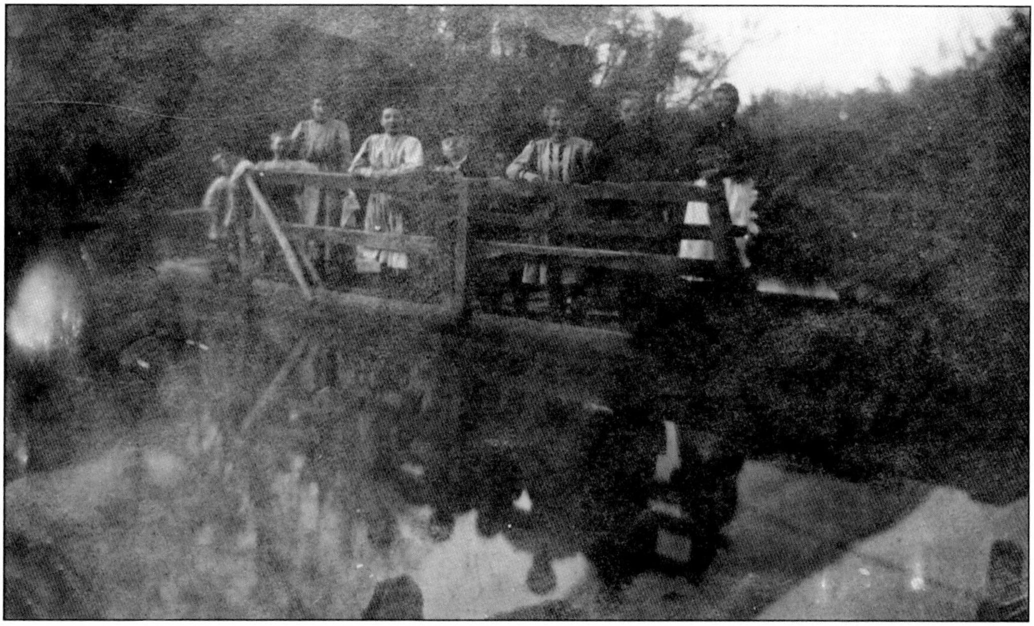

FERRY BOAT AT BUFFALO HOLE. Buffalo Hole is located on Old River near Chisholm Lake. Pictures on pages 73–77 show a family camping trip at Buffalo Hole. The trip was about two to three weeks long, and families took large tents, cook stoves, beds, mosquito netting, and food of all kinds, including chickens in a coop and the family milk cow. They would hunt and fish and enjoy the great outdoors. (Courtesy of Joyce Henson.)

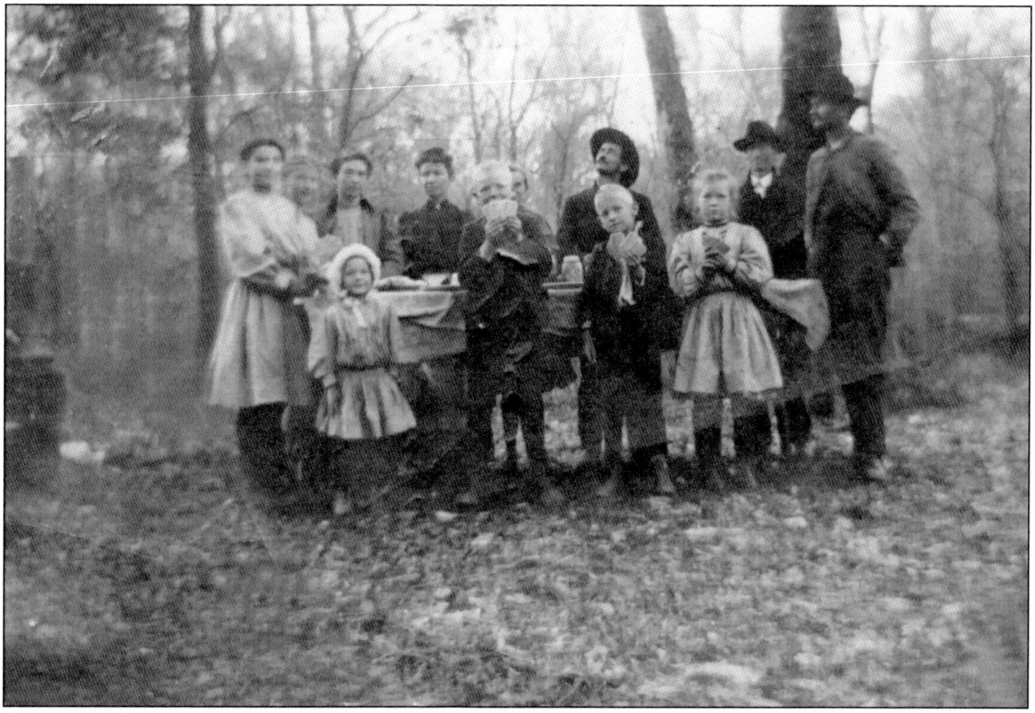

CHILDREN PLAYING CARDS. Pictured are the Chambers and Arwood children playing cards while camping at Buffalo Hole on Old River. (Courtesy of Joyce Henson.)

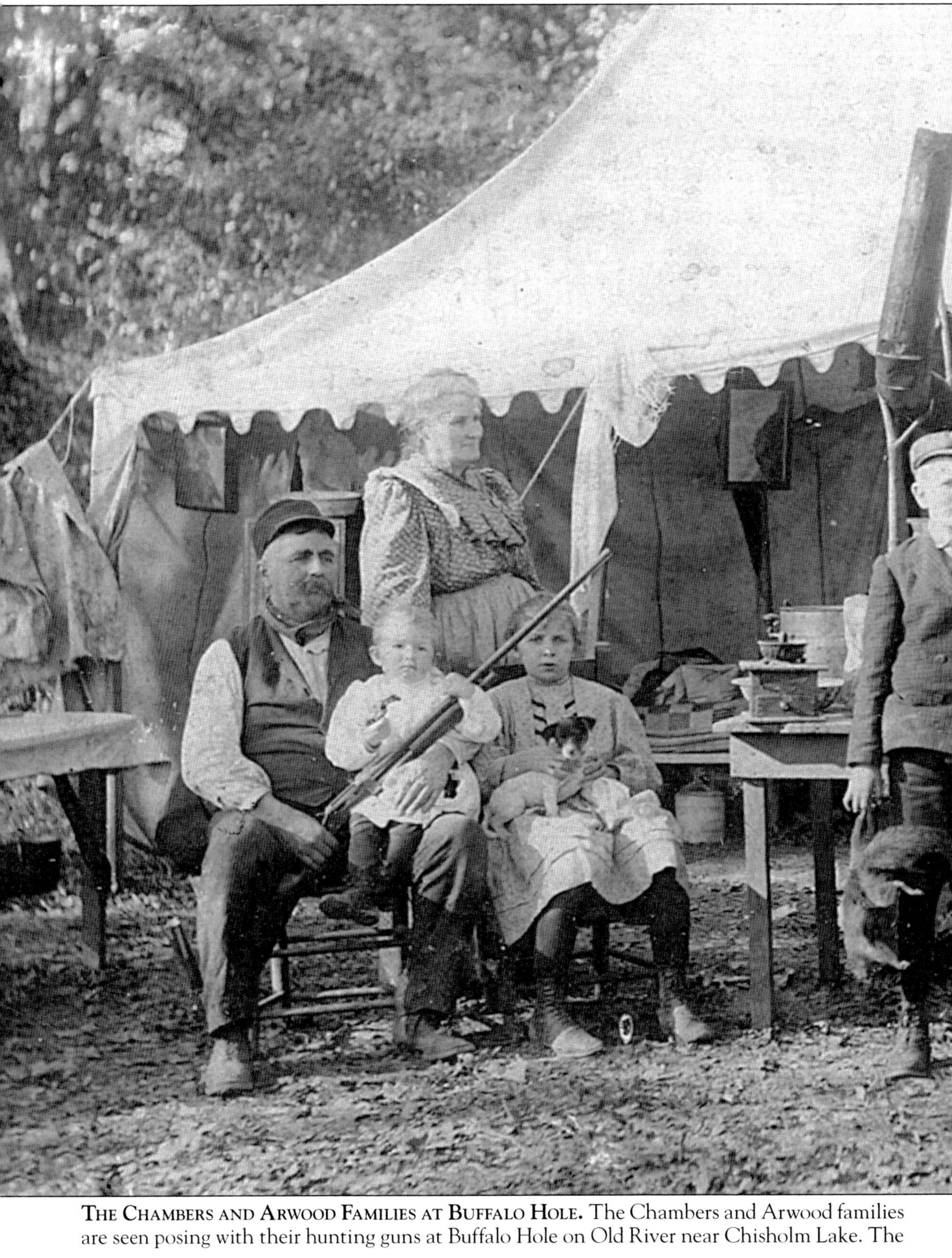

The Chambers and Arwood Families at Buffalo Hole. The Chambers and Arwood families are seen posing with their hunting guns at Buffalo Hole on Old River near Chisholm Lake. The

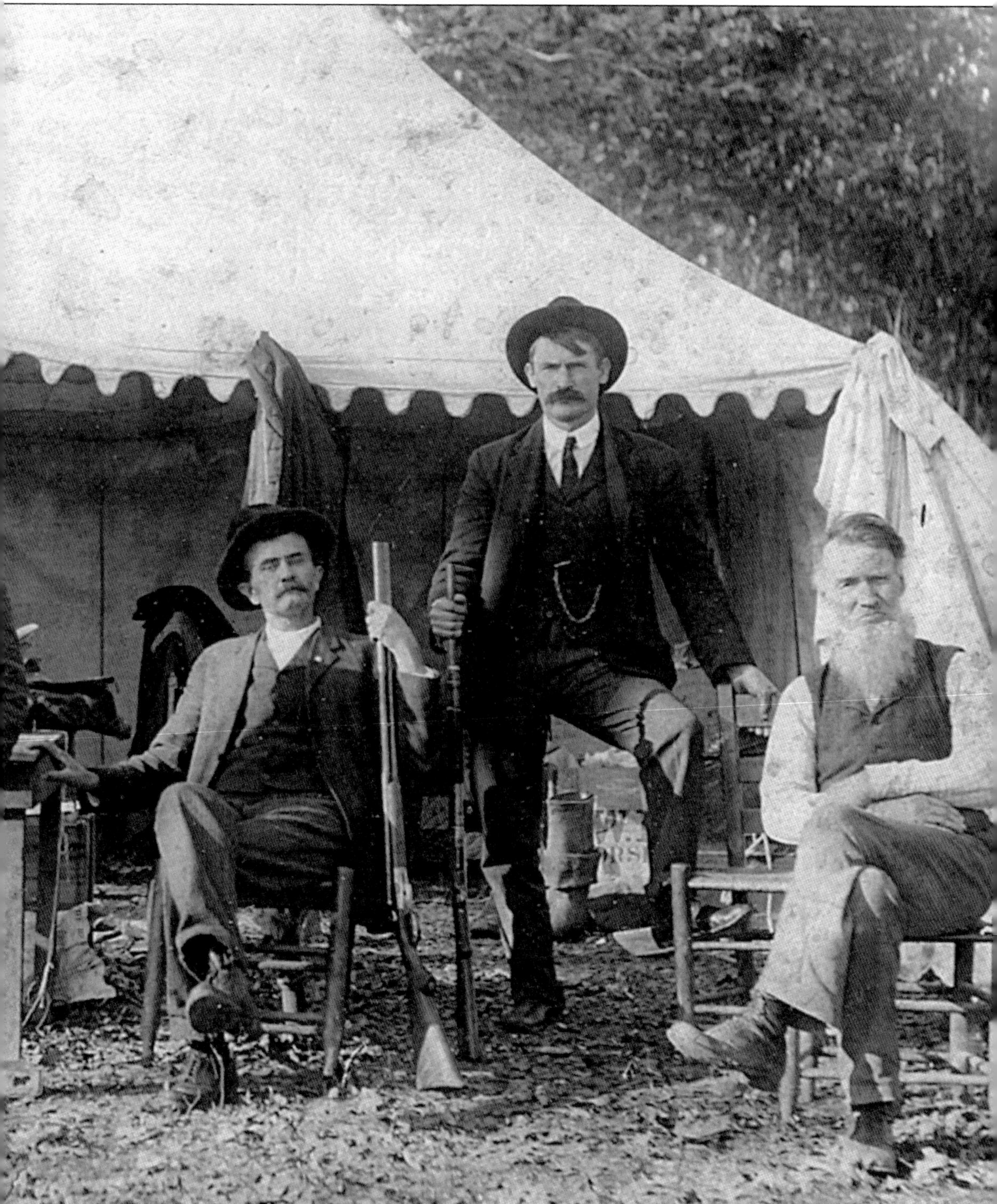

boy at center holds a squirrel from a hunt. (Courtesy of Joyce Henson.)

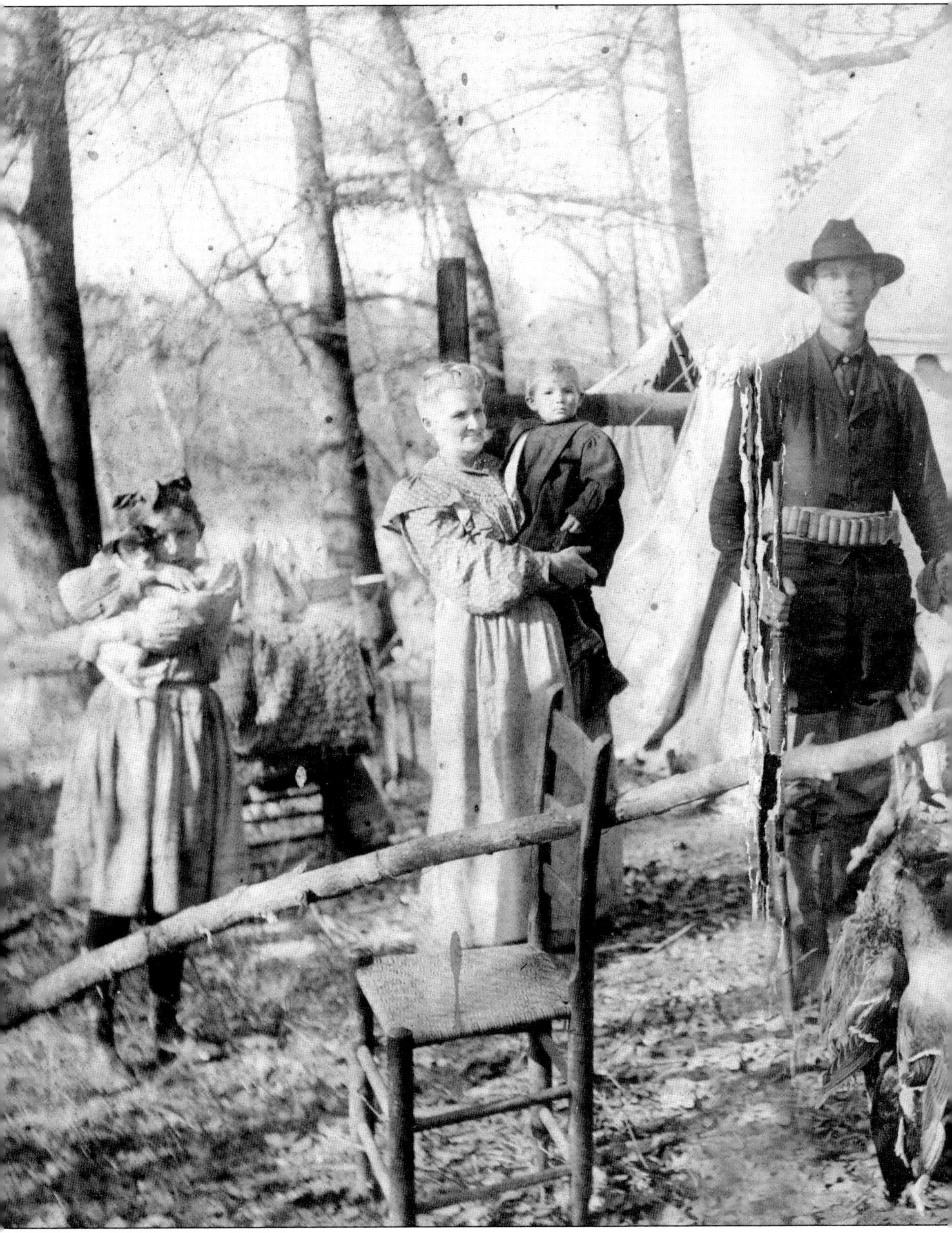

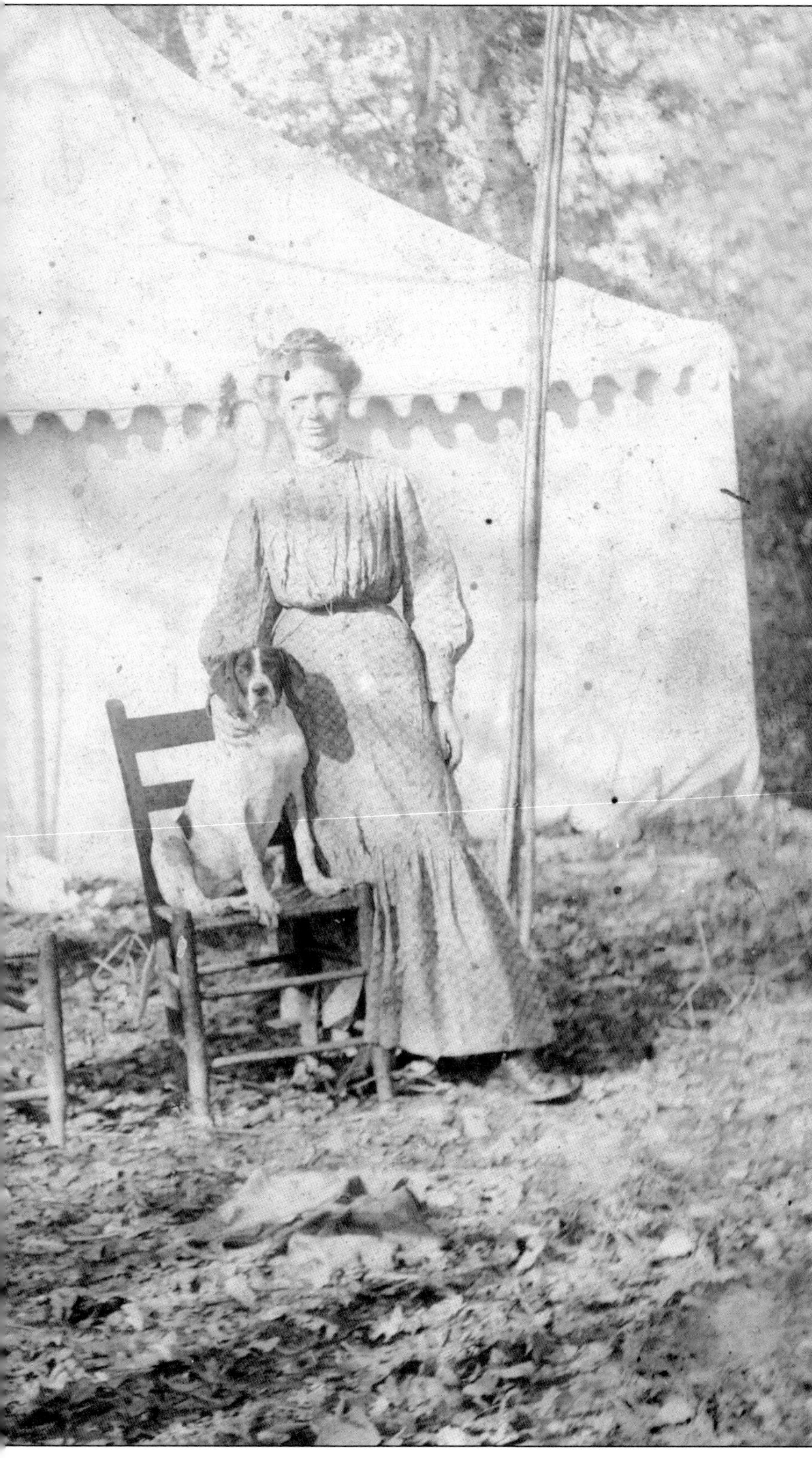

Camping and Hunting at Buffalo Hole. Pictured at far right are Ada and Fletcher Lusk. Notice the geese on the pole in front of the picture and hunting dogs sitting on chairs. (Courtesy of Joyce Henson.)

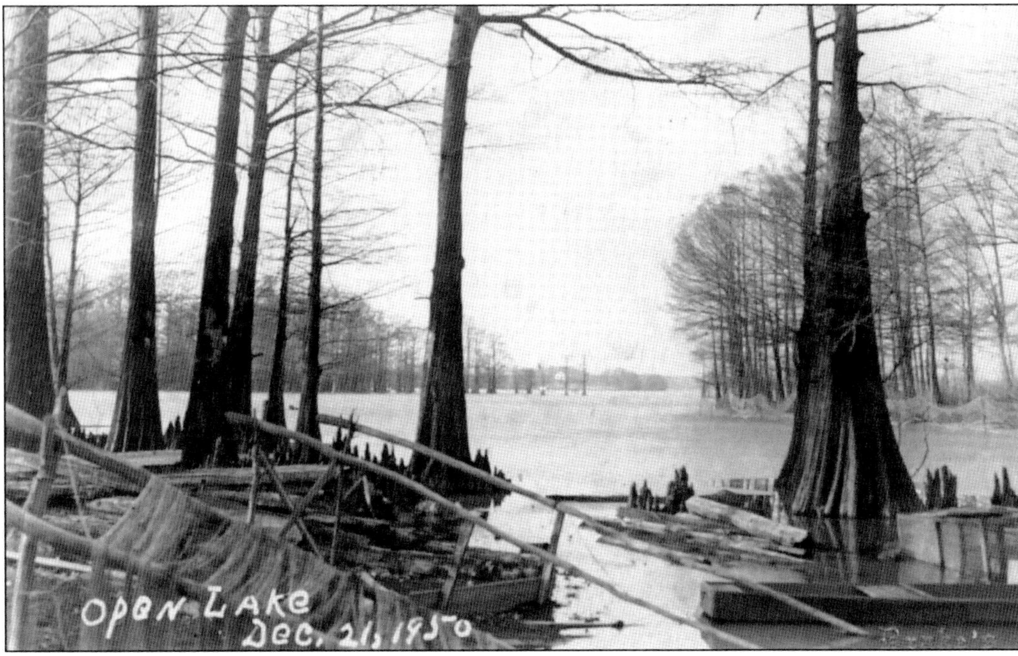

Open Lake, December 21, 1950. This scene shows picturesque Open Lake, a favorite spot in Lauderdale County to fish and duck hunt. It is now privately owned by club members. (Courtesy of Charly Cubine.)

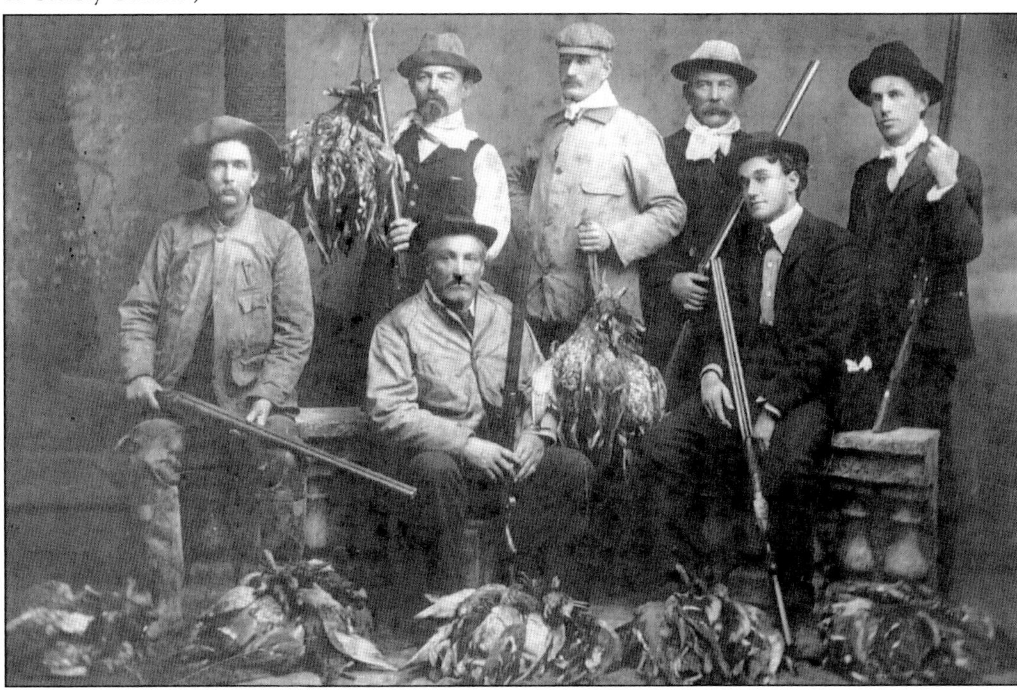

Duck Hunting on Open Lake. A group of duck hunters pose for this c. 1880 photograph with the day's kill of mallard and susie ducks from Open Lake. The only known person is H.B. Moorer (center, in the back row) of Henning. This group hunted with the Little Lake Hunting Club. (Courtesy of Emily Suggs.)

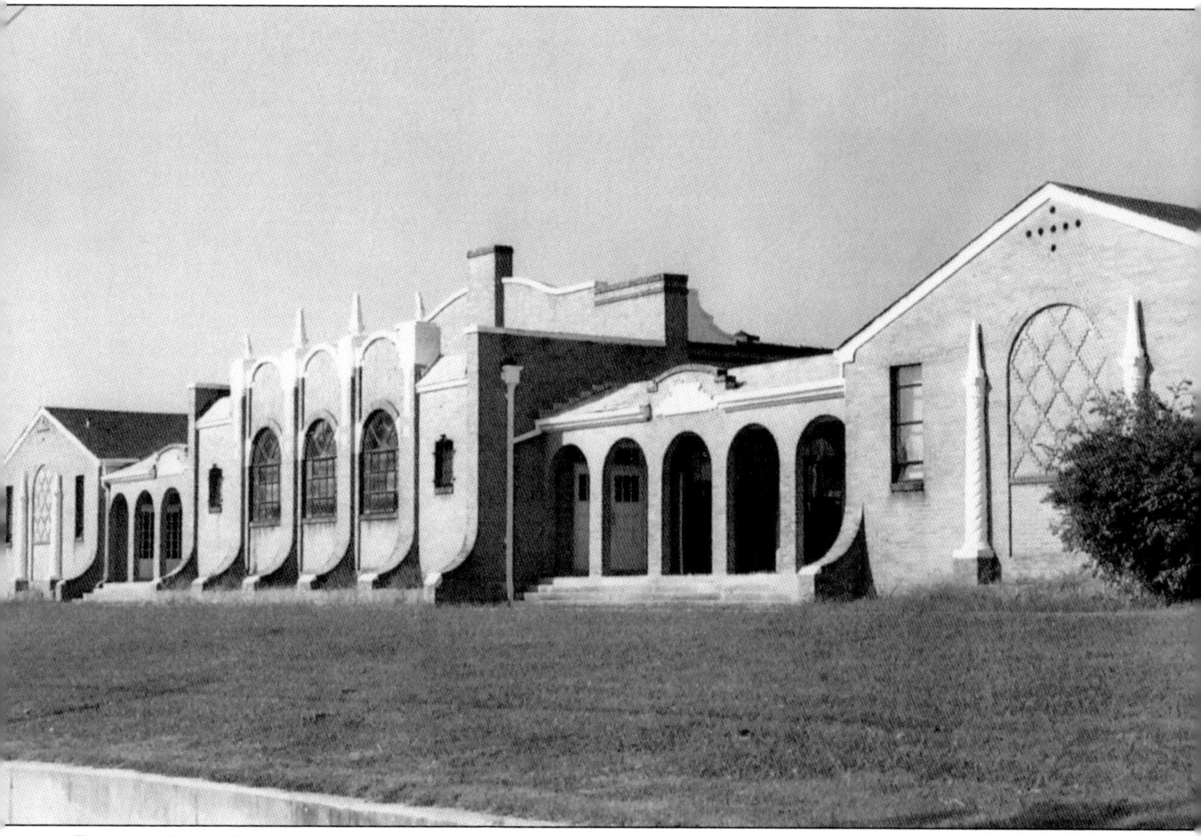

Ripley High School. Built in 1926, this school had already chartered a Beta Club and new coach Irvin "Tiny" Knee had started a football and track program by 1927. (Courtesy of Evelyn Stewart.)

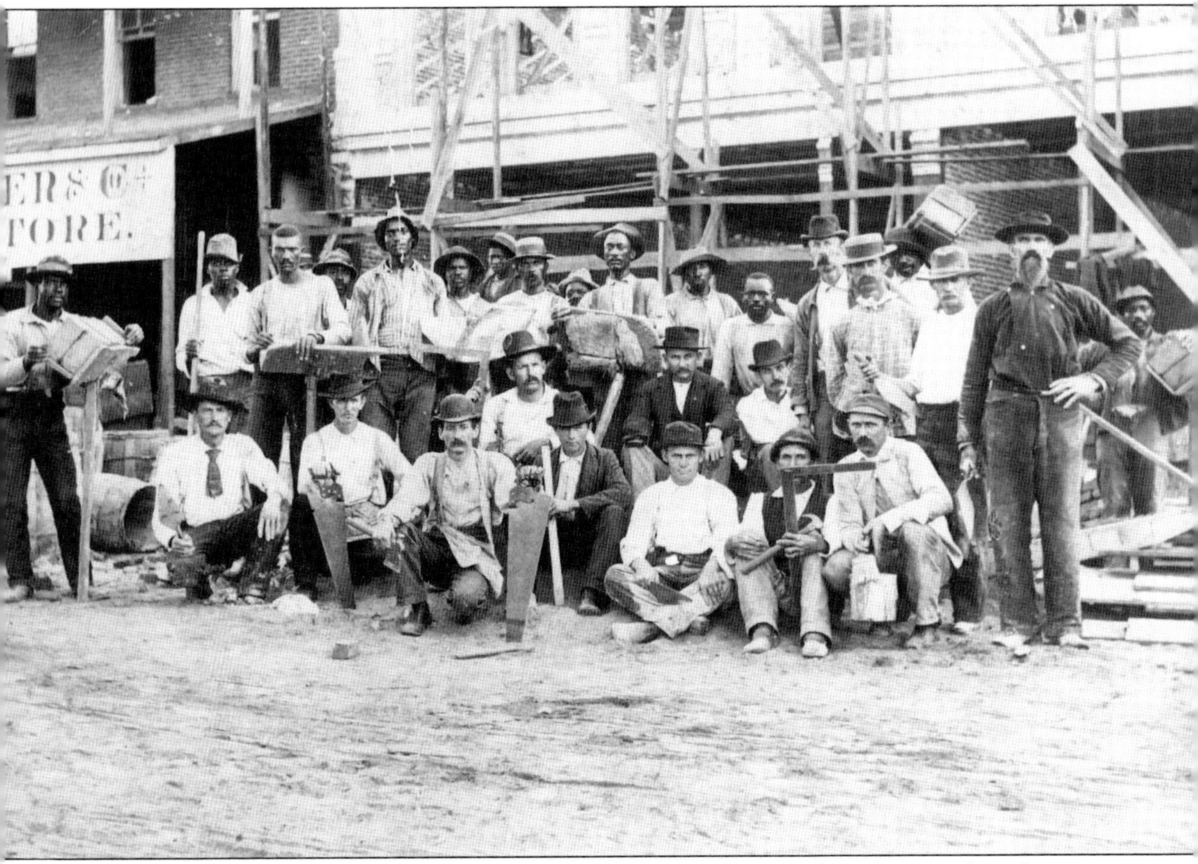

Construction Workers in Ripley. Workers, with their tools, pause for a photograph in downtown Ripley. Construction was in progress on the Maurice Miller & Company Store and William Tucker's buildings on the east side of the square.

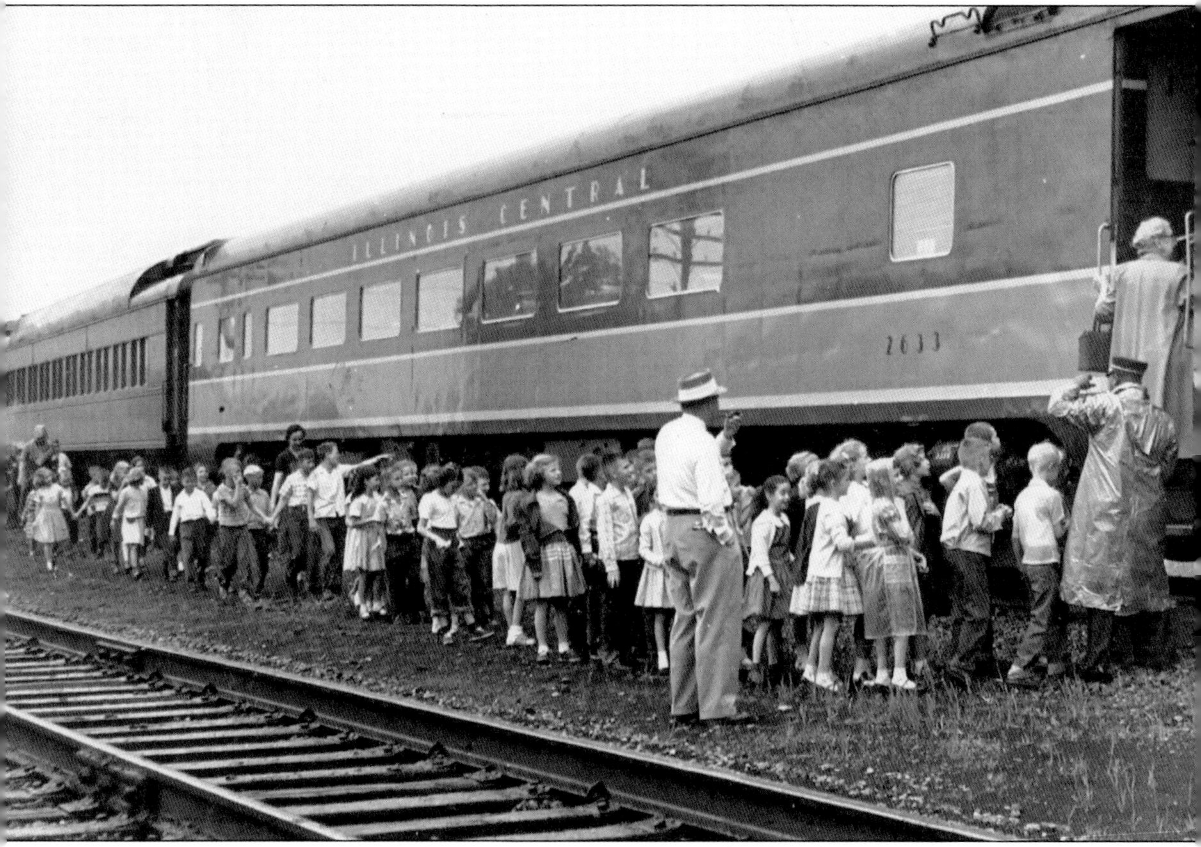

SCHOOLCHILDREN BOARDING A TRAIN. Ripley Grammar School students are seen boarding an Illinois Central Train in Ripley. The field trip took them to Dyersburg and back in 1955. The teacher on the steps of the train car is Kathleen Givens. (Courtesy of Terry Ford.)

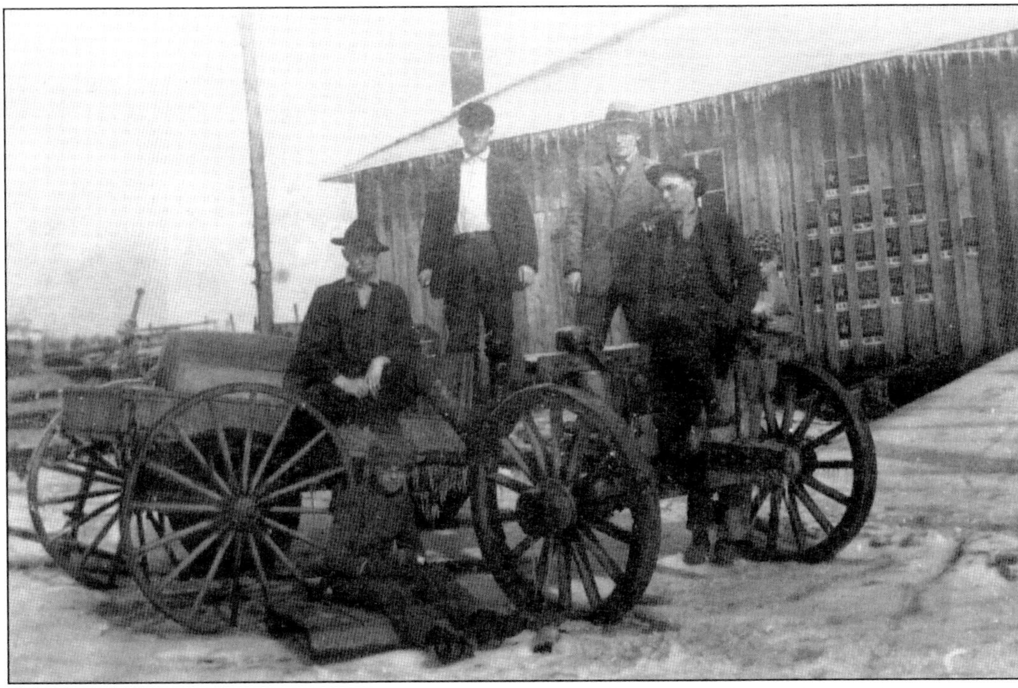

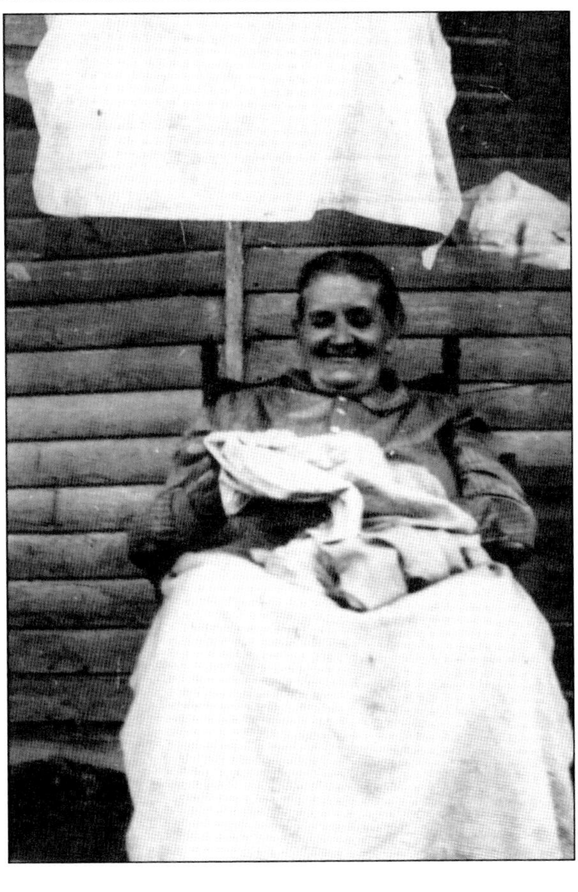

CHAMBERS FARM SCENE. Family members are seen posing with equipment on a winter day in the Edith community. All family members worked hard and played hard. They raised farm animals and a large vegetable garden for their food. They worked in the fields, worshipped together, and remained close-knit families in their small communities. (Courtesy of Joyce Henson.)

MATT SANFORD. Mrs. Sanford spends a few relaxing moments doing hand stitch work in the Central Community in 1919. (Courtesy of Joyce Henson.)

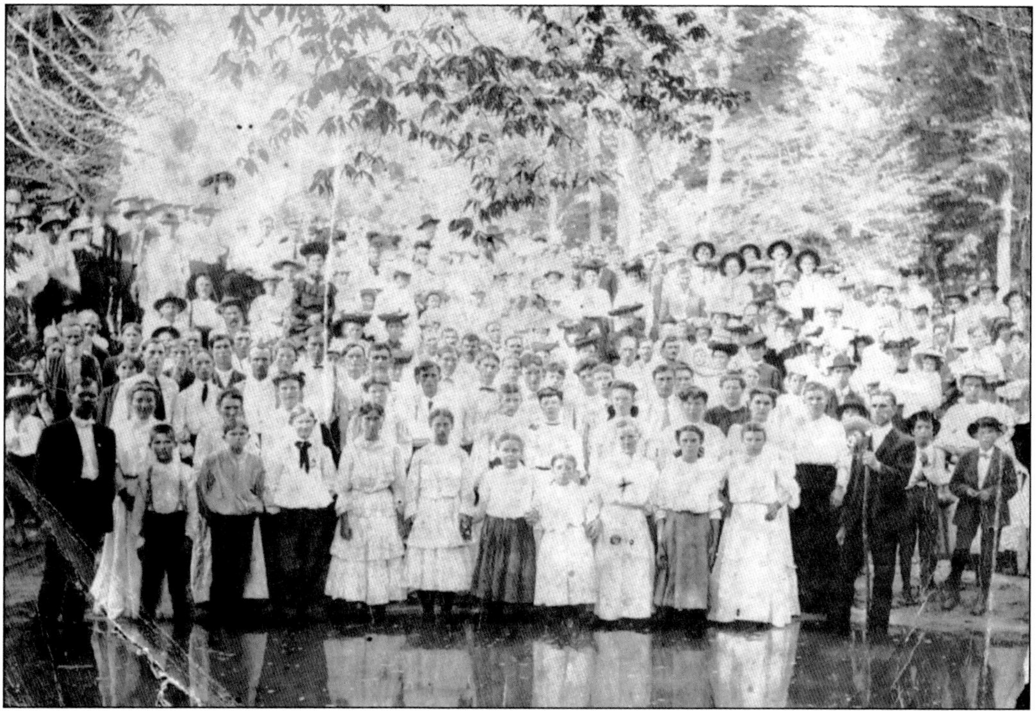

Church Baptism Group. A large group attends and participates in a baptism in Lauderdale County.

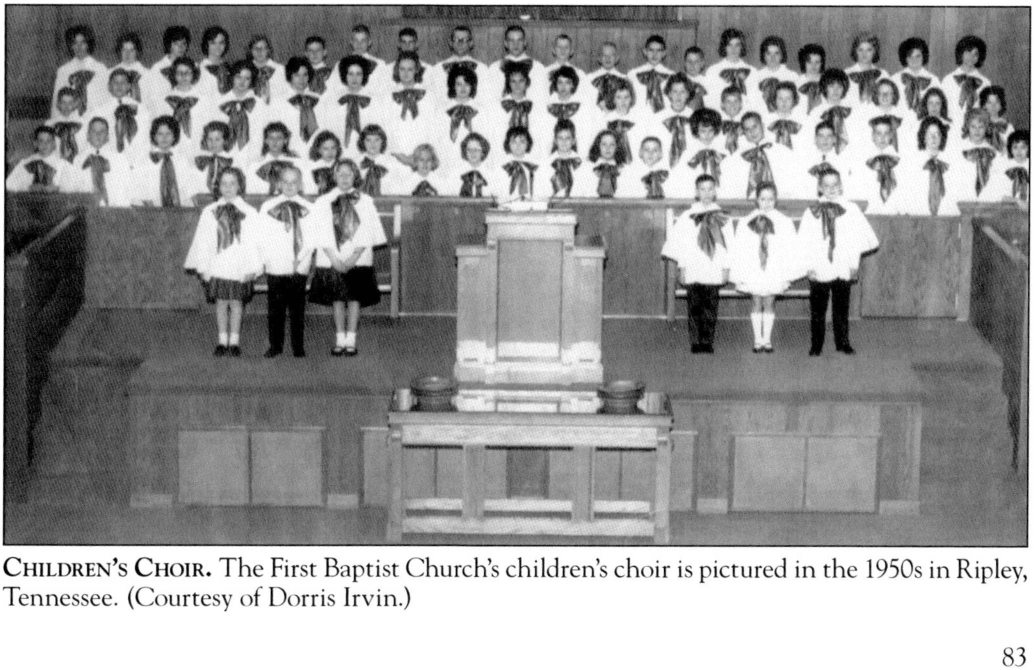

Children's Choir. The First Baptist Church's children's choir is pictured in the 1950s in Ripley, Tennessee. (Courtesy of Dorris Irvin.)

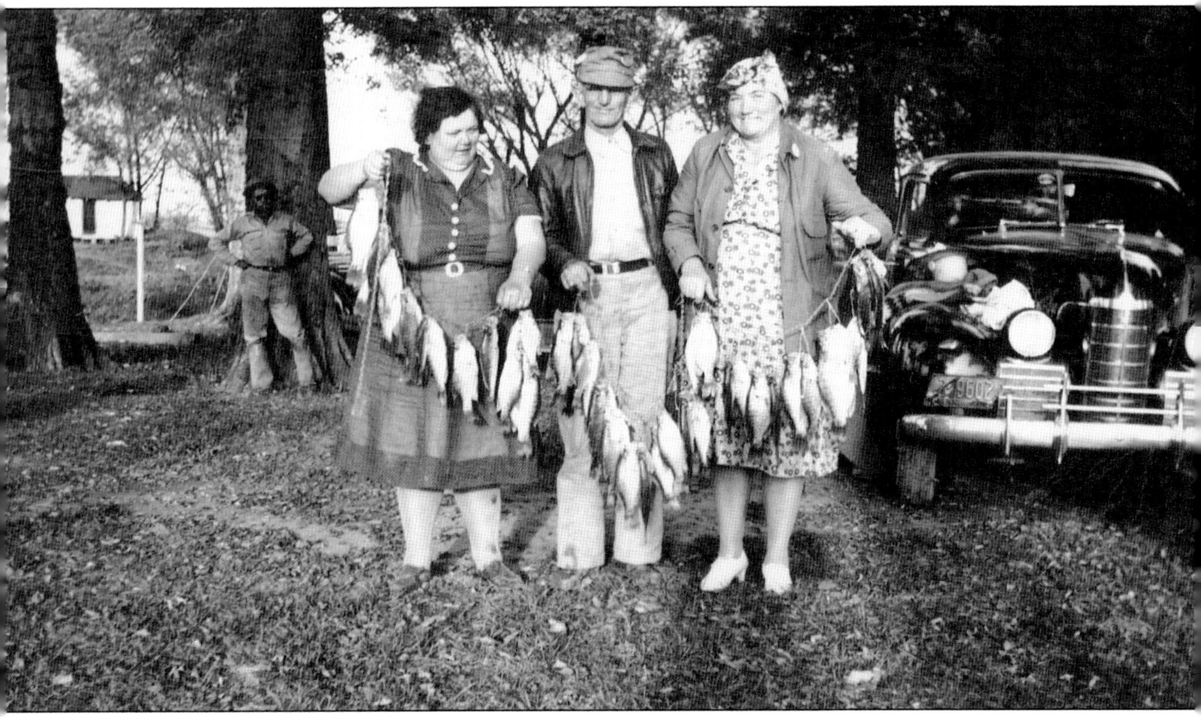

CRAPPIE CAUGHT AT OPEN LAKE. This group of guests, after renting a wooden boat and paying a small fee, has a fine string of crappie fish caught in beautiful Open Lake in the 1950s. (Courtesy of Joyce Henson.)

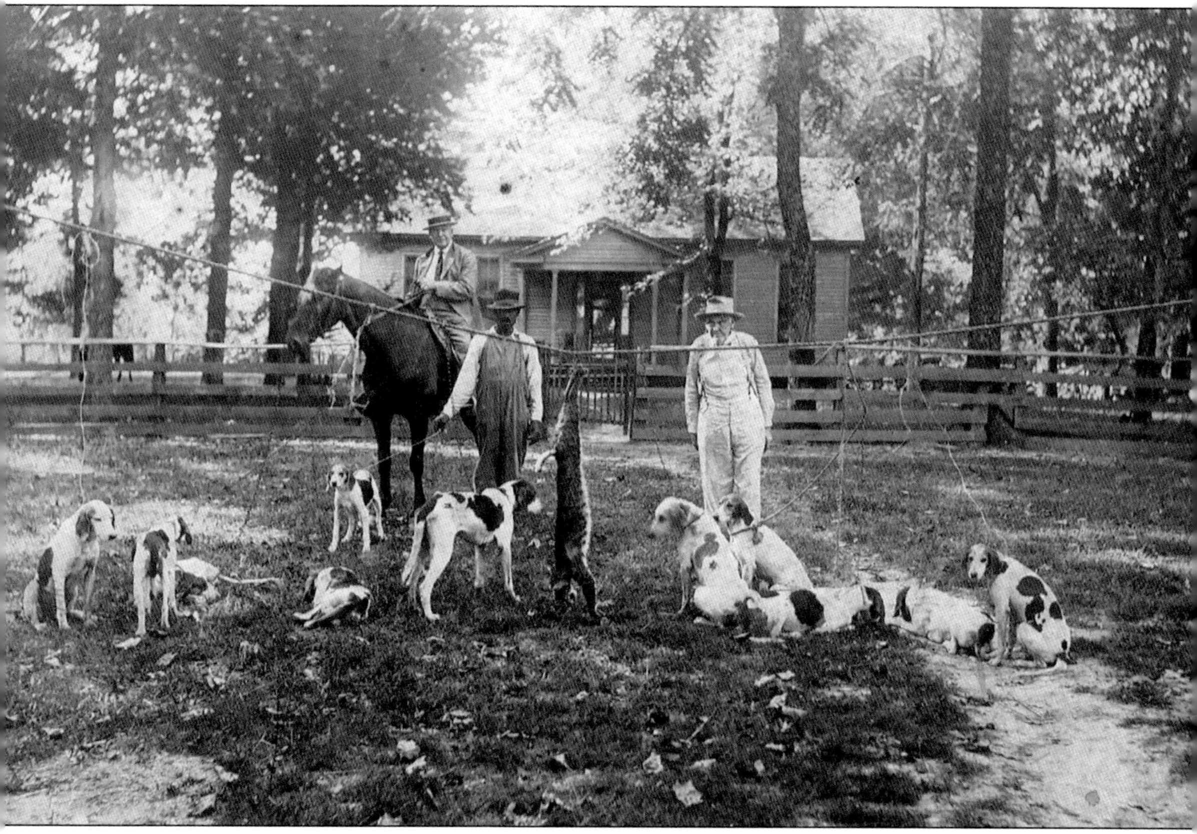

Walker Hounds Resting after a Hunt. These hounds are seen resting in front of Ed Sanford's home after a hunt in the Conner-Marys Chapel community. A large bobcat is suspended from the rope line. (Courtesy of Tom Scott Jr.)

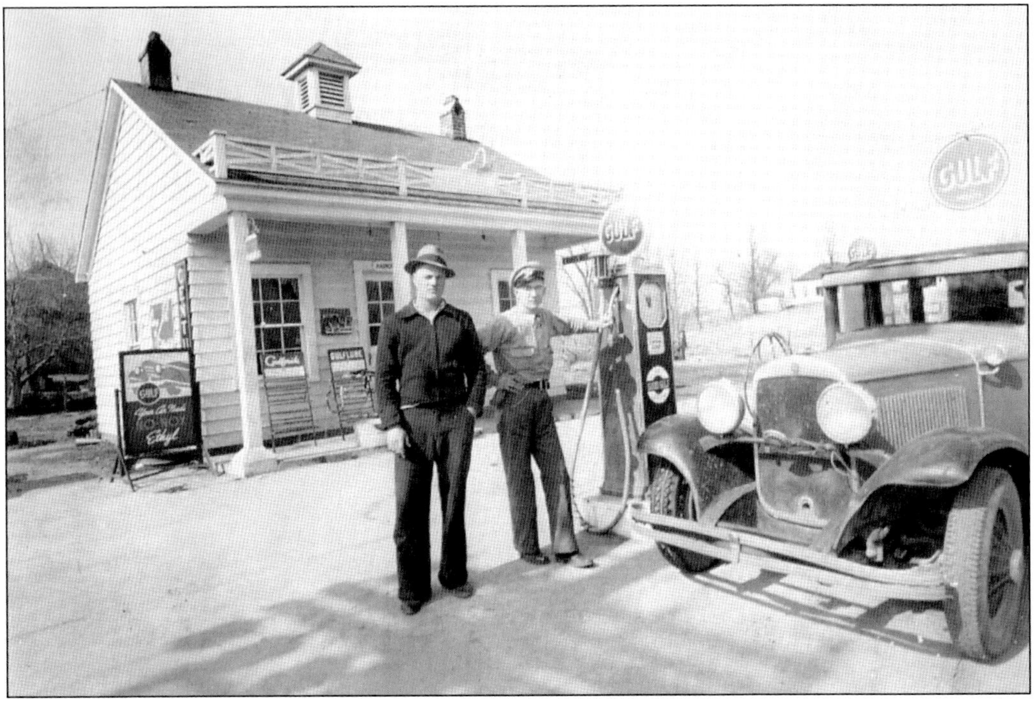

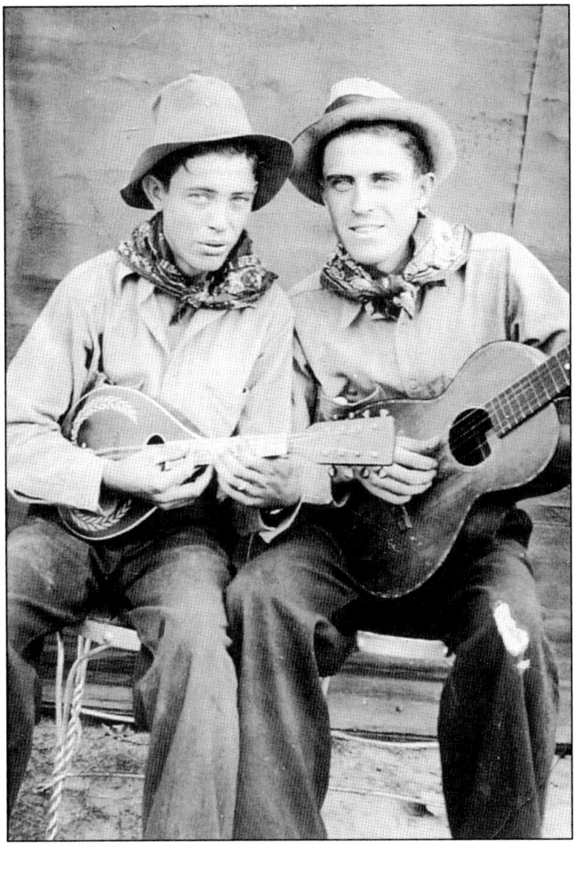

GULF OIL SERVICE STATION, 1940. Pictured are, from left to right, Willis Powell and Harmon Burks (owner) in Henning, Tennessee. (Courtesy of Margie Glenn.)

MAKING MUSIC IN HALLS. Two young men are pictured with their instruments in Halls, Tennessee. Tennessee was the birthplace of country string music, and Lauderdale County groups played for church events, Saturday night crowds, and for their families. The county is known for its gospel, blues, and country music. (Courtesy of Tommy Simmons.)

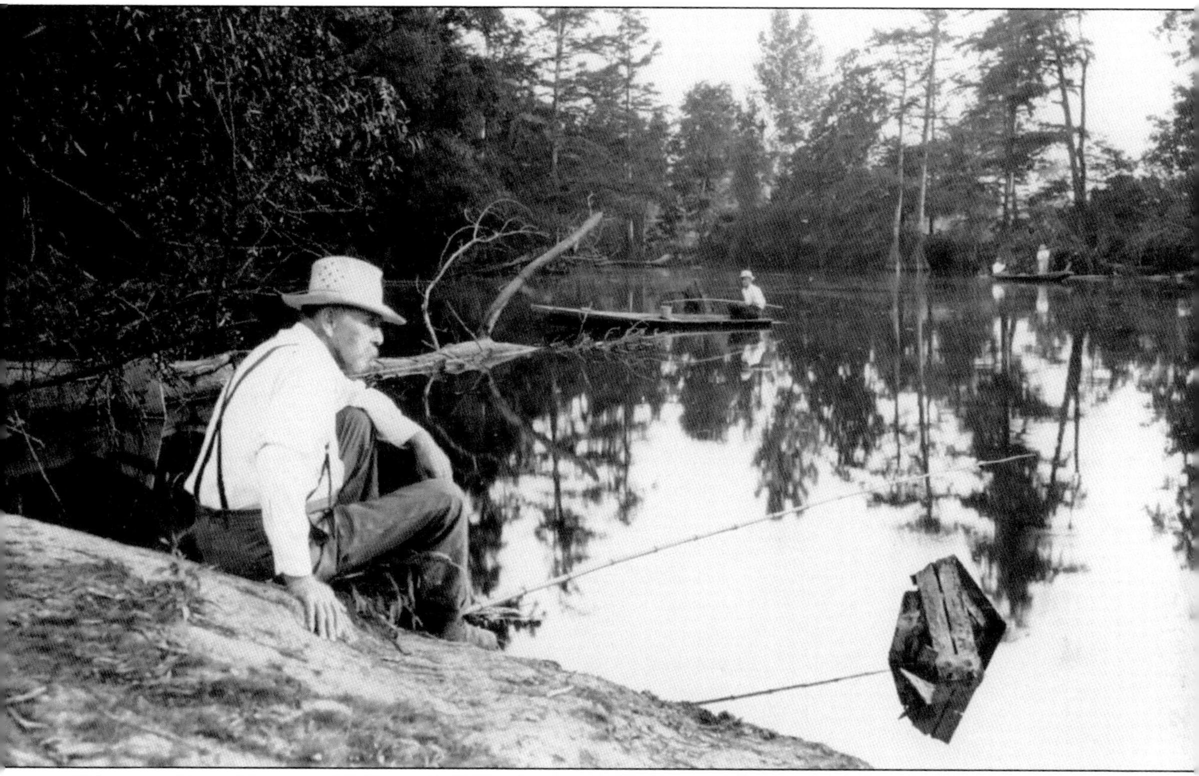

William Ball Drake. William Ball Drake is seen fishing and spending a day seated on the dirt bank of Cypress Hole, located near Open Lake in Lauderdale County, Tennessee. His day's catch probably consisted of bream, crappie, and catfish. (Courtesy of Tricia Drake.)

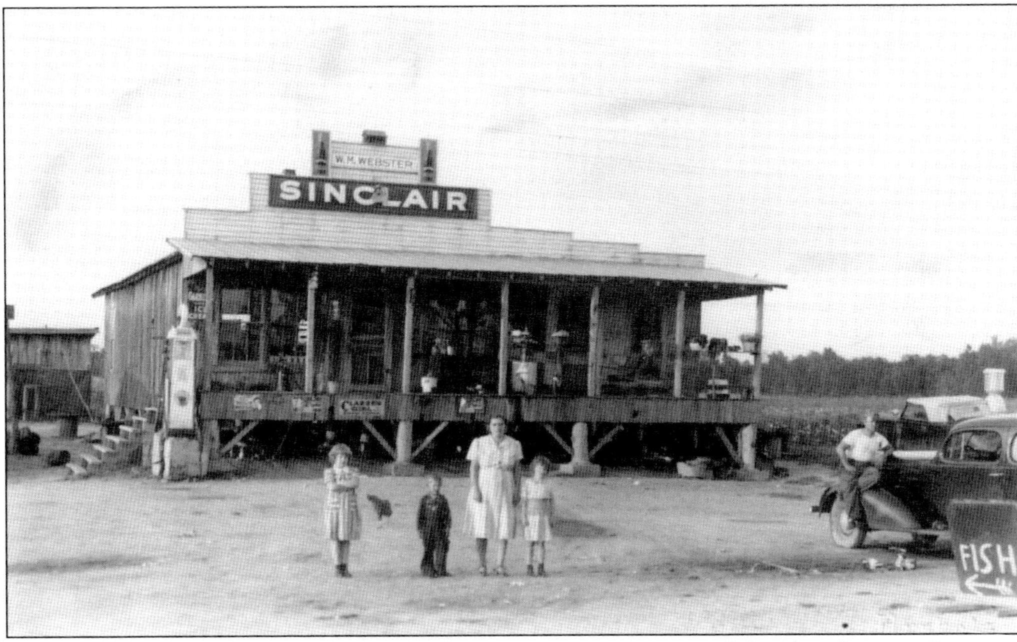

Webster's Grocery Store. William Webster's Grocery Store and Sinclair Service Station is pictured in the Ashport community in 1948. Pictured are, from left to right, Wanda, William, Dorothy, Linda, and W.M. Webster. Located near the Mississippi River, the sign in the bottom right-hand corner advertises fish for sale. (Courtesy of William Webster.)

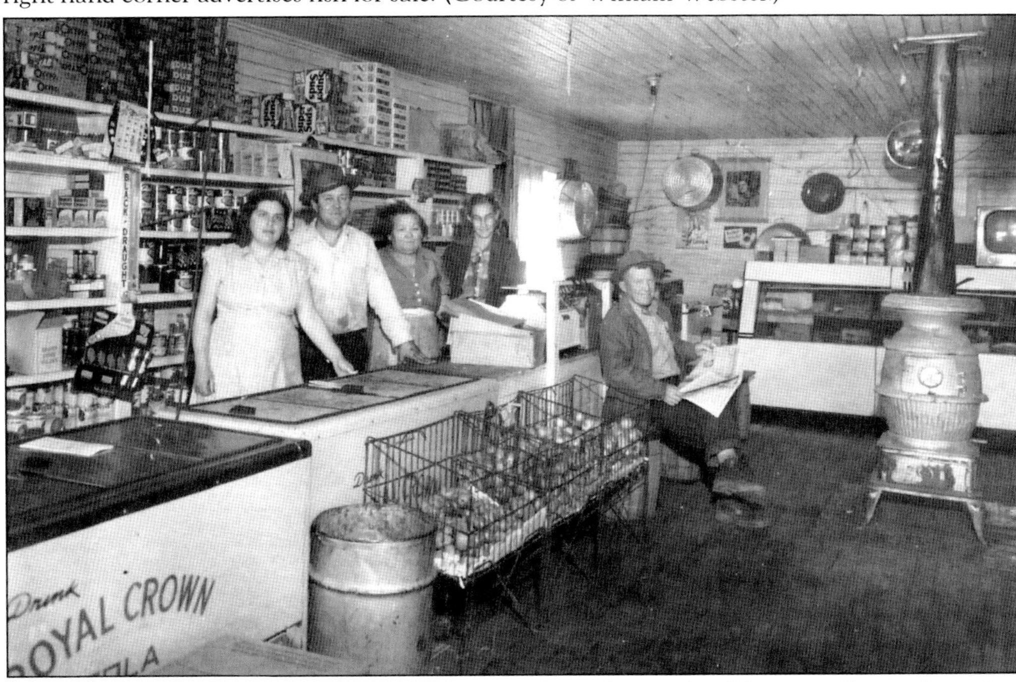

William Webster's Grocery Store. This scene shows the inside of the store. Pictured are, from left to right, Dorothy Webster, W.M. Webster, Zeffie Collins Webster, Annie Kirkpatrick, and Collie Osteen. Every small community had a grocery store. It was also a meeting place to share news of births and deaths and to discuss the crops and weather. (Courtesy of William Webster.)

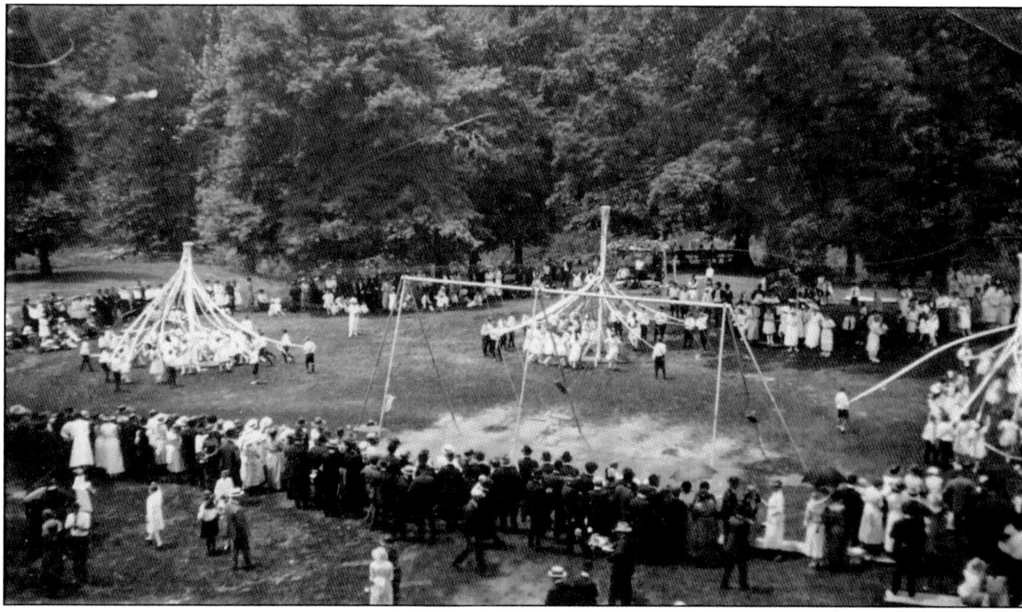

DANCING AROUND THE MAYPOLES. Ripley schoolchildren dance around the maypoles at the end of the school year. Children were awarded blue ribbons for meeting certain criteria in health, such as good nutrition and cleanliness. (Courtesy of Jenny Wren Nunn.)

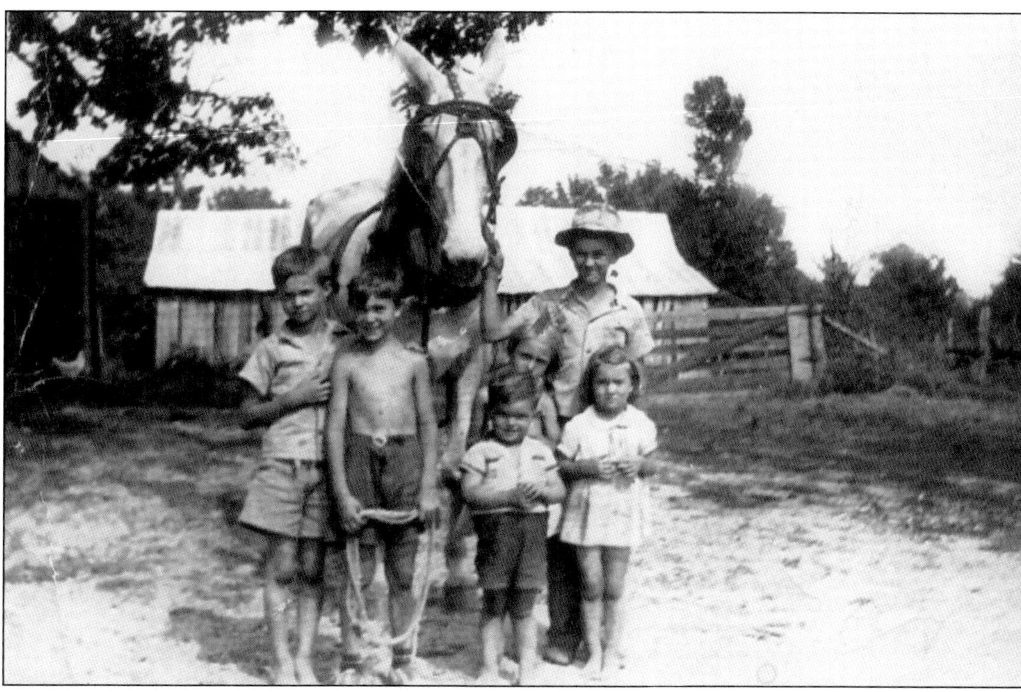

PLAYING AT NANKIPOO. These children are playing in the Nankipoo community in 1942. Pictured are, from left to right, Dudley Belton, Gene Olds, Lowell Tillman, Patsy Belton (partially hidden), Dotsy Olds, and Billy Olds (in rear). A summer day, an old mare, bare feet, and suntanned faces are all components of a wonderful childhood in Lauderdale County. (Courtesy of Carol Woodley.)

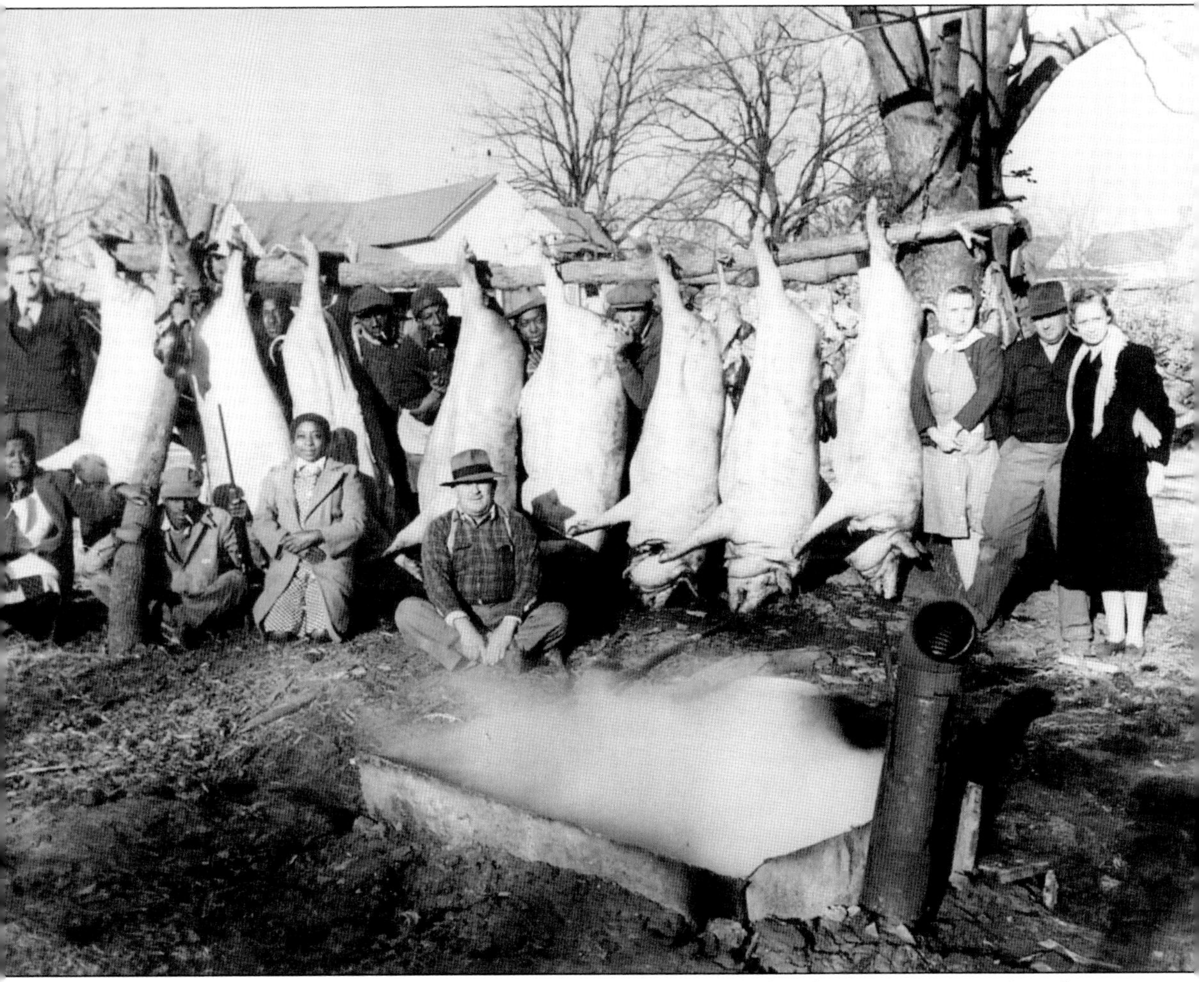

HENDERSON FAMILY WINTER HOG KILLING. Processing pork for their winter meat, Henderson family members in the Ashport community are pictured with workers. From left to right are (first row) Rose Johnson, unidentified, Gladys Walker, and Jap Henderson; (second row) Alvin Haynes, Albert Walker, unidentified, Leonard Mackaway, Richard Walker, Buck Bonds, Rosa Henderson, Guy Tucker Henderson, and Luvenia Henderson. (Courtesy of Beth Ables.)

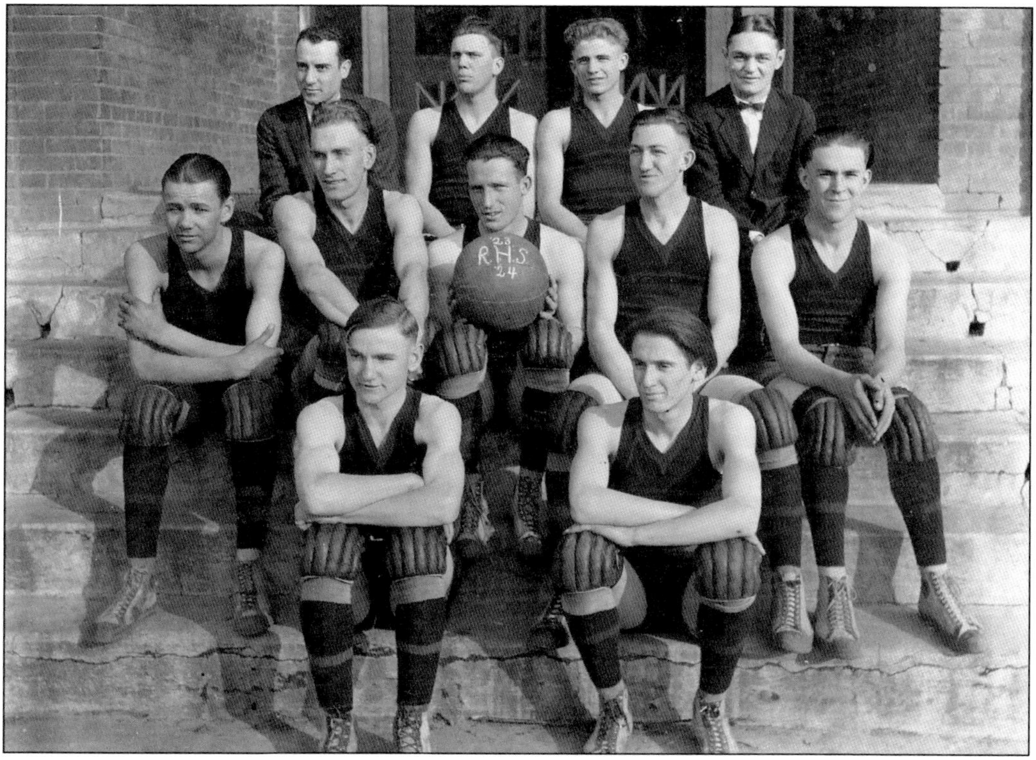

Basketball Team. This muscular group of young men played on the Ripley High School basketball team during the 1923–1924 school year. They are pictured with their coach.

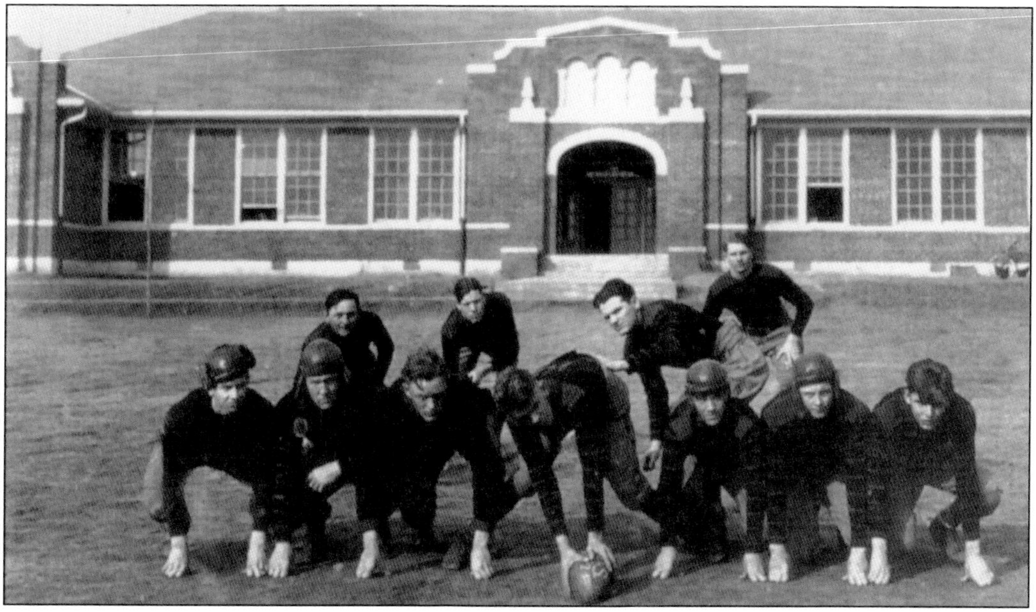

Halls High School Boys' Football Team, 1924. Pictured in front of the Halls High School are, from left to right, (first row) Laverne Jones, Reginal Scott, Jim Sumerlin, C.S. Whittaker, Lloyd Hart, Foster Moore, and Allen Massengill; (second row) Paul Jordan, Bill Sugg, Ellis Jordan, and Lloyd Hellen. (Courtesy of Tommy Simmons.)

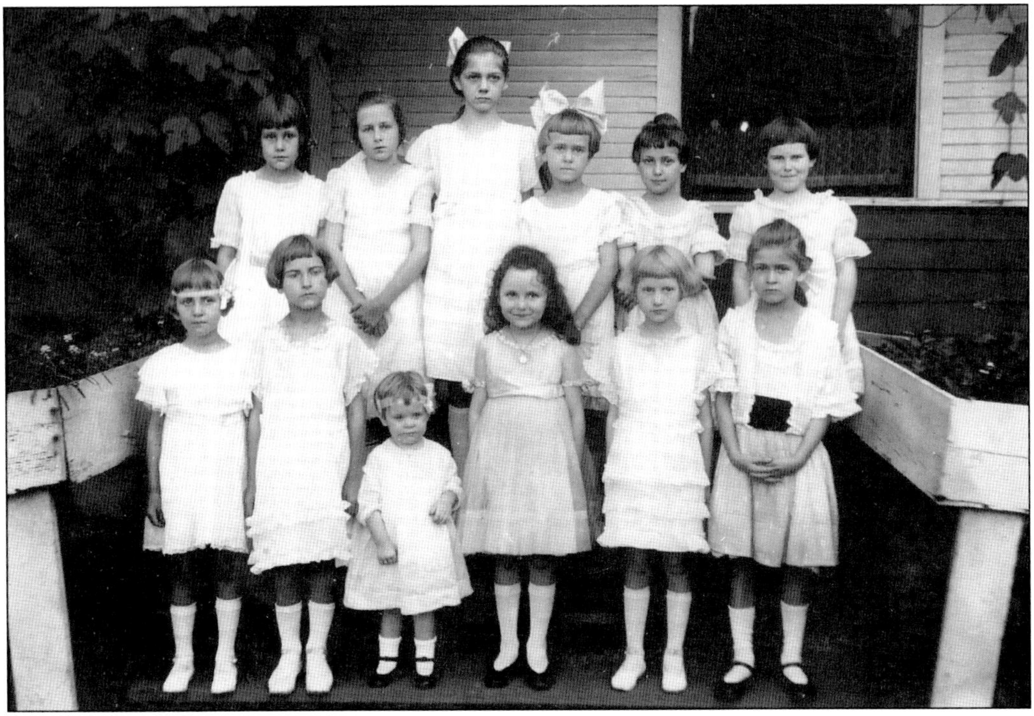

DOROTHY WALKER PALMER'S NINTH BIRTHDAY PARTY IN RIPLEY, 1921. Pictured are, from left to right, (first row) Ruth Carney, Genieve Tarrant, Mary Lou Johnson, Dorothy Walker, Evelyn Carney, and Nettie Johnson; (second row) Catherine Foust, Virginia Chapman, Marie Frances Bell, Elizabeth Miller, Dorothy White, and Rebecca Morris. (Courtesy of Terry Ford.)

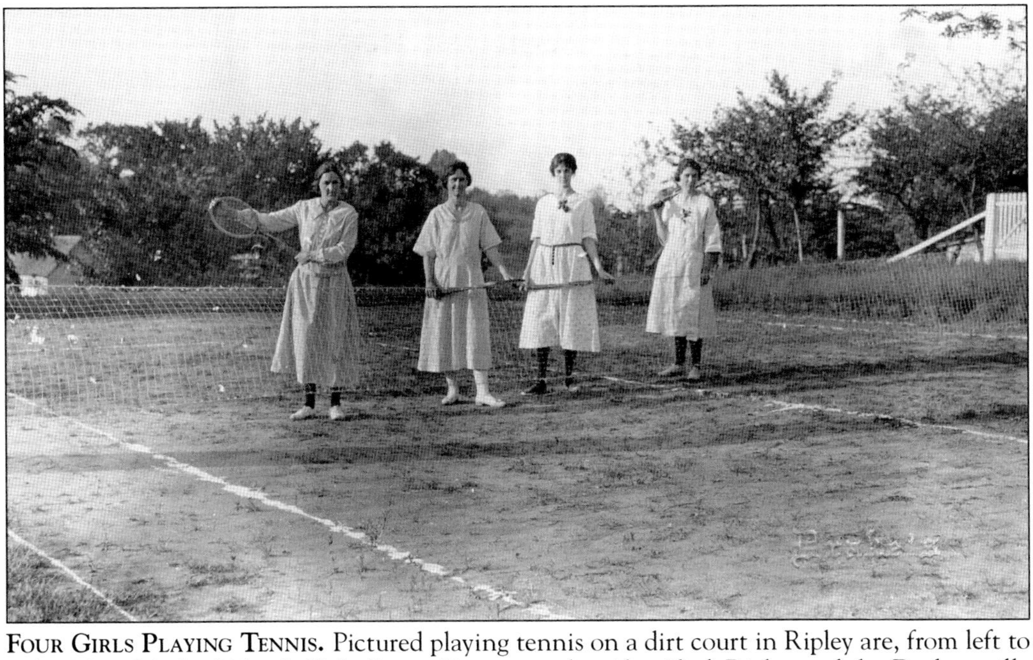

FOUR GIRLS PLAYING TENNIS. Pictured playing tennis on a dirt court in Ripley are, from left to right, Mary Mosby, Velmah Holt, Rivers Everett, and unidentified. Ripley and the Durhamville communities had private tennis courts. (Courtesy of Terry Ford.)

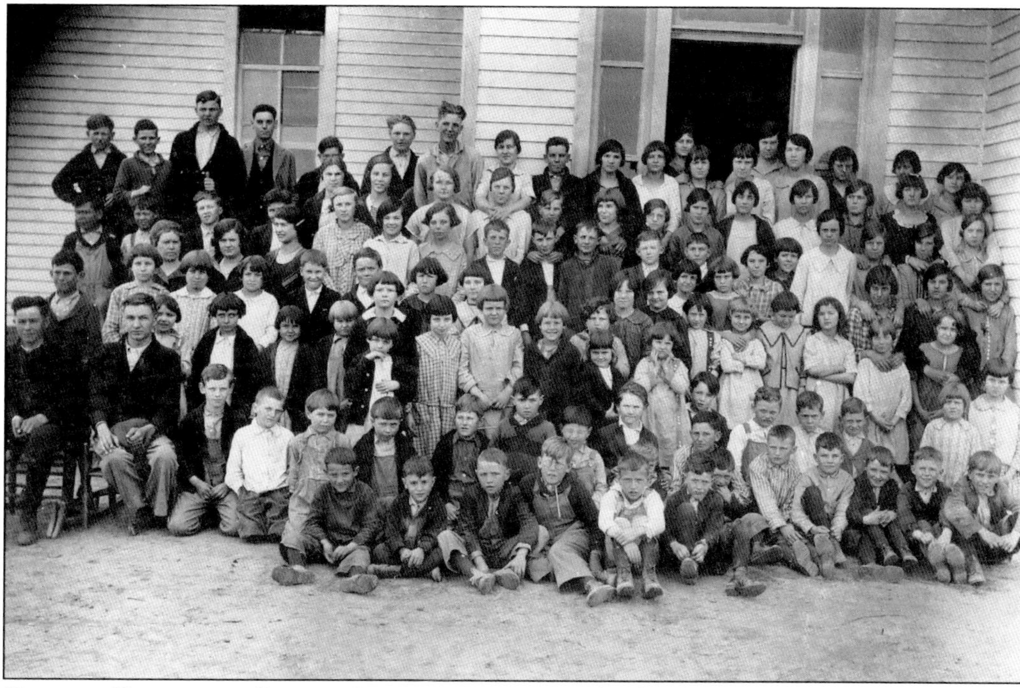

Central Community School Group, 1920s. Central School was formed in 1912 by merging the former small community schools of Stonewall, Cole Creek, and Thompsons. The school was named for its "central" location.

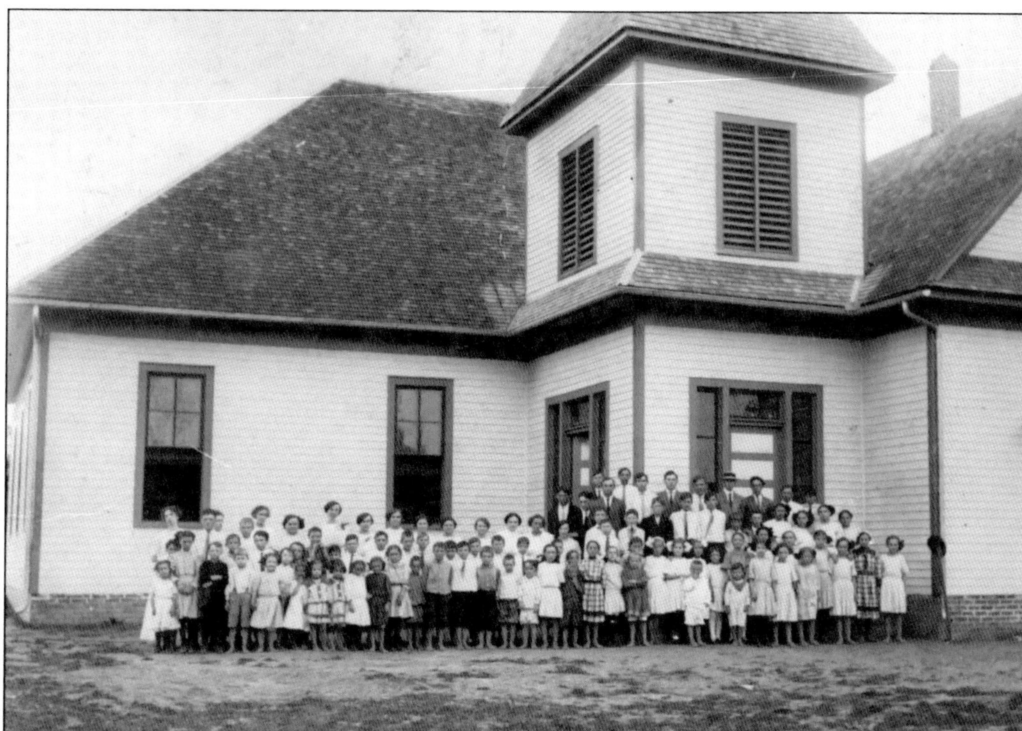

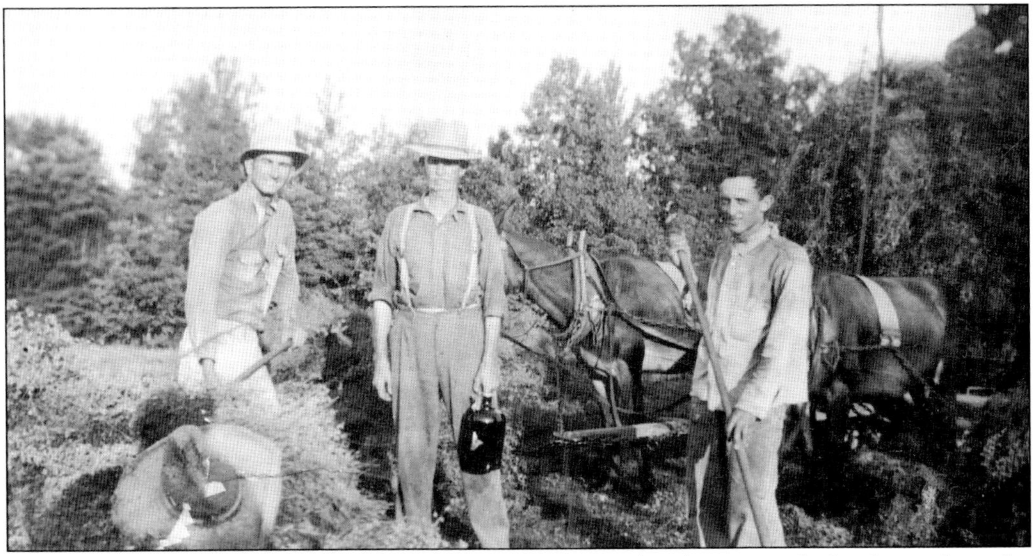

Chambers Farm Harvesting Time, 1930s. The men and mules are ready for the work in the fields in the Edith community in Lauderdale County, Tennessee. Note the brown water jug. (Courtesy of Joyce Henson.)

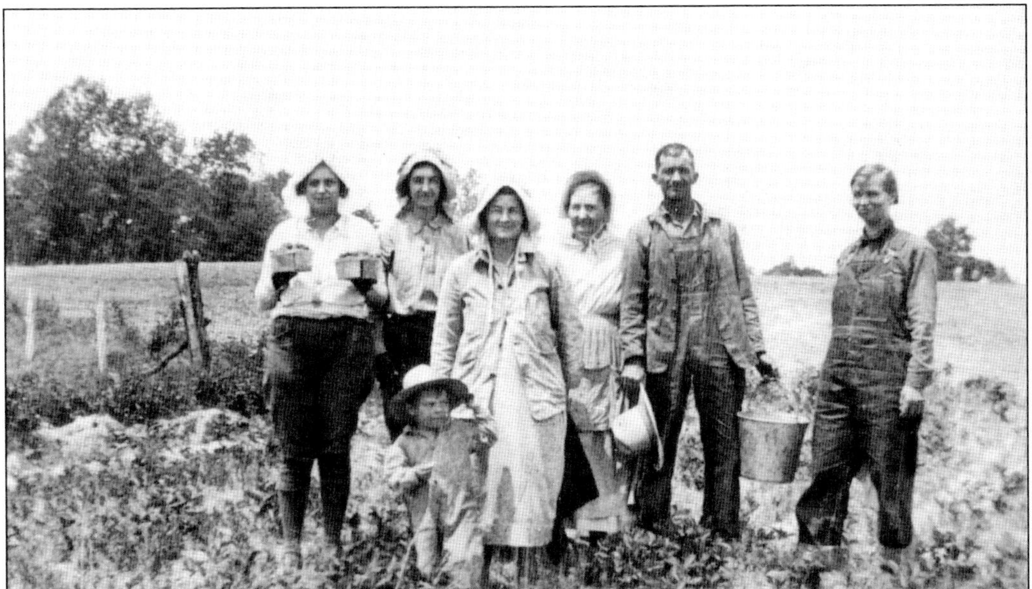

Picking Strawberries. Family members are seen picking strawberries on the Alf Chambers farm in the Edith community. (Courtesy of Joyce Henson.)

Winnie Bell, Choctaw Indian. Choctaw communities in Ripley and Henning are the outgrowth of two Choctaw families that came from Philadelphia, Mississippi, to Lauderdale County in the 1950s to pick cotton in Lauderdale County.

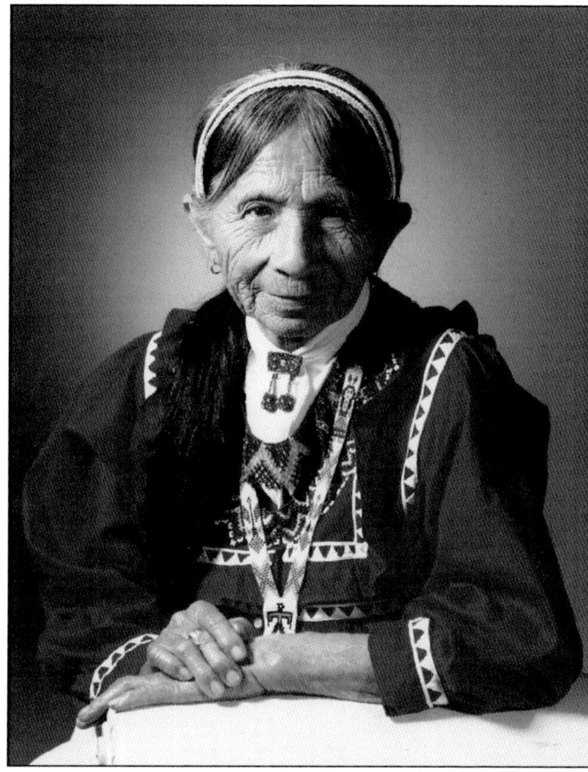

Wednesday Book Club Program. Pictured are Winnie Bell, Barbara Anthony, and Carol Walker. In Ripley in the 1960s, Winnie Bell presented a program to the Wednesday Book Club regarding her Choctaw Indian heritage and showed numerous handmade items. Petite and charming, Winnie was loved by citizens of Lauderdale County.

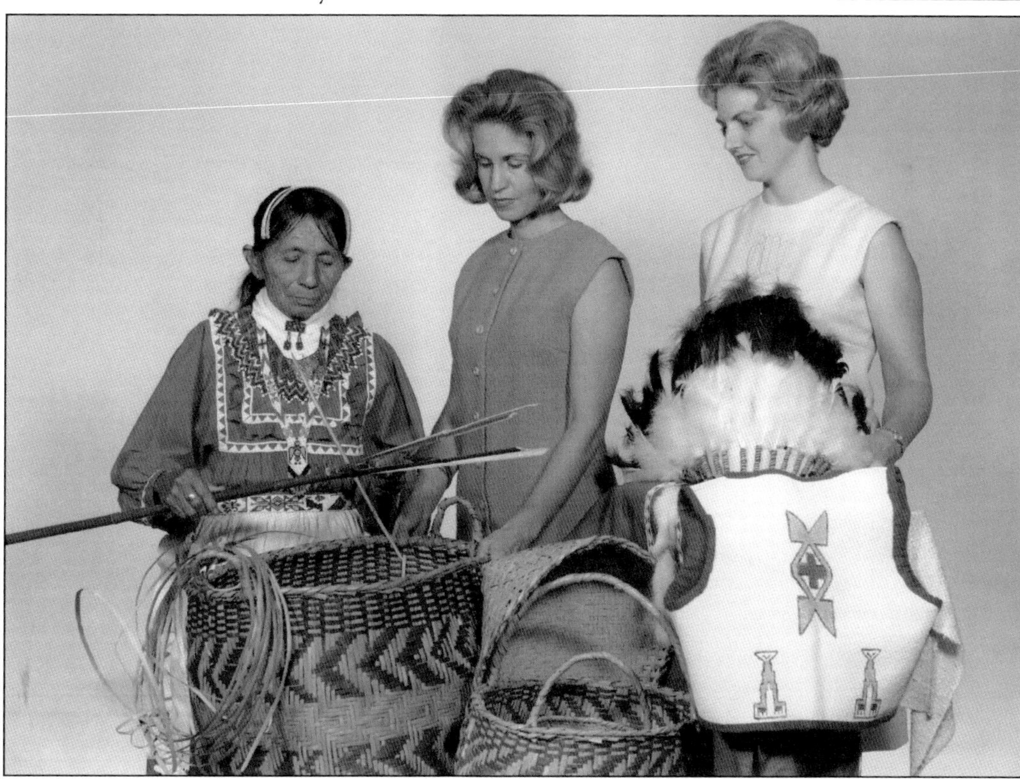

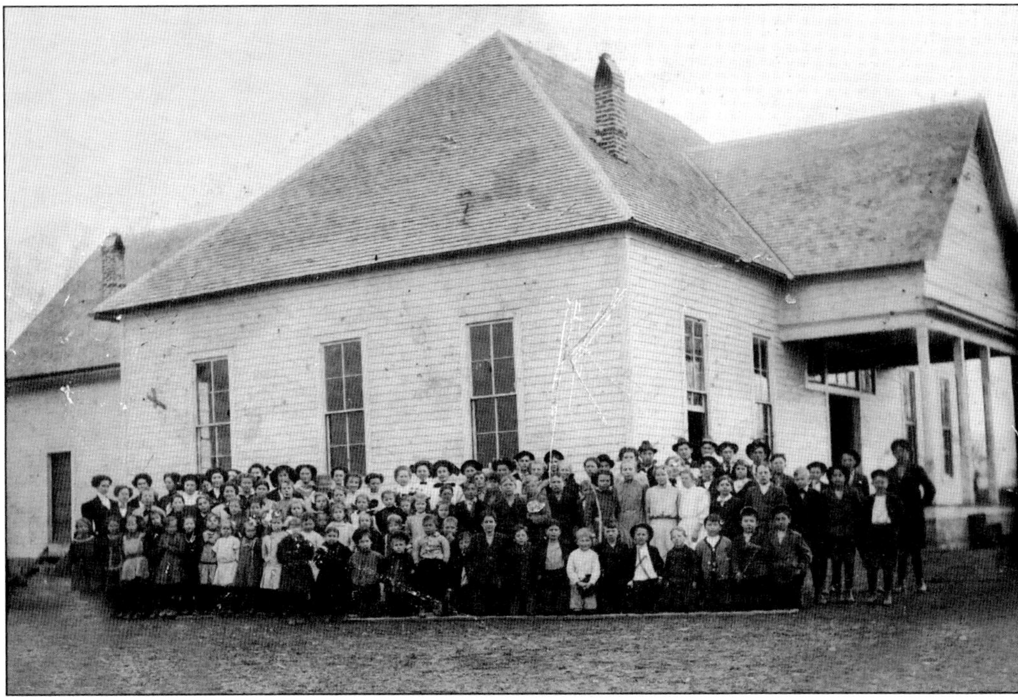

CENTRAL SCHOOL GROUP. This group photograph shows all the schoolchildren assembled outside the school building.

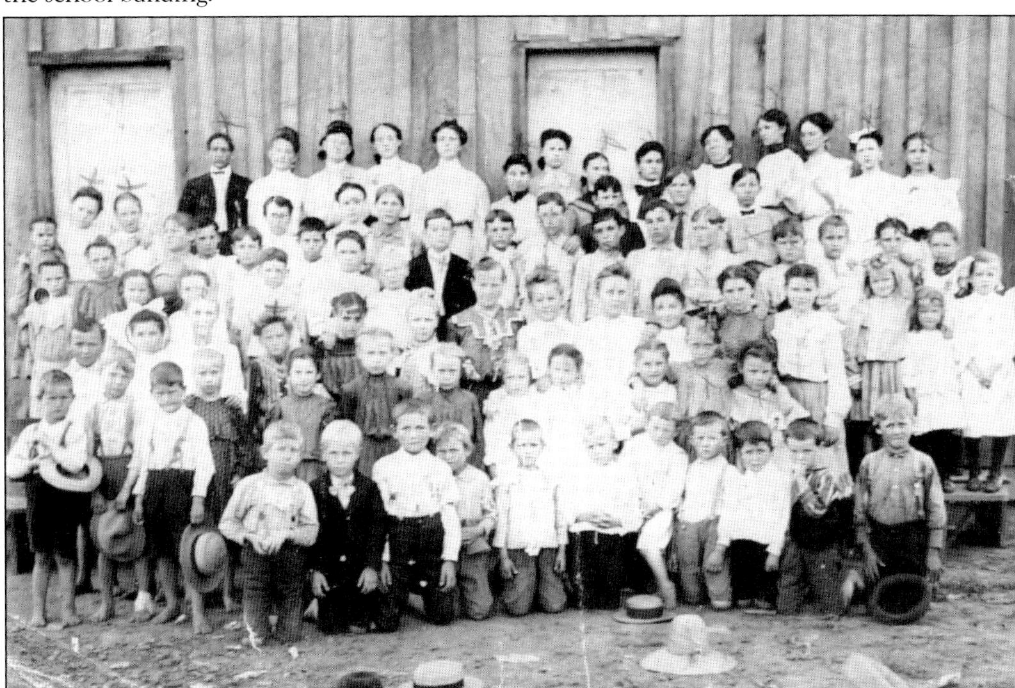

LAUDERDALE COUNTY SCHOOL GROUP. This group of finely dressed young men and women attended a Lauderdale County School. Several young men are seen holding their hats, but if one looks closely, several hats are visible on the ground in front of them.

Ann Chambers in Her Garden, Edith community. Ann Chambers's son Jack is hiding in the green beans. Gardens were a part of every family's home, providing fresh vegetables for the summer and canned vegetables for the winter. (Courtesy of Joyce Henson.)

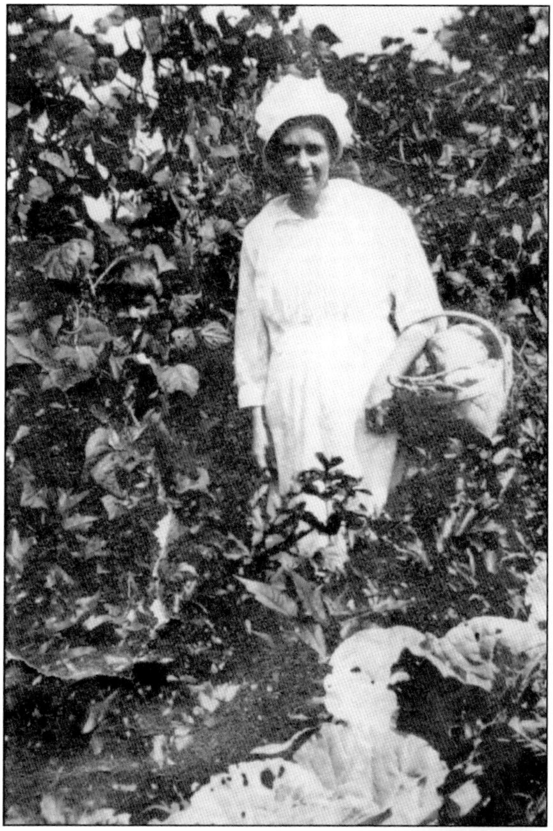

The Alf Chambers Family Digging Potatoes. The family is pictured with several bushels of freshly dug potatoes from its garden in the Edith community in 1957. (Courtesy of Joyce Henson.)

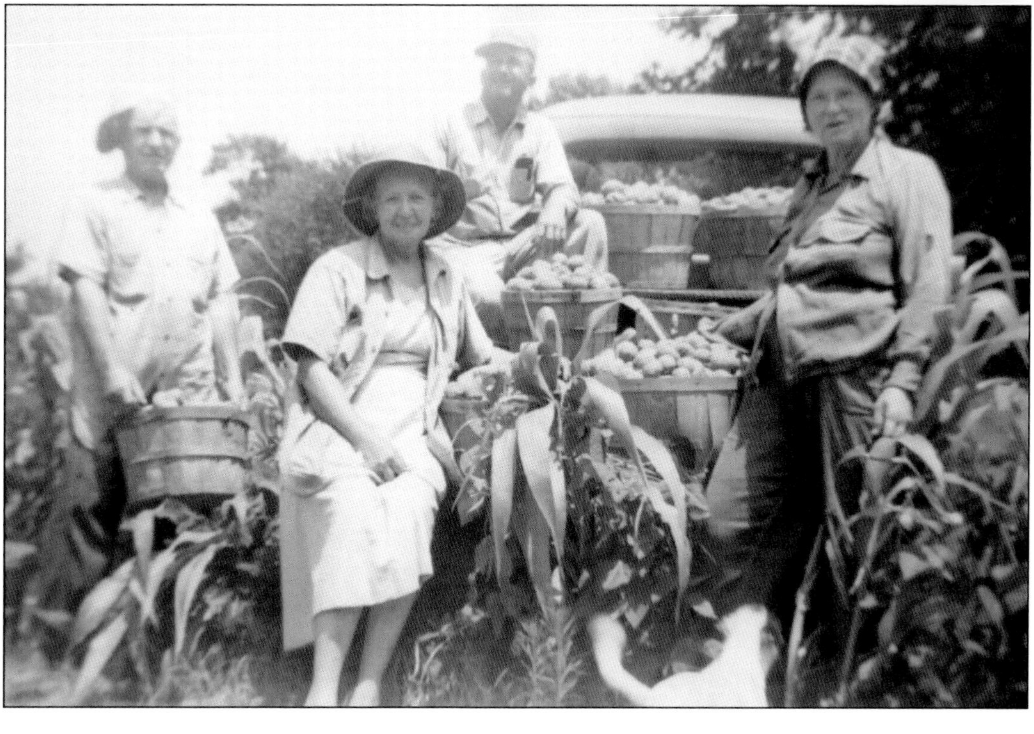

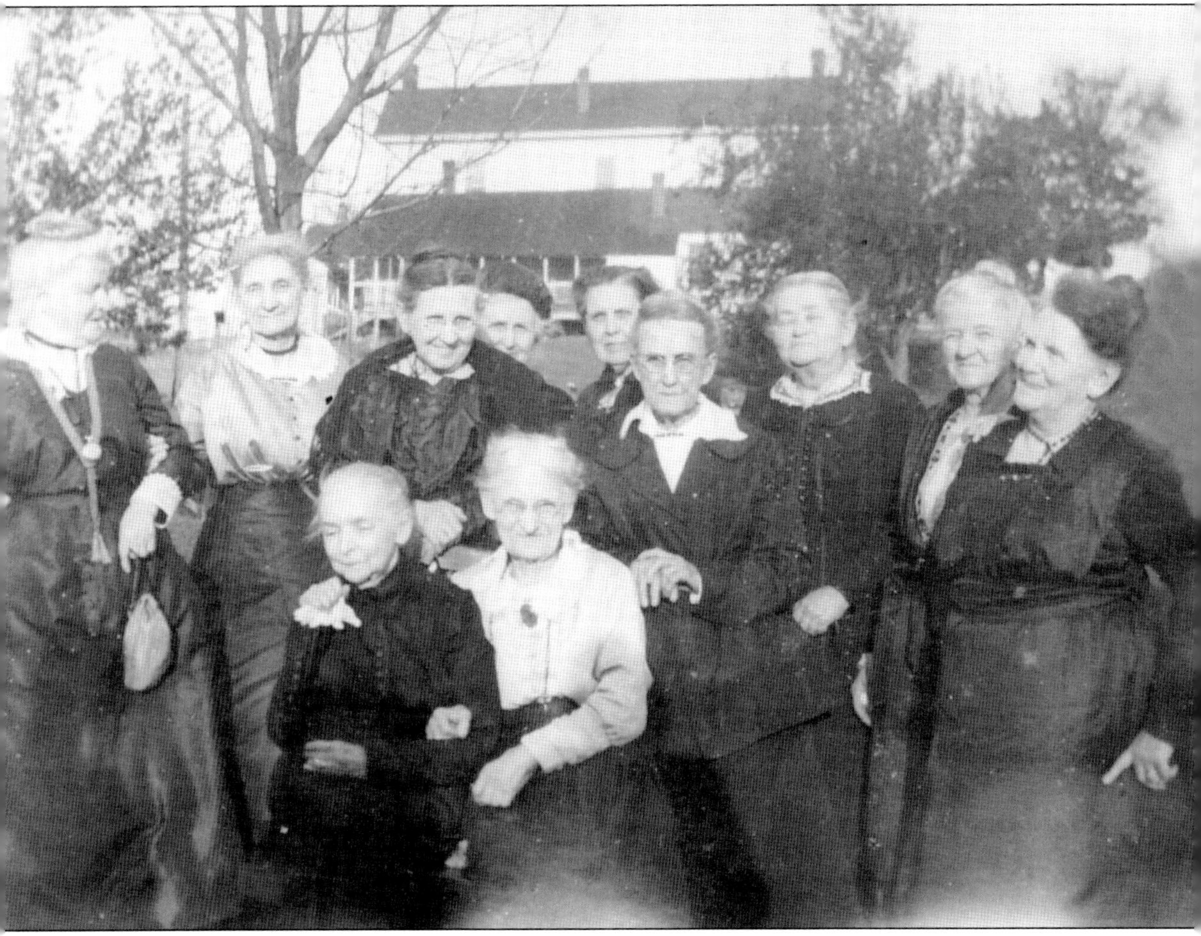

BIRTHDAY PARTY FOR MRS. C.E. JACKSON. Mrs. Jackson, who is seated on the left, was known as "Little Mam." She is seen here in Ripley, Tennessee, in 1920. (Courtesy of Terry Ford and Susan Scott.)

PICKING COTTON. Jessie Lou Chambers Arwood is seen picking cotton in the Edith community in 1918. A cotton sack held about 80–100 pounds of picked cotton. (Courtesy of Joyce Henson.)

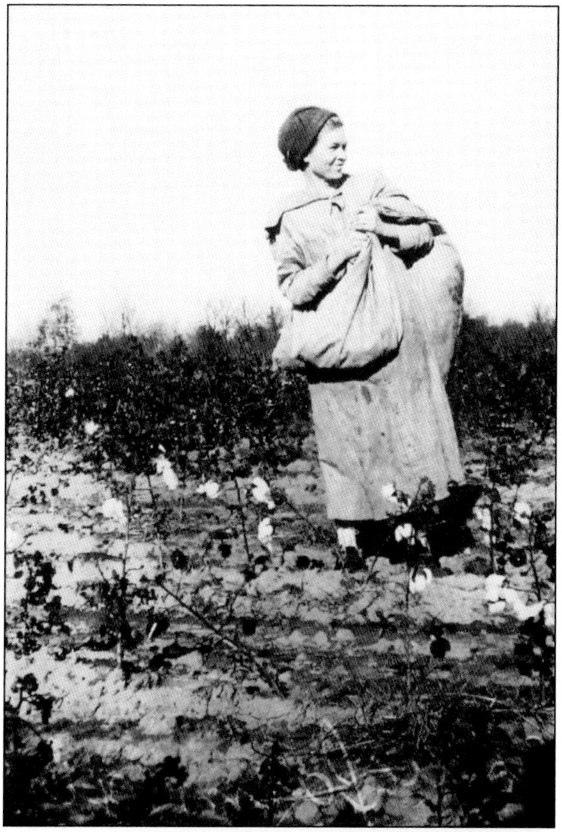

PICKING STRAWBERRIES AT WHITEFIELD. A group is shown after picking strawberries in the Whitefield community. Note the crates of strawberries on the right side of the picture. Families and community groups joined together to pick the harvest normally in the months of May and early June. (Courtesy of Marian Russell.)

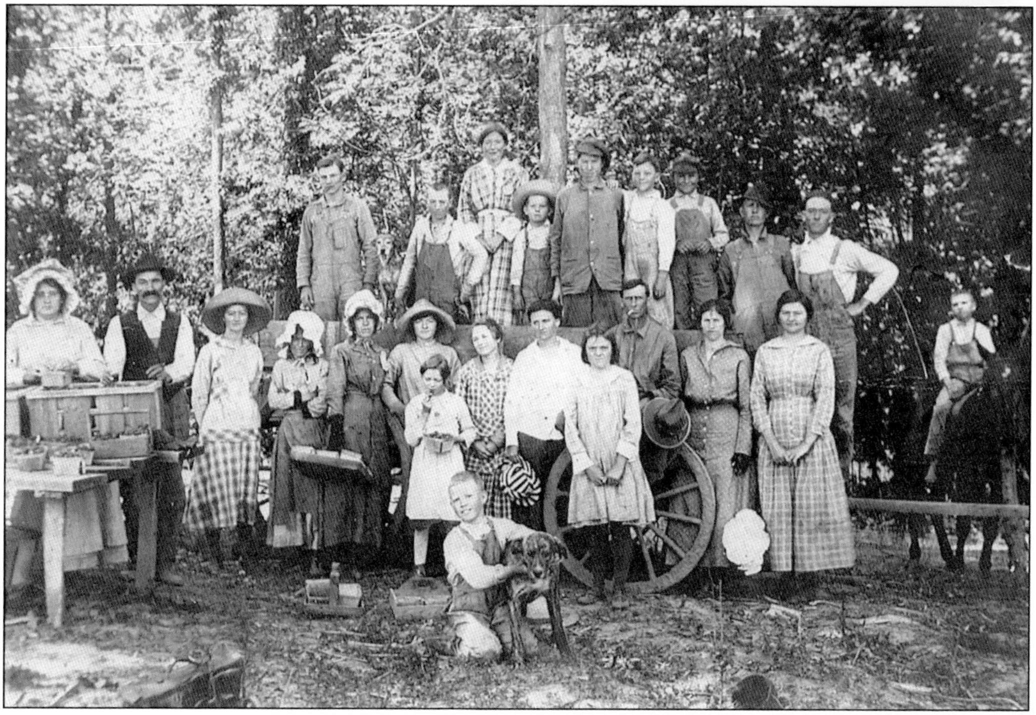

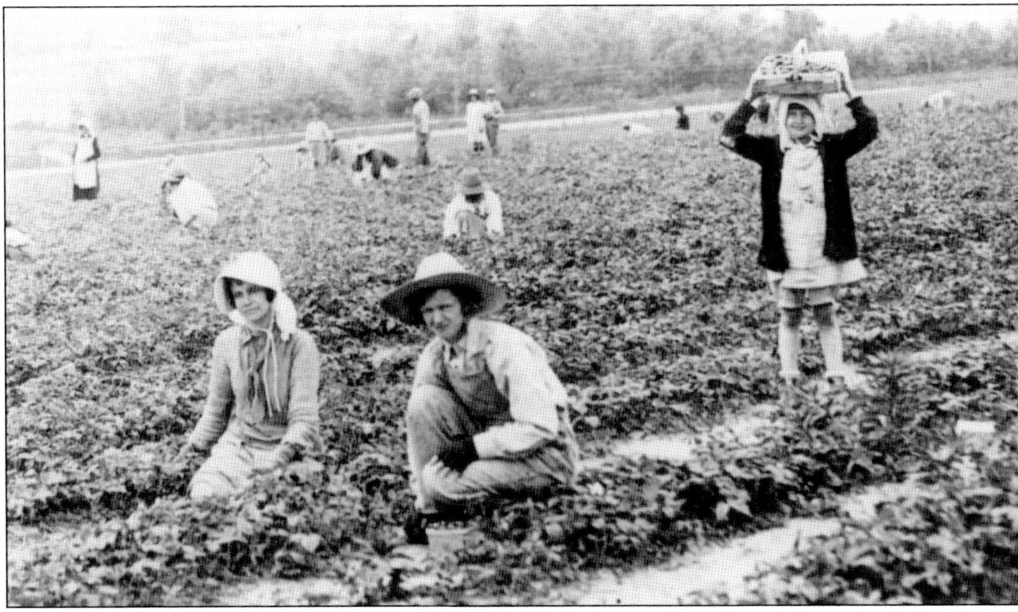

Strawberry Patch in Gates. With the coming of the railroad, it became profitable to grow perishable crops, and Lauderdale County was at the forefront of strawberry production in the South. In 1911, strawberry pickers earned 2¢ a quart. More than 200 freight car loads were shipped from the county in 1914. Each train car held 480 crates, and each crate held 24 quart baskets. (Courtesy of Bettie Davis.)

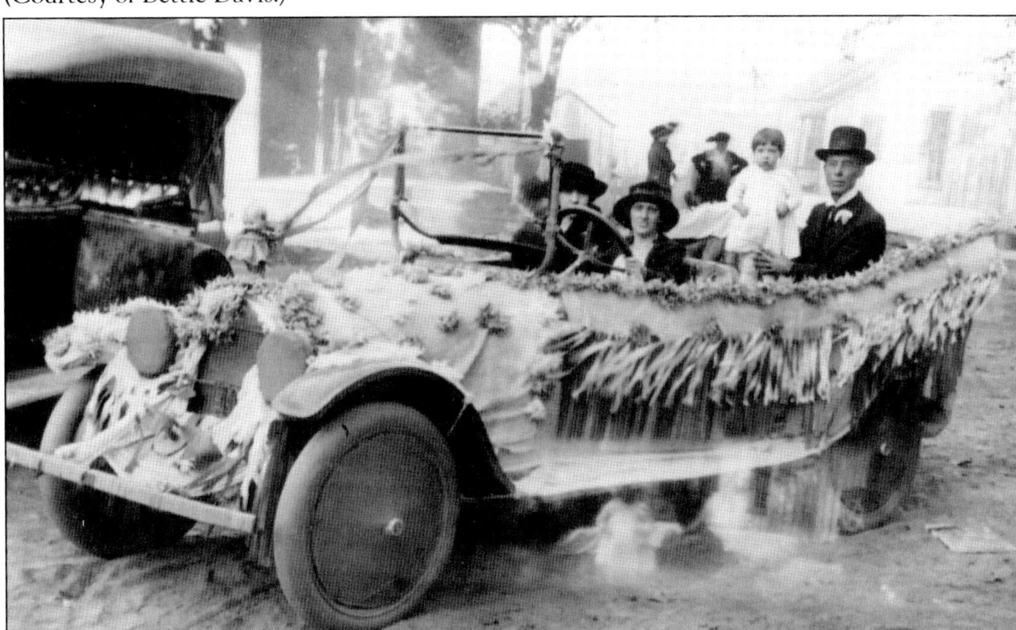

Car Decorated for an Agricultural Fair. Gates, Tennessee, held an agricultural fair in October 1921. This car was owned by Mr. and Mrs. F.B. Bradford. "Miss Stell" Bradford, teacher, is seated at the steering wheel. Also in the front is Miss Bruce Campbell, teacher. In the back seat is Rev. W.H. Haste, principal of the high school and pastor of the Baptist church, with his daughter Rebekah Haste. (Courtesy of Bettie Davis.)

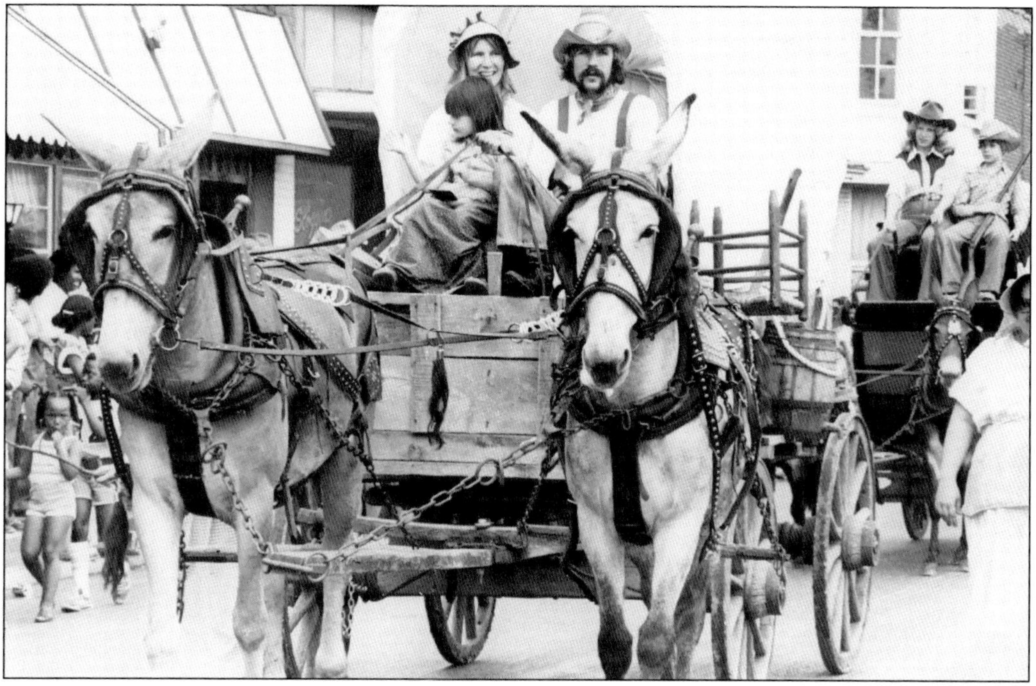

Todd Uniform Employees. Todd Uniform employees are seen participating in a Heritage Day Parade in Henning, Tennessee, in the 1990s. Distribution centers and manufacturing plants of Todd Uniform provided many jobs to the area, and the company was known for being involved in community projects.

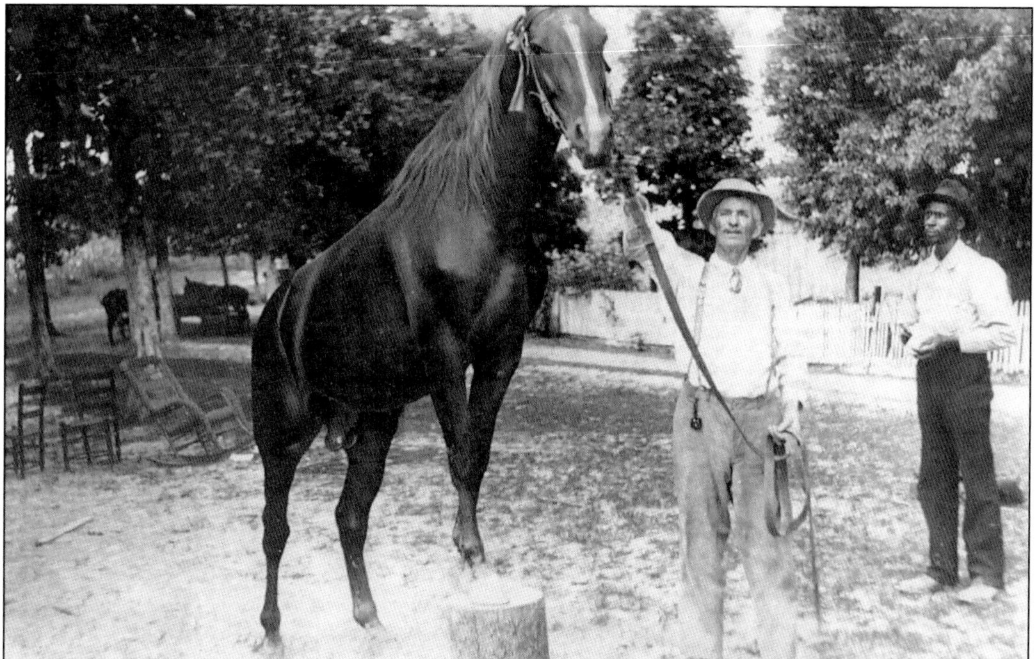

Will Leggett with His Prized Horse, Woodville Community. Will was known for training horses and made money doing so. (Courtesy of Dale Collins.)

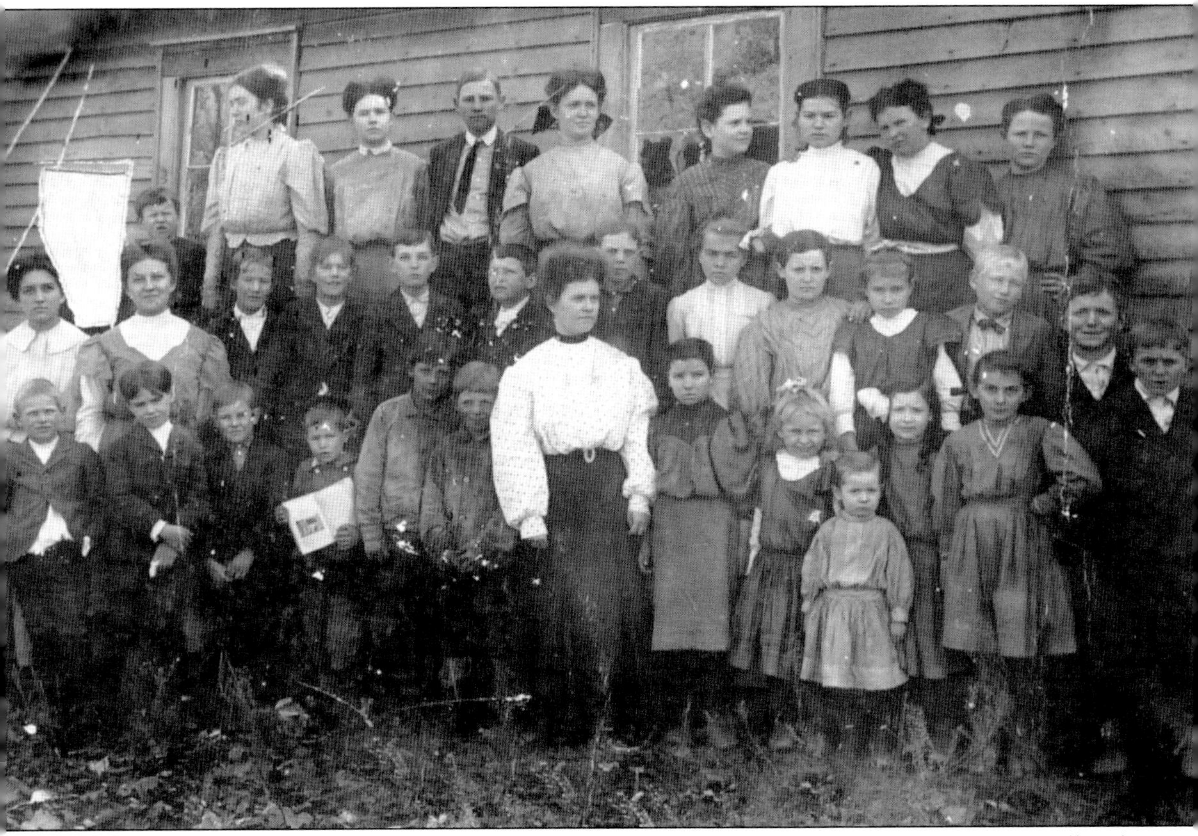

CHESTNUT BLUFF SCHOOL GROUP, EARLY 1900S. Lauderdale County's early schools were small and community oriented. Pictured in the center wearing the white blouse is teacher Sarah Elizabeth Martin. This group of schoolchildren contained many members of the Martin and Steelman families. (Courtesy of Anna Katherine Pippin.)

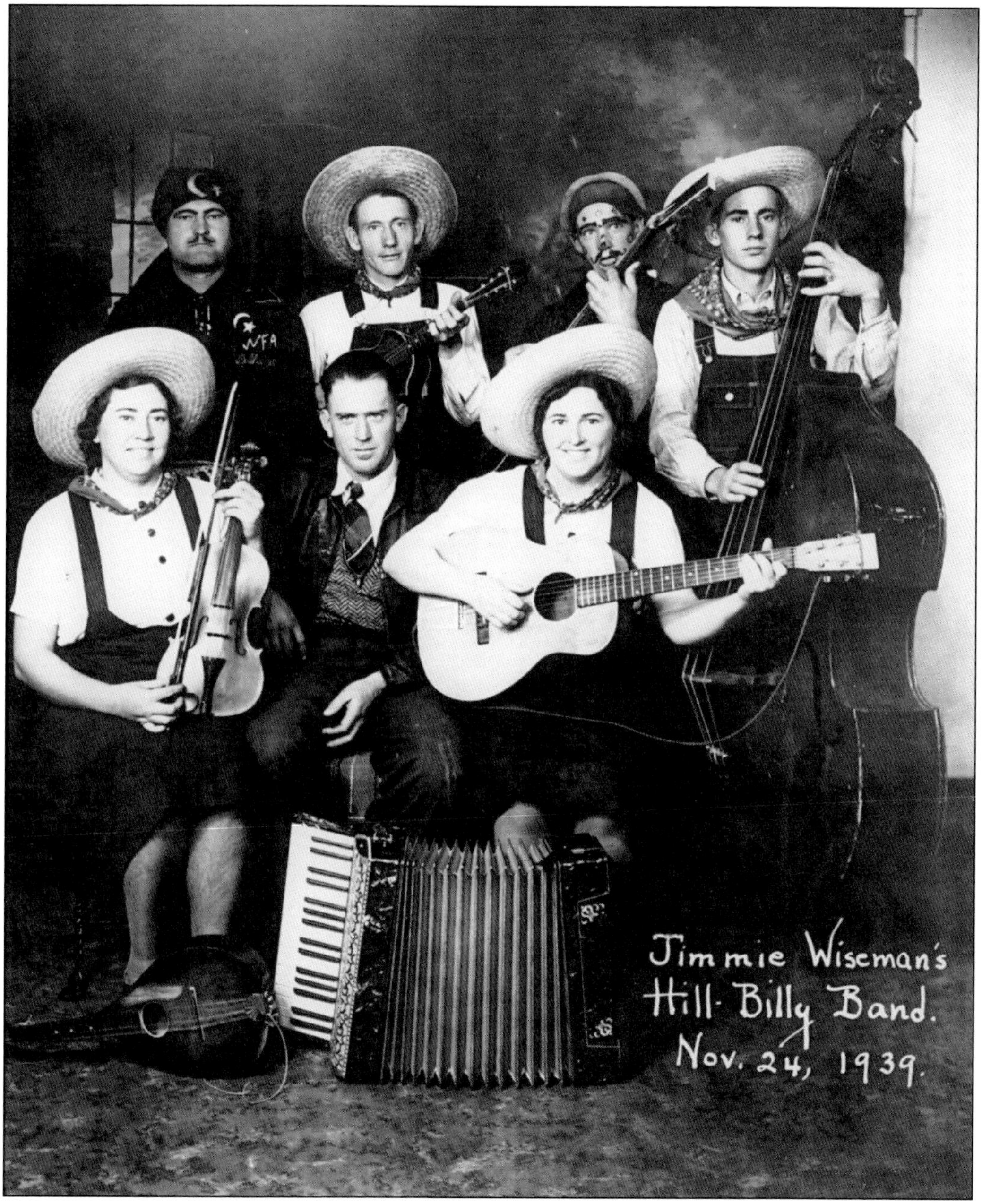

JIMMIE WISEMAN'S HILLBILLY BAND, NOVEMBER 24, 1939. Pictured from left to right are (first row) Robbie Wiseman Jones, Basil Jones, and Mary Sue Wiseman Butner; (second row) Bill Blake, Bill Butner, James Northcott, and James Wiseman. The Butner and Wiseman families were well known for their music all over Lauderdale County. (Courtesy of Bill Butner.)

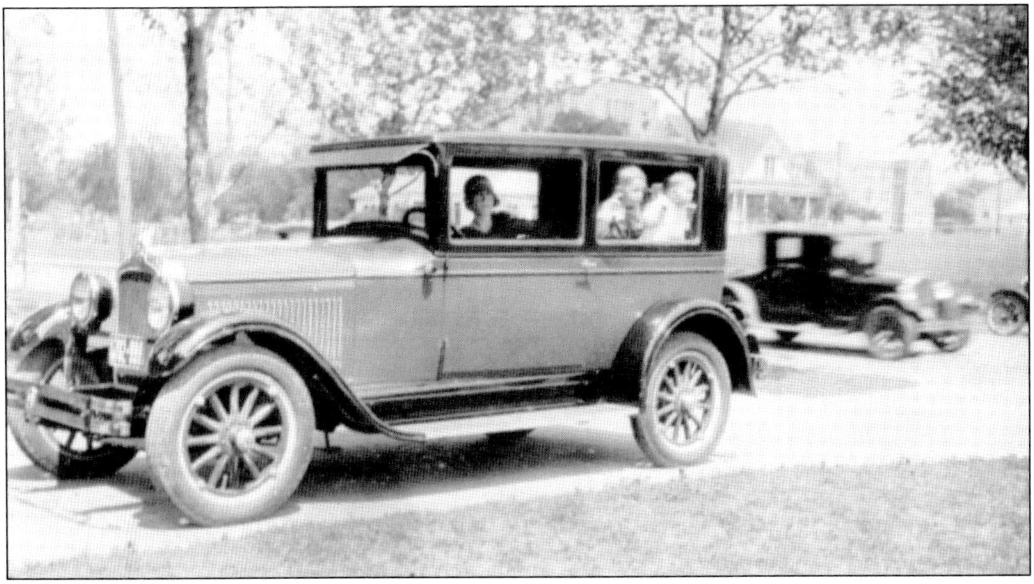

Bondurant Family Members Enjoying a Ride in Ripley. Families with automobiles were considered prominent members of the community. The Bondurants were relatives of Dr. Gus Lusk.

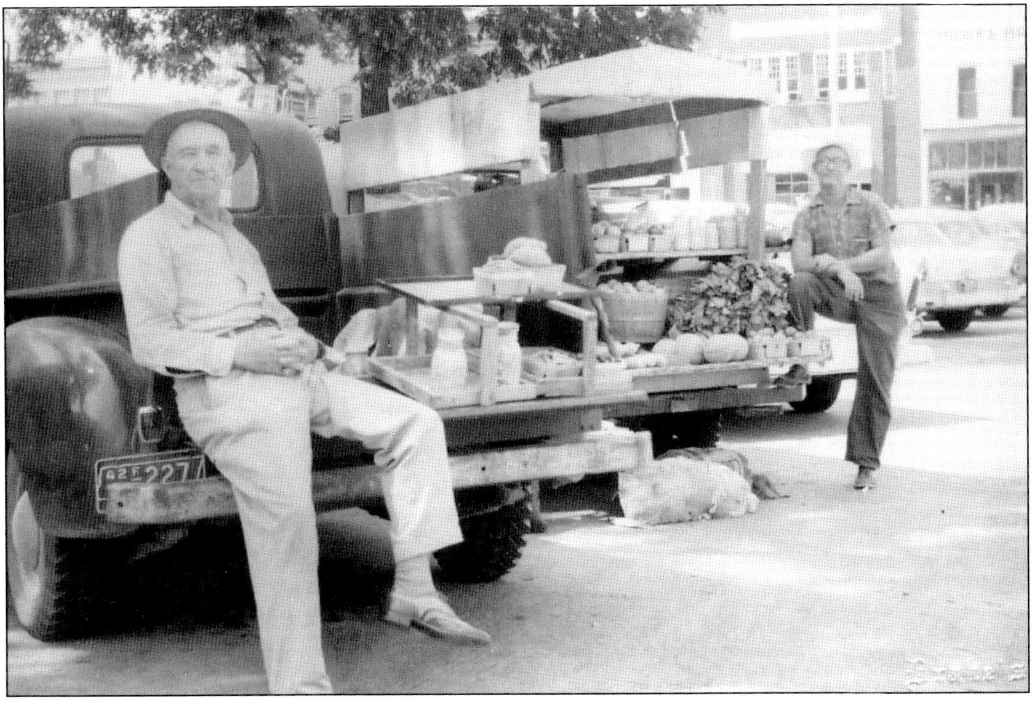

Farmers' Market in Ripley. Farmers sell their produce at a farmers' market in Ripley, Tennessee. Still a common sight in Lauderdale County, the farmers sell vegetables and fruit and varieties of canned jars of goods. (Courtesy of Susan Weiber.)

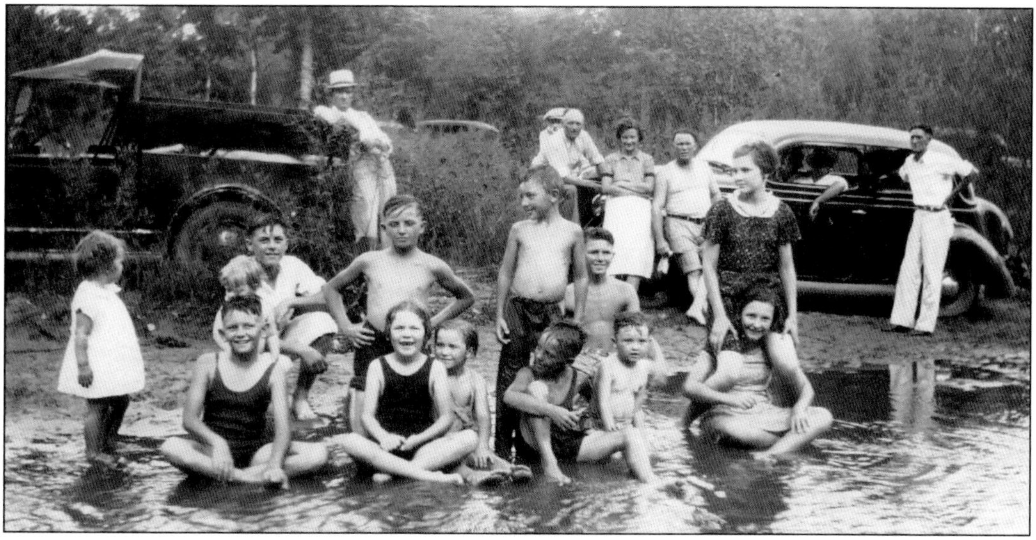

W.E. Crews Family at Knob Creek, 1935. Families often went swimming in the creek after church on Sundays. (Courtesy of Joyce Henson.)

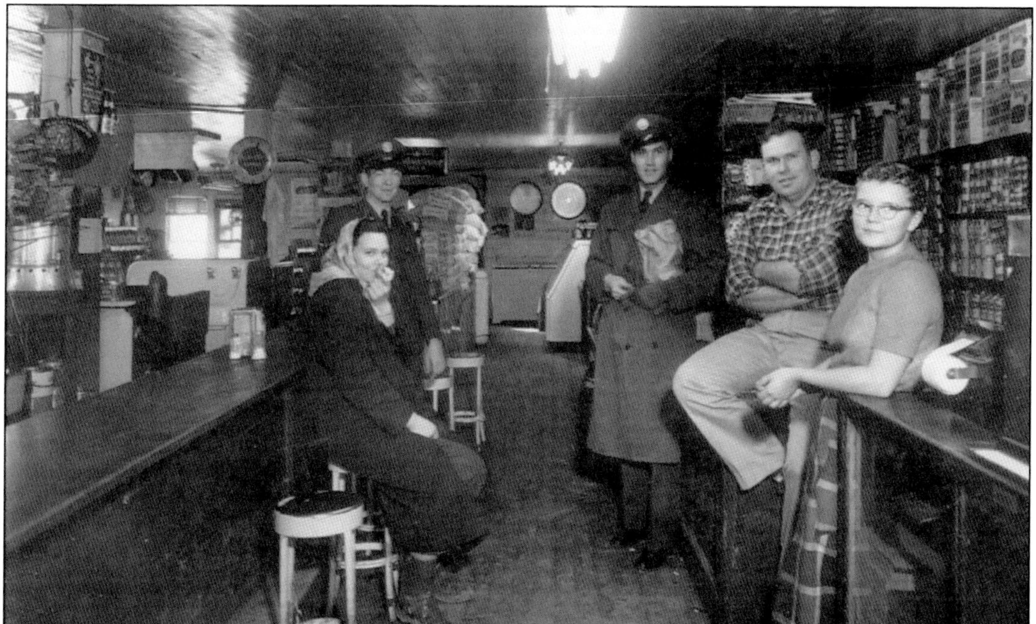

Leonard Simpson and Charles Nelson on Military Leave. This group is shown at Jap Henderson's Grocery in the Gold Dust community in 1951. Pictured are, from left to right, Helen Nelson Barham, Leonard Simpson, Charles Nelson, Billy Davis, and JoAnn Proctor Davis. (Courtesy of Gilbert Simpson.)

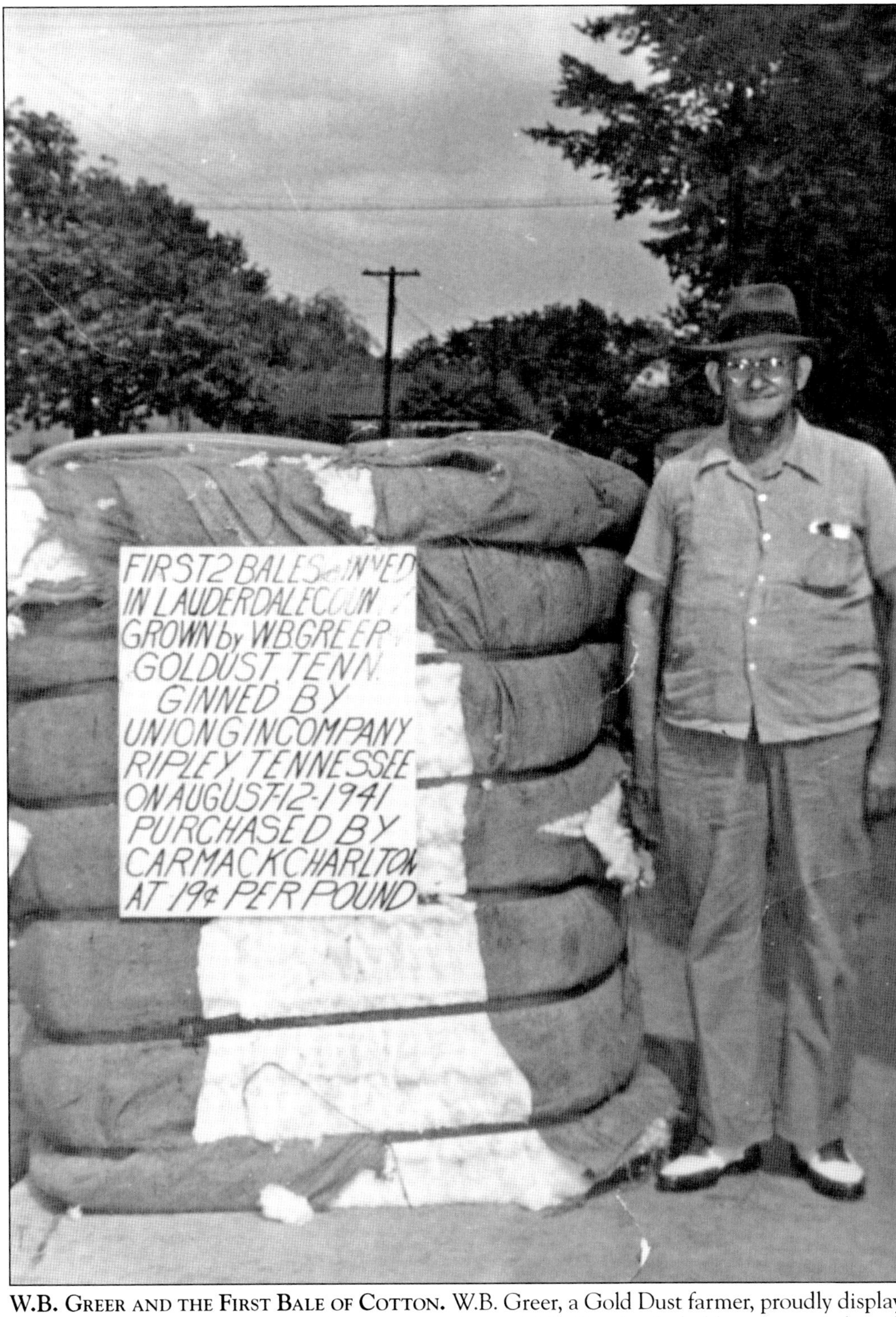

W.B. GREER AND THE FIRST BALE OF COTTON. W.B. Greer, a Gold Dust farmer, proudly displays the first bale of cotton in Lauderdale County in August 1941. The banks held a contest and would display the bale of cotton in the lobby. (Courtesy of Rose Rhodes.)

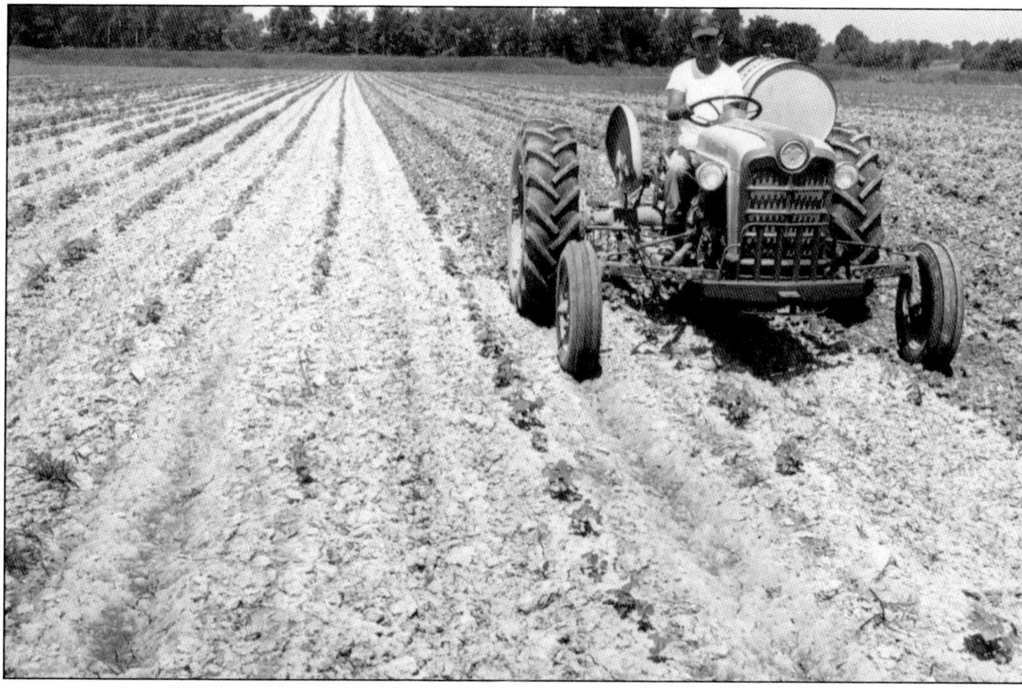

Norman Burks Farm. The Norman Burks farm was located in the Forked Deer bottoms of Lauderdale County. Roger Harris is shown on the farm tractor spraying the crop in the fields in preparation for a good yield.

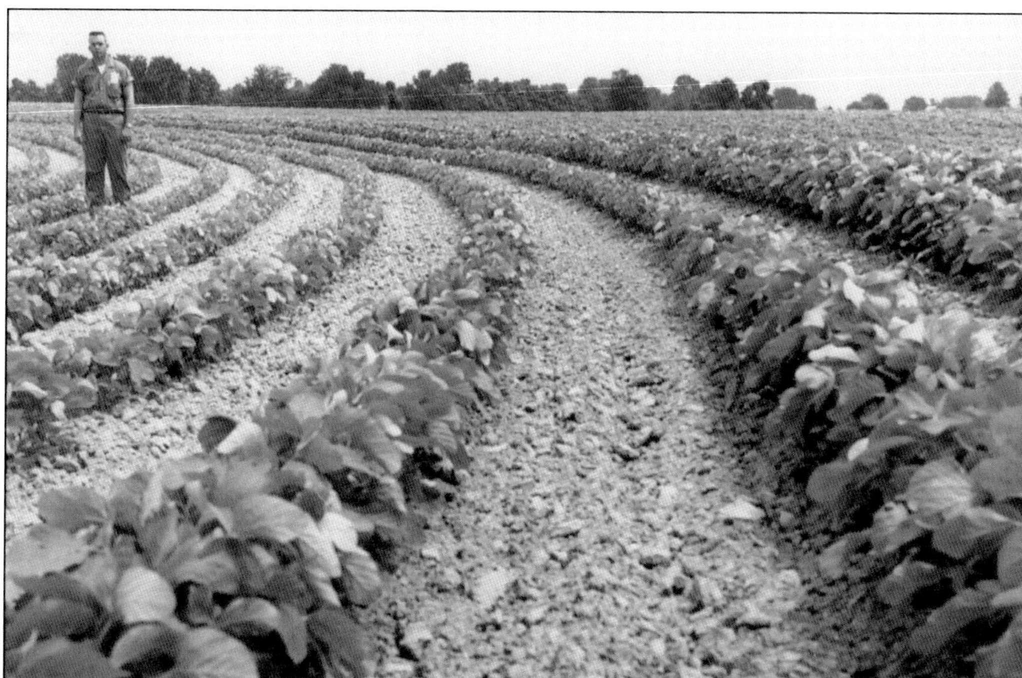

Byron Escue Farm. Byron Escue looks over his soybean field in the Durhamville community. Soybeans, now one of Lauderdale County's largest crops, are still grown by the Escue family.

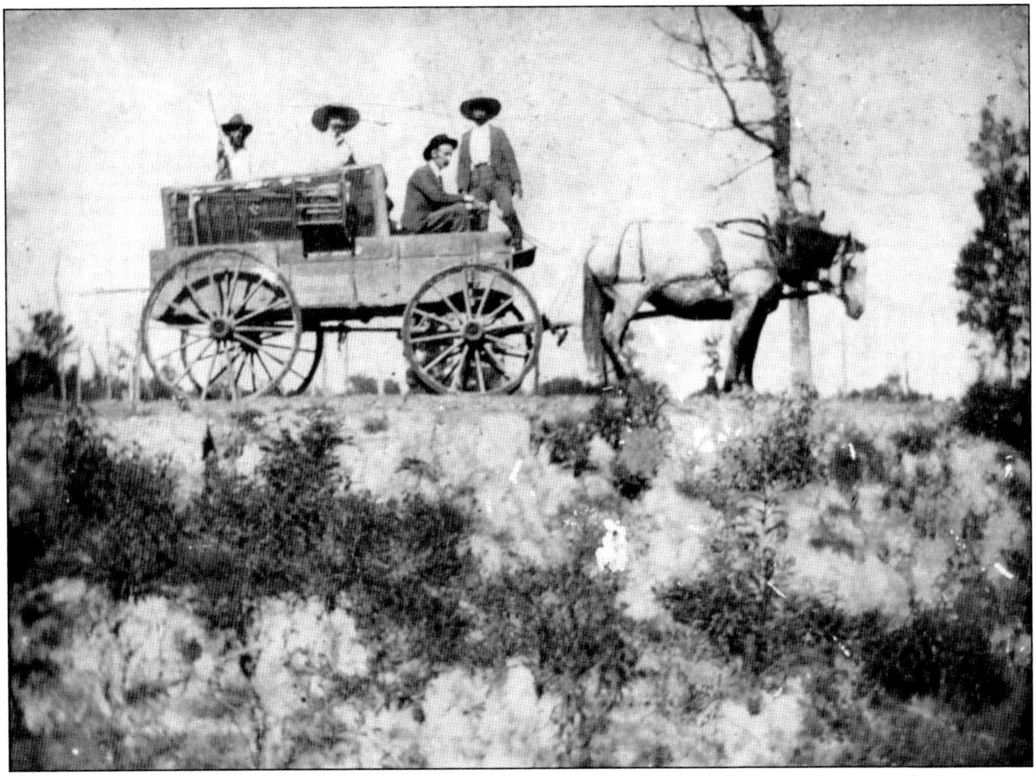

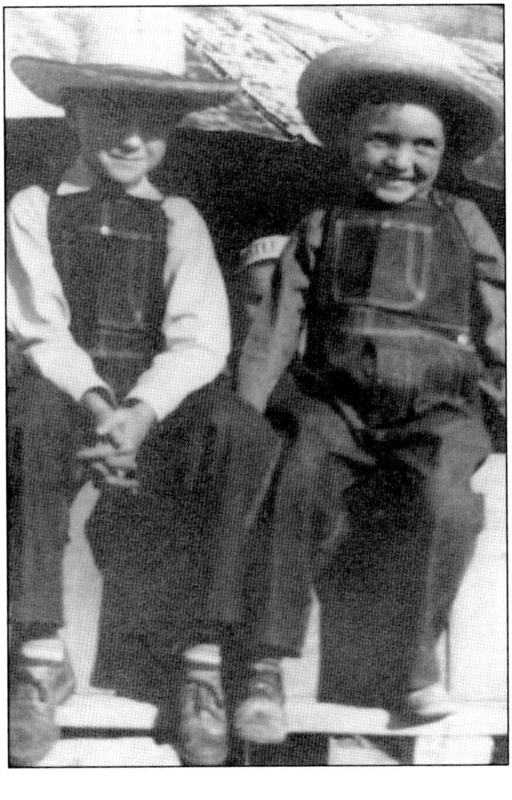

Driving Mrs. M.F. Given Sr.'s Household Goods. Pictured above, a wagonload of furnishings belonging to Mrs. M.F. Given Sr. are being transported from her home in Ripley to her cabin at Chisholm Lake. Chisholm Lake cabins were often a secondary home, and citizens spent time hunting in the area, fishing on the lake, and just "getting away." (Courtesy of Terry Ford.)

Fishing on a Summer Day. Brothers Ed Shelby (left) and Larry Shelby get ready to go fishing at Fish Trap and Long Hole on Cole Creek in Lauderdale County in August 1940. (Courtesy of Larry Shelby.)

Three

These Days

Lauderdale County remains to this day primarily an agricultural community. Soybeans, cotton, corn, and wheat remain the mainstay of area farmers. Tomatoes, another prominent crop and one that Ripley and Lauderdale County are famous for, are a very important part of the agricultural economy. Although not as many acres are produced now as before because of the intensive labor involved, the tomatoes produced are shipped nationwide. This beautiful red fruit is honored, as are the farmers, each year with the annual Tomato Festival, held each July. These types of events, which feature lots of activities including contests, carnivals, tastings, and so on, attract tourists to the area. Tourism is a means of economic development that the county has begun to concentrate on. Lauderdale County is blessed to be home to Fort Pillow State Park, the Alex Haley Home and Museum in Henning, and the Veteran's Museum located on the former World War II Army Air Base in Halls. The county is an outdoorsman's paradise for hunters and fishing. Open Lake, Chisholm Lake, and the Mississippi River are just some of the many favorite spots.

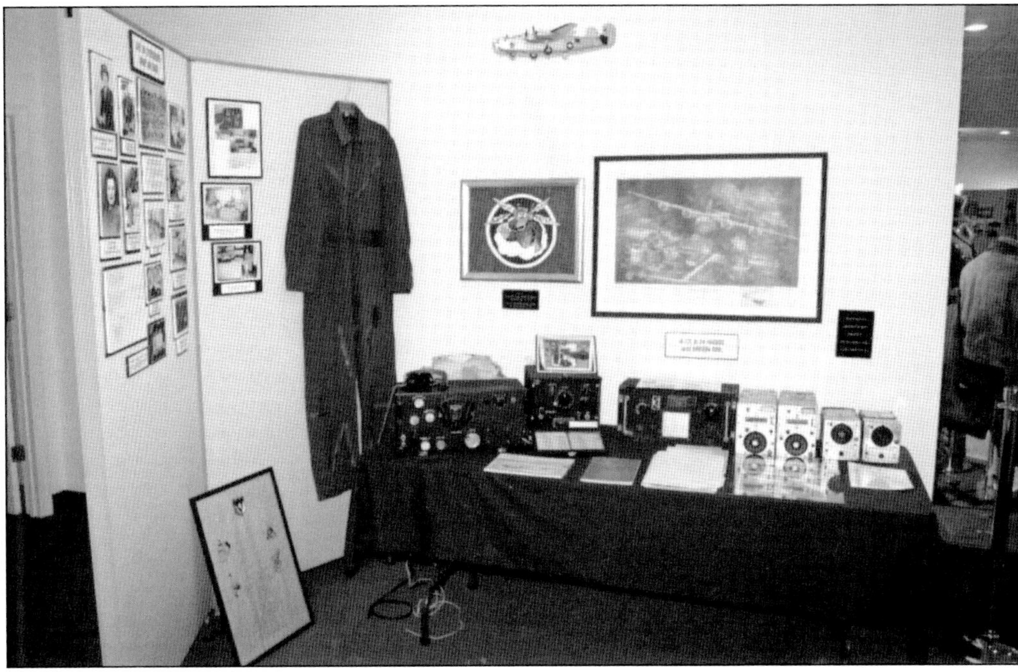

Veteran's Museum. Displays inside the Veteran's Museum in Halls, Tennessee, include uniforms, radio equipment, medals, a Nazi typewriter, and Norden Bombsight vaults, among thousands of other items. (Photograph by Amie Vanderford; courtesy of the author.)

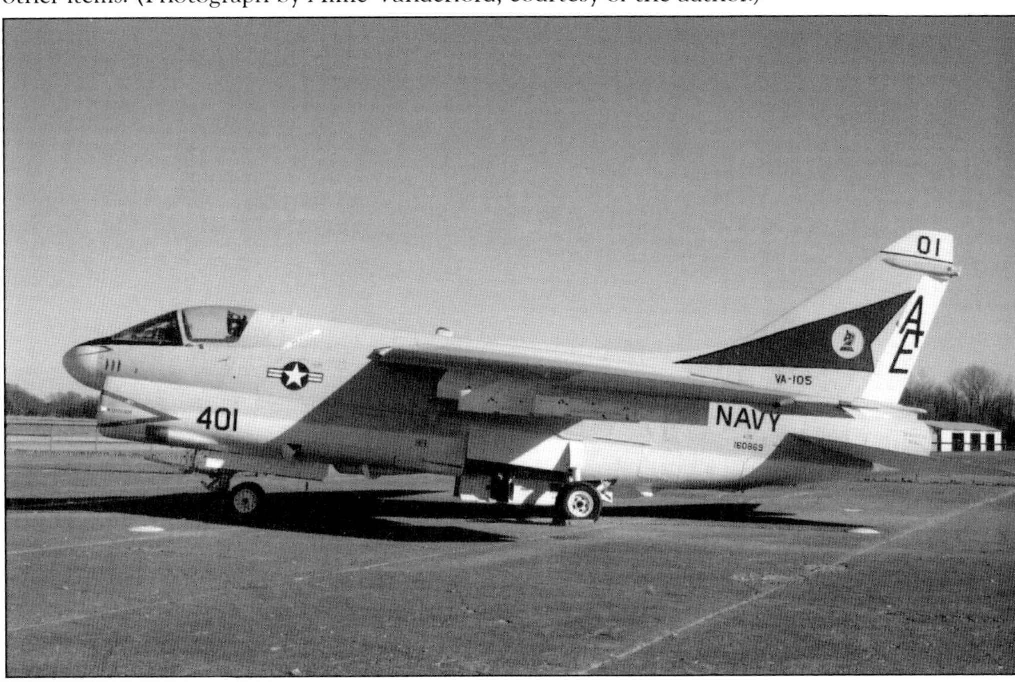

AE Corsair Navy Plane at the Veteran's Museum. This AE Corsair Navy plane is also at the museum. A recent addition is a Sea Knight Marine helicopter, which saw service in the Vietnam War. It is only one of two available for public viewing. (Photograph by Amie Vanderford; courtesy of the author.)

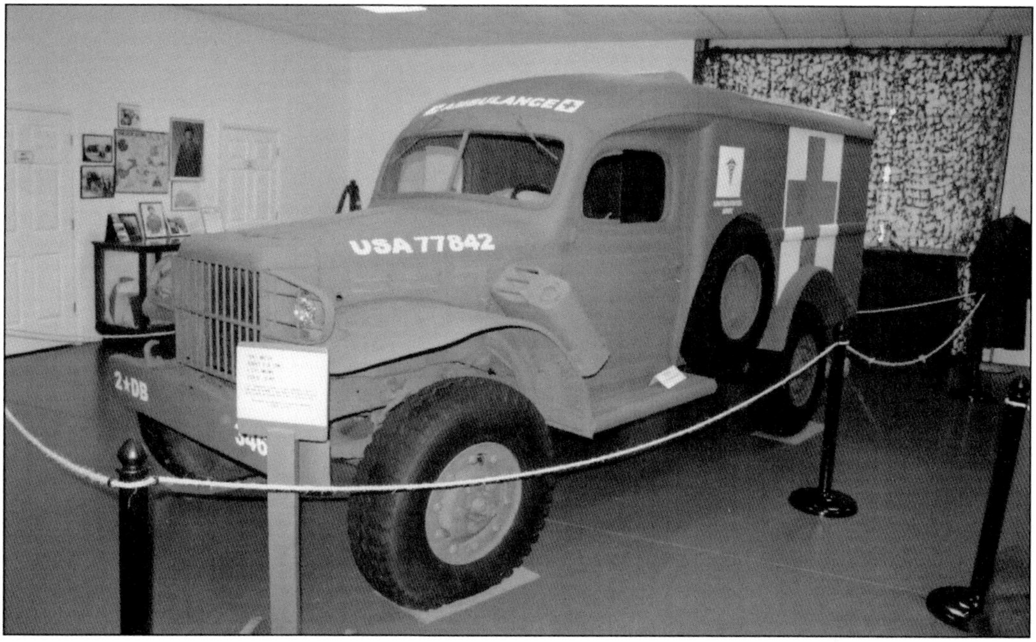

World War II Ambulance Veteran's Museum. A collection of military vehicles, including this World War II ambulance that saw service in France, is on display inside the Veteran's Museum. (Photograph by Amie Vanderford; courtesy of the author.)

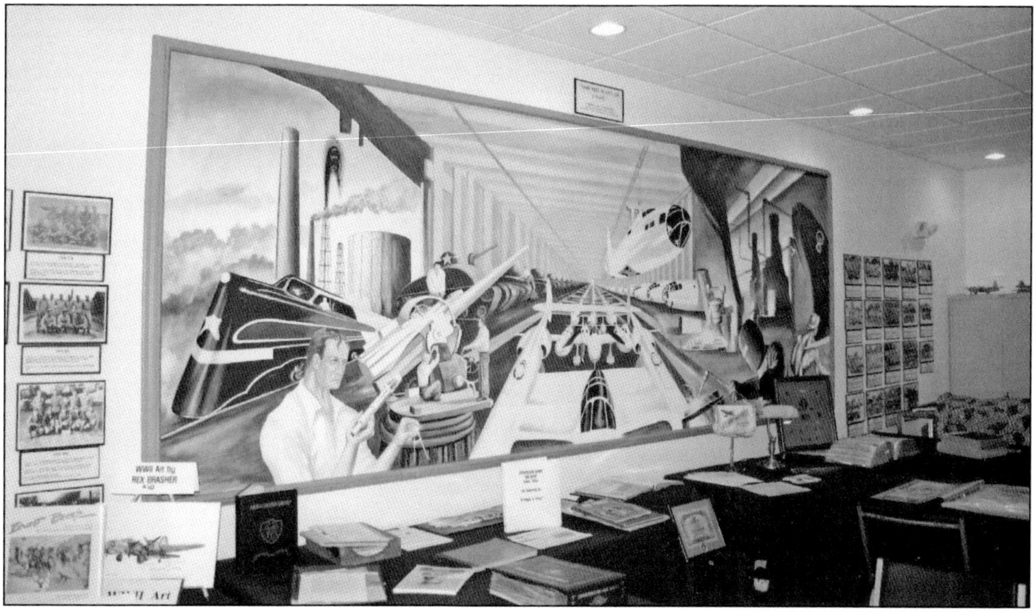

The Veteran's Museum and Air Show in Halls. Located at Arnold Field in Halls, Tennessee, the Veteran's Museum honors the service of Lauderdale County veterans of all wars. Features at the museum include World War I and World War II exhibits, with displays from Korea, Vietnam, and Desert Storm. The museum is housed on the former site of the World War II B-17 training base, which was operational from 1942 to 1945. An annual air show features vintage planes on display and acrobatic flying maneuvers. This photograph depicts one of the three murals painted by artist Ernie Berke. (Photograph by Amie Vanderford; courtesy of the author.)

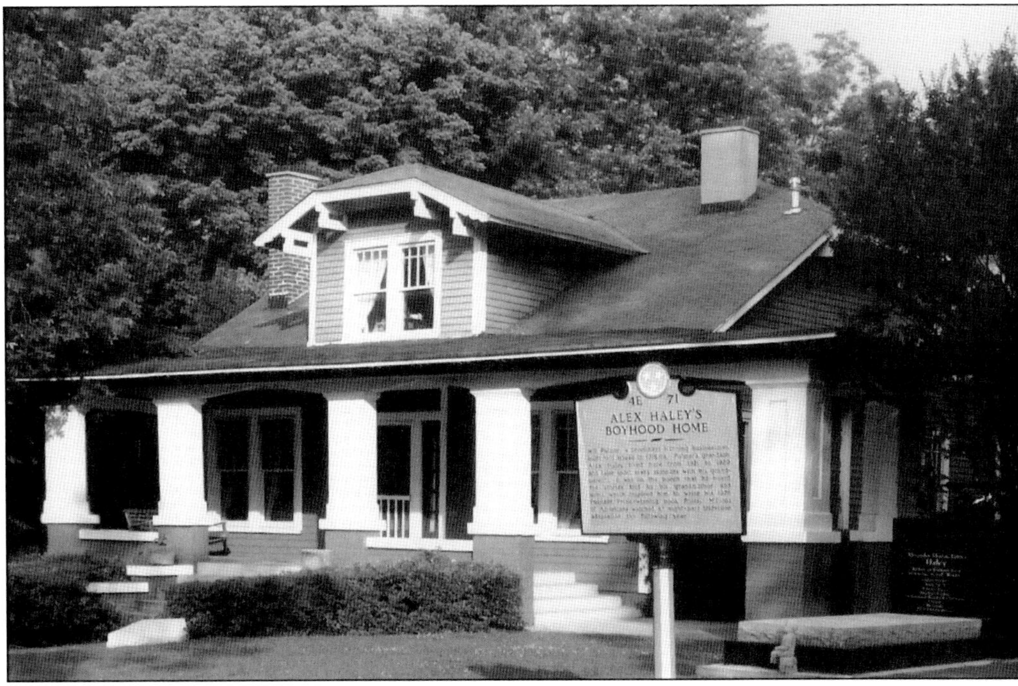

Alex Haley Home and Museum in Henning. "Will Palmer, a prominent Henning businessman, built this house in 1918–19. Palmer's grandson Alex Haley lived here from 1921 to 1929 and later spent many summers with his grandparents. It was on the porch that he heard the stories told by his grandmother and aunts which inspired him to write his 1976 Pulitzer Prize–winning book *Roots*. Millions of Americans watched an eight-part television adaptation the following year." The home is in the National Register of Historic Places.

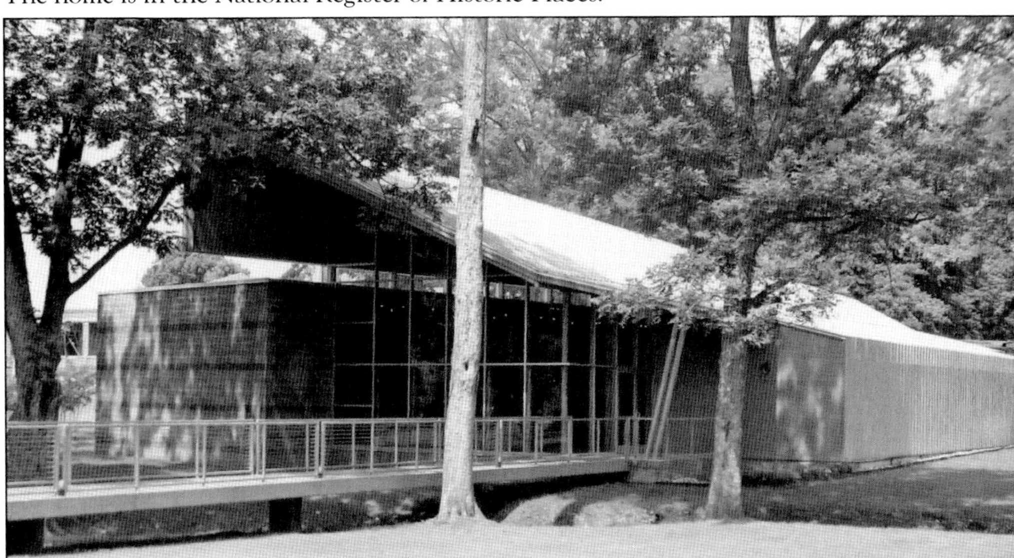

Alex Haley Interpretive Center in Henning. The Alex Haley Interpretive Center is located behind the childhood home of Alex Haley and houses displays and collections of Alex Haley's life. The center was dedicated in August 2010. The center's design has a boardwalk entrance and is shaped like a slave ship (*Roots*).

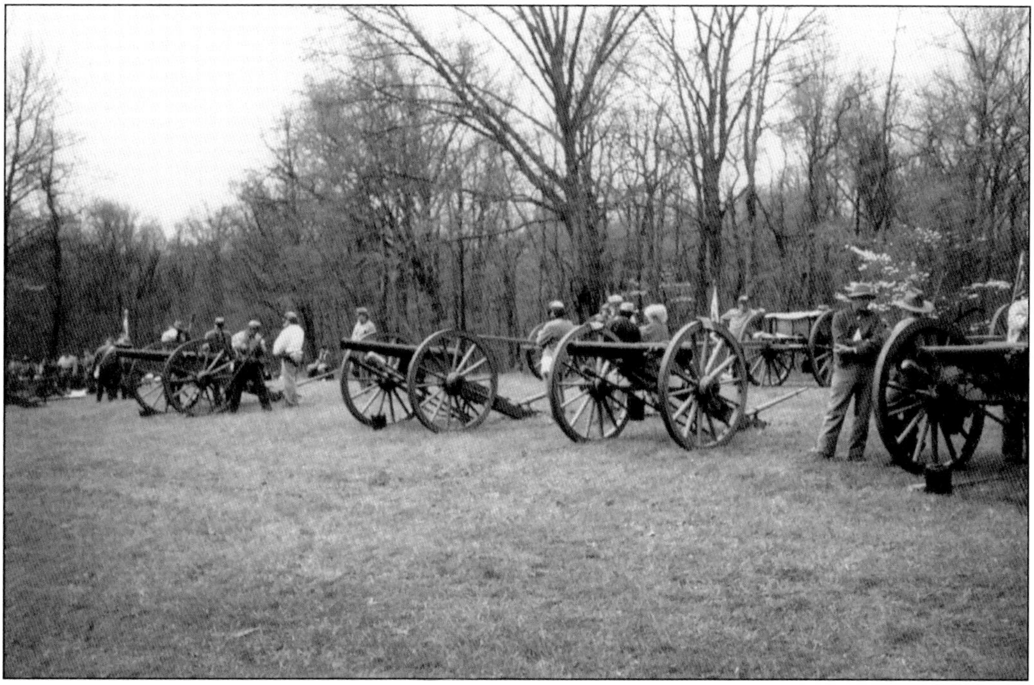

Fort Pillow Battle Reenactment. This reenactment occurs each year at Fort Pillow State Park, located off Tennessee Highway 87. The park offers camping, wildlife observation, hiking trails, a Mississippi River overlook, and fishing. This park was created atop the majestic bluffs of the river and is located where the historic battle was fought.

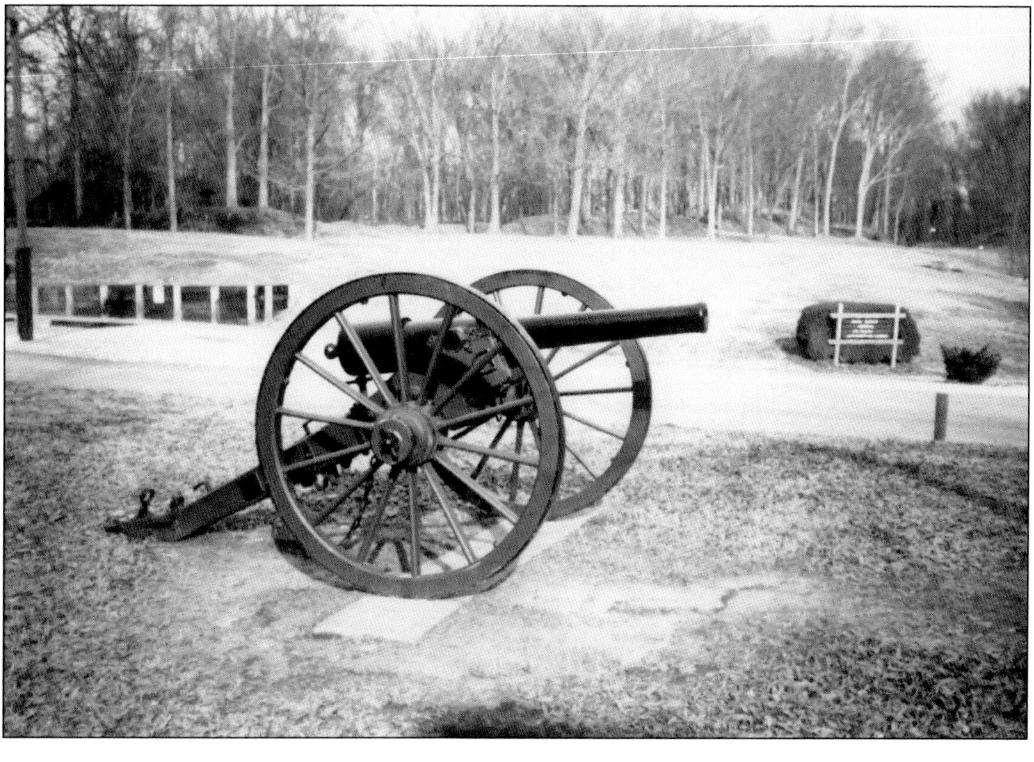

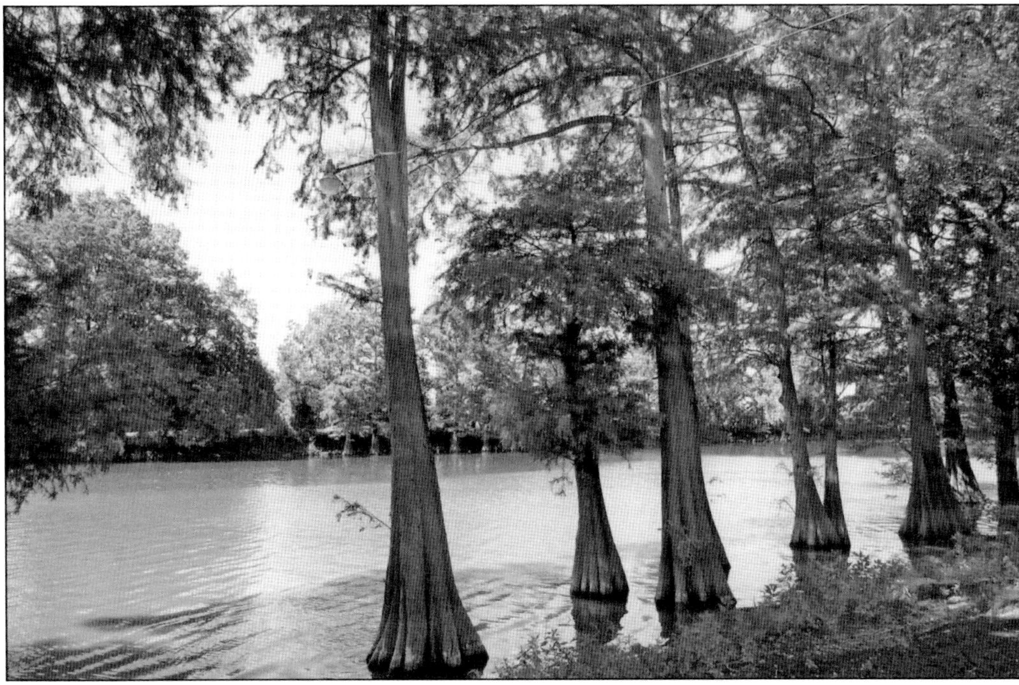

SCENIC CHISHOLM LAKE. Chisholm Lake was originally known as Clear Lake or Boyd Lake. The lake was renamed for early settler William H. Chisholm. (Courtesy of Joe Morris.)

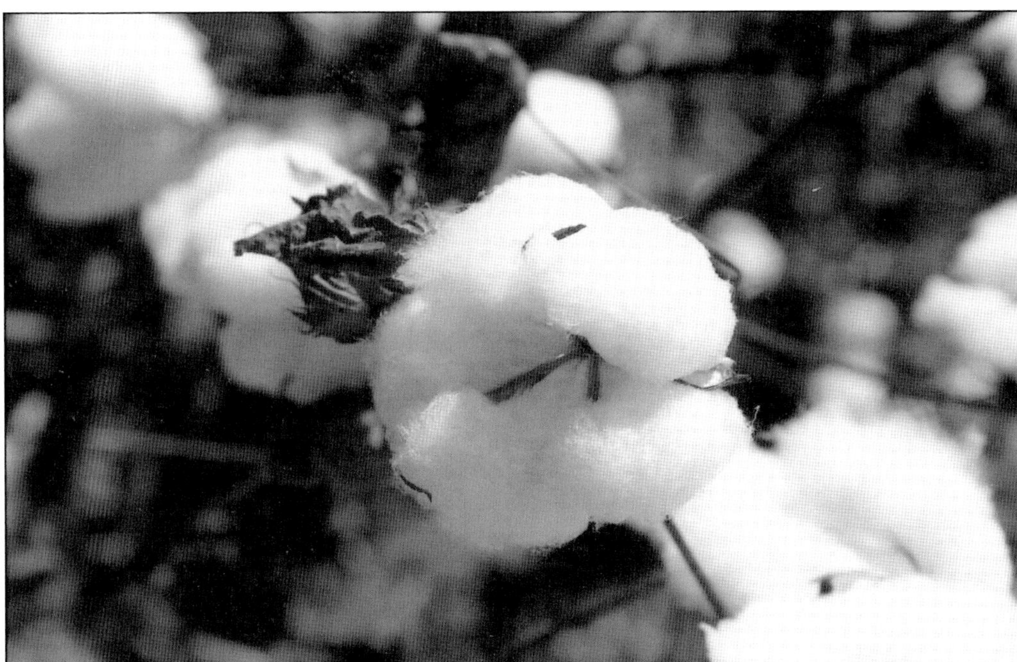

COTTON CROP. In the early days, cotton was known as "white gold" and was one of the main agricultural crops in Lauderdale County. (Courtesy of Linda Caldwell.)

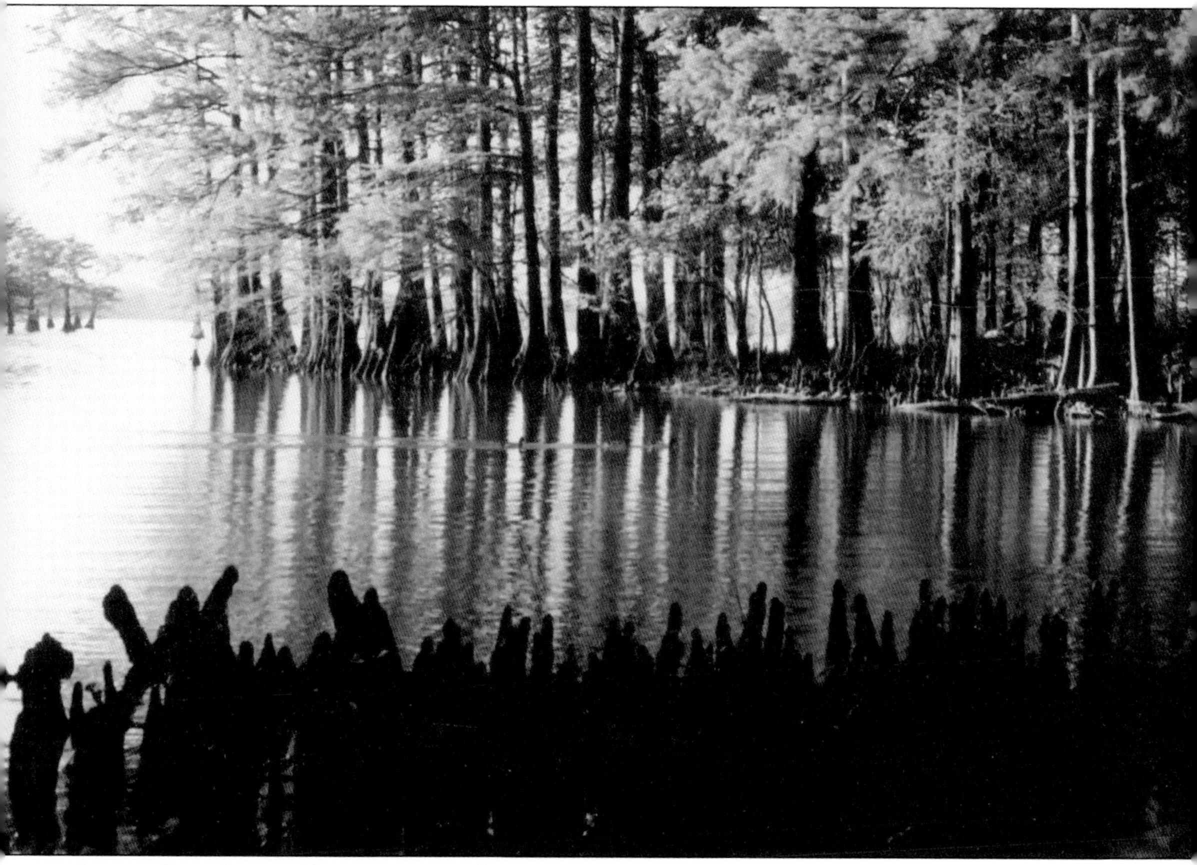

Scenic Open Lake. The massive earthquake in 1811 in West Tennessee is said to have increased the size of Open Lake. (Courtesy of Joe Morris.)

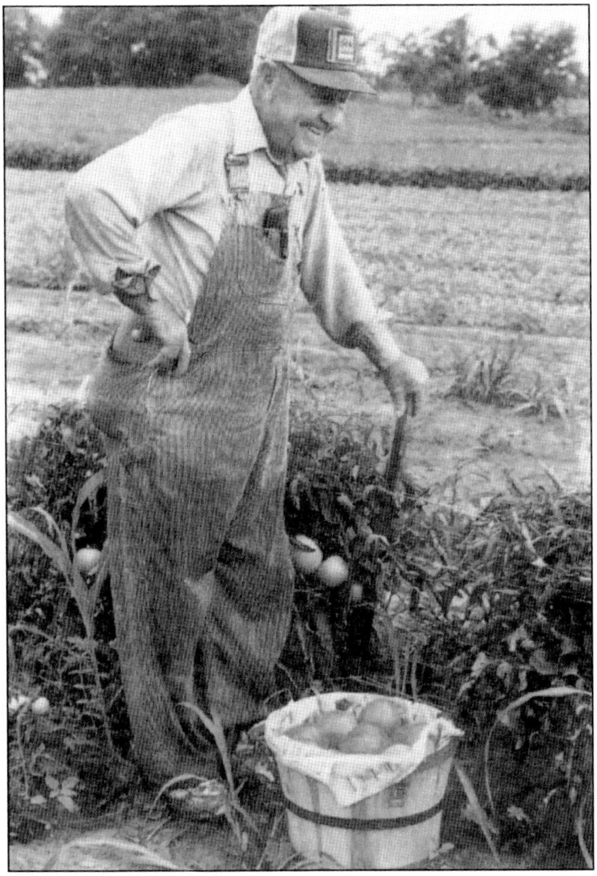

PICKING TOMATOES. Pete Tims, Whitefield farmer, takes a break from picking tomatoes on his farm. The famous Ripley Tomatoes and the county's tomato growers are saluted with a celebration the weekend following the fourth of July each year. Ripley Tomatoes are a sought-after favorite throughout the eastern United States and are grown on 1,200 acres in Lauderdale County. (Courtesy of Mike Tims.)

TOMATO FARMERS PETE AND WAYNE TIMS, 1996. Pete Tims (left) and his son Wayne (right) are pictured with "Mountain Spring" tomatoes from their farm in the Whitefield community. The Timses are well known for their produce all over West Tennessee. (Courtesy of Mike Tims.)

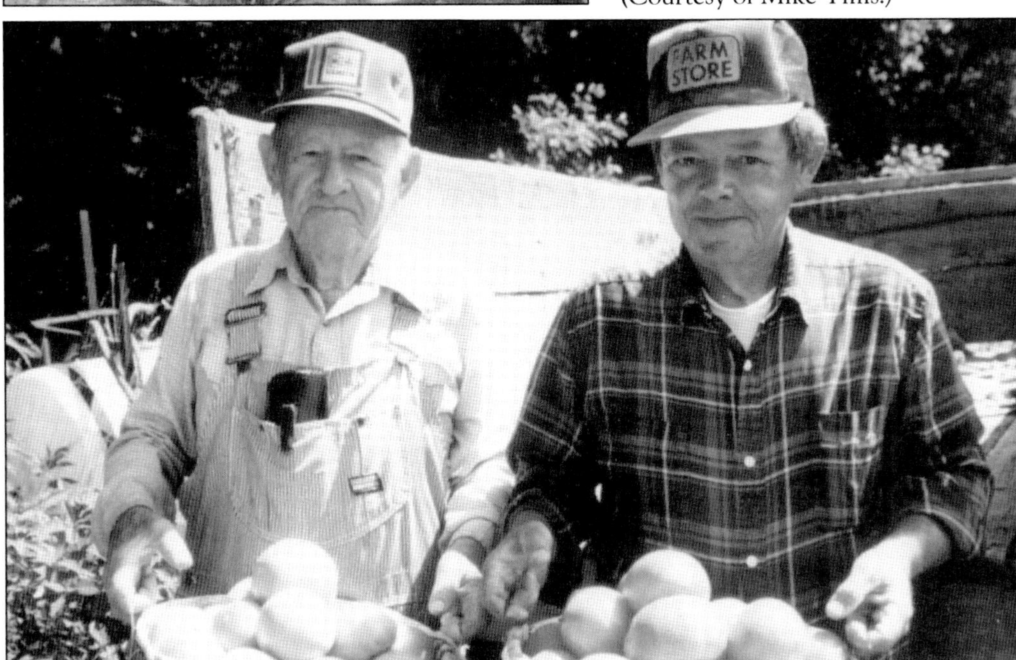

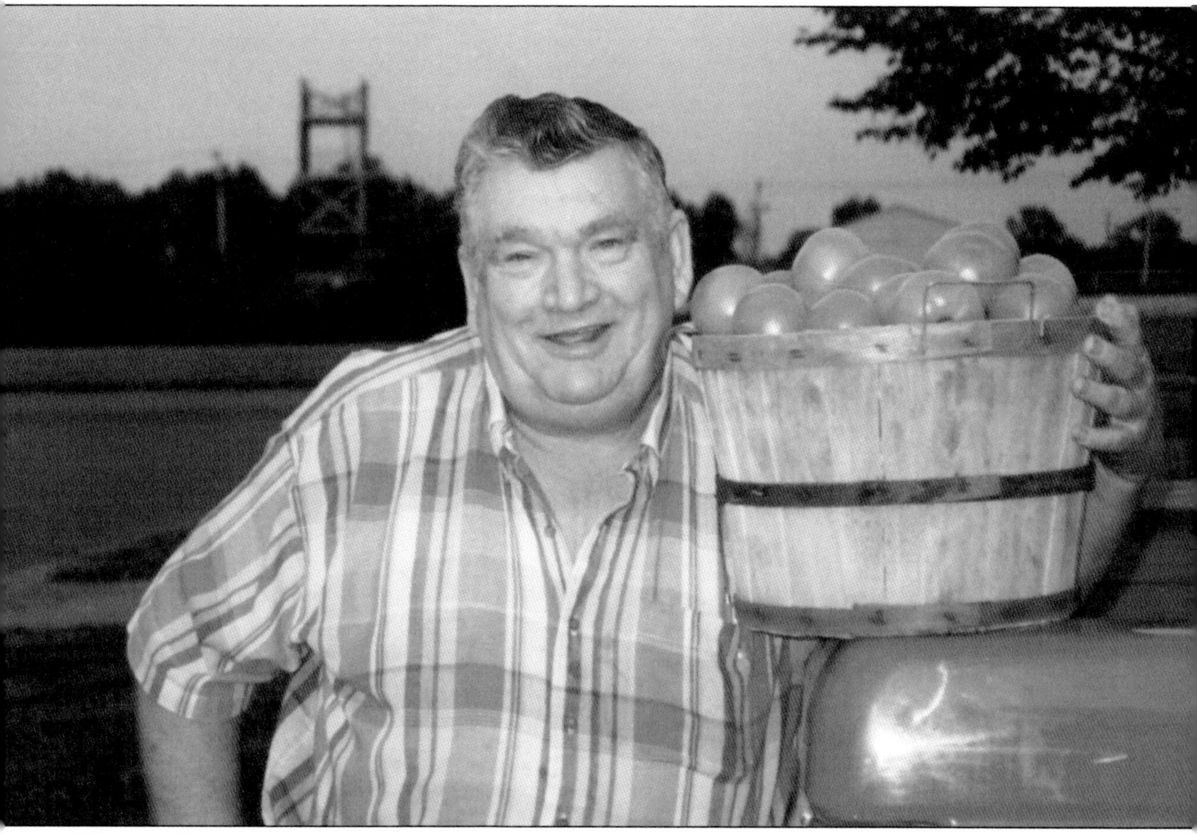

William Daniels Jr. Coming from the Garden. William Daniels Jr. is pictured coming in from his garden with a basket of tomatoes in Henning, Tennessee, in July 1994. Tomatoes are grown in gardens, in truck patches, and commercially on 1,200 acres throughout the county. Tomatoes and other produce are sold at many roadside markets throughout the county. (Courtesy of Beverly "Sissy" Steelman.)

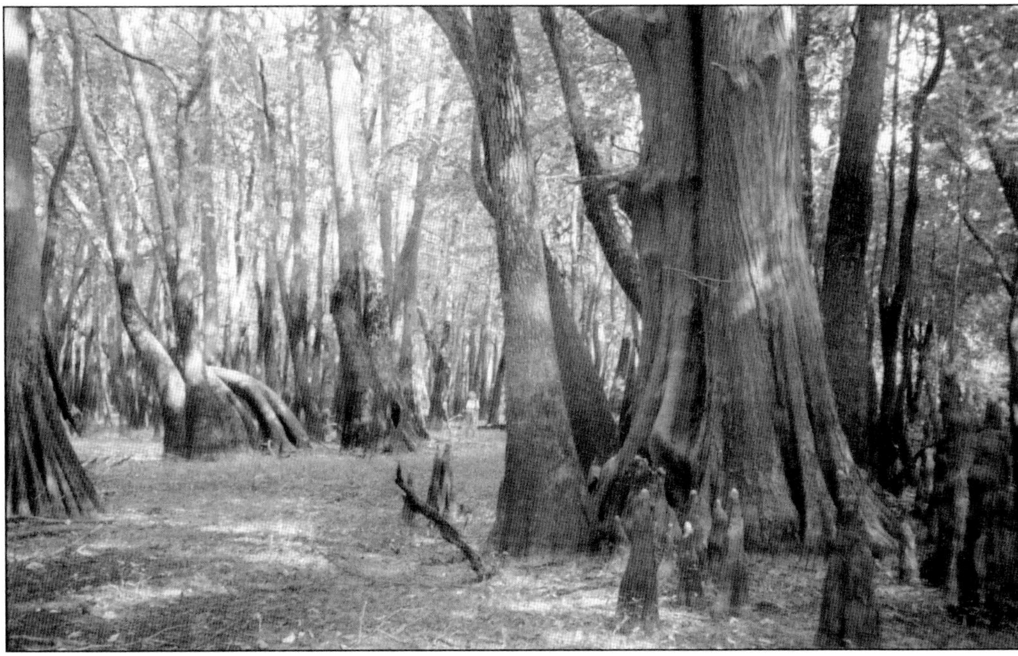

BERTHA MORRIS AT ROUND POND, 2000. Bertha Morris (at center in the back of the photograph) stands among her old growth cypress trees on Round Pond in the Chisholm Lake bottoms. The cypress trees will grow in water and have cypress knees that help the trees breathe. (Courtesy of Joe Morris.)

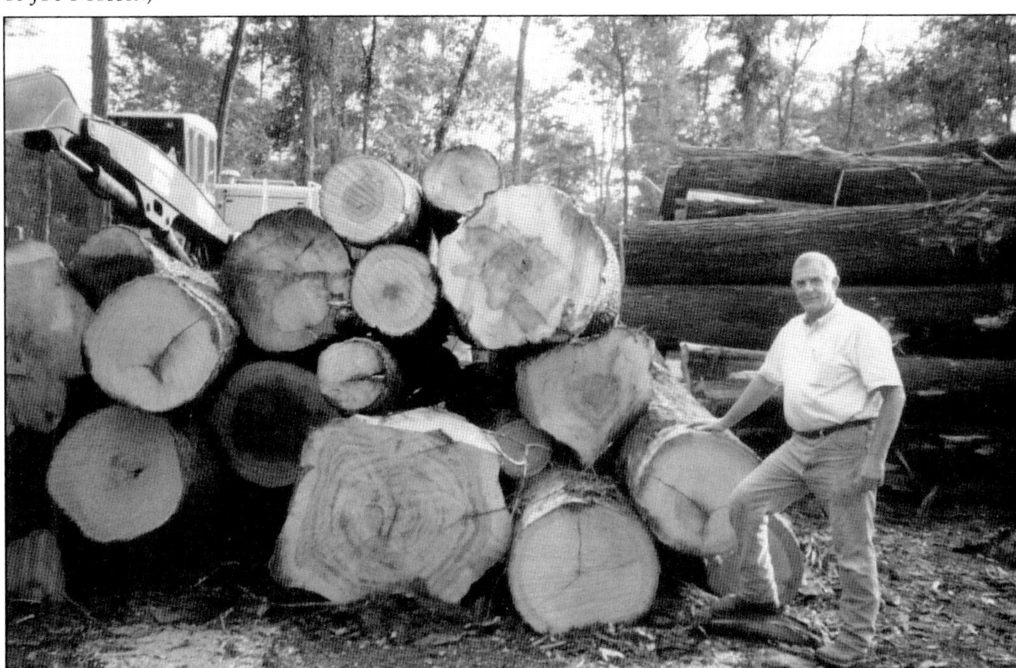

JOE MORRIS REVIEWING LOGS. Joe Morris is seen reviewing logs from a timber project at Long Pond and Yonka Pond in the Chisholm Lake bottoms. The timber industry is still active in Lauderdale County. (Courtesy of Joe Morris.)

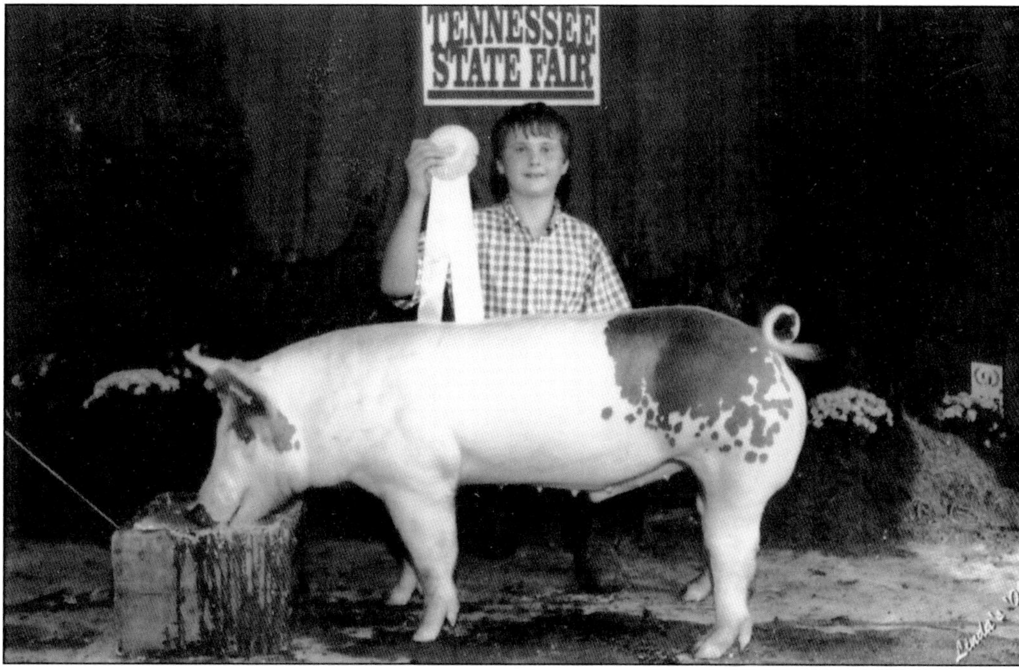

RESERVE GRAND CHAMPION MARKET HOG. Chad Lewis, a Halls Junior High student, shows off his Reserve Grand Champion market hog at the Tennessee State Fair in 2009. Halls High School has an active Future Farmers of American organization. (Courtesy of University of Tennessee Extension Service.)

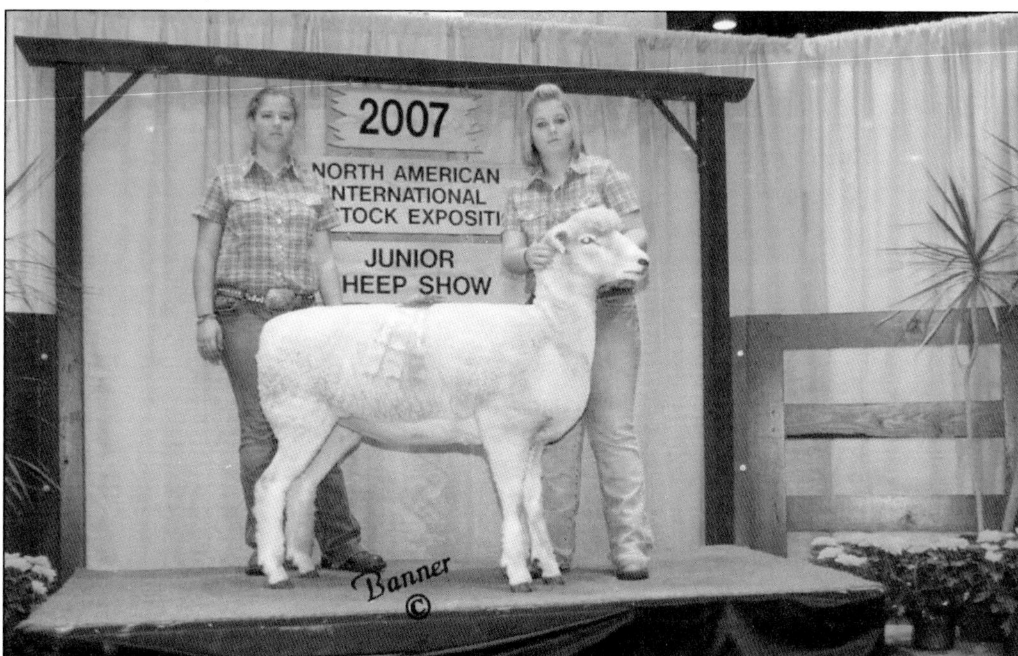

GRAND CHAMPION SHEEP. Carley and Kirby Cherry, Halls High School students, show off Naile, a 2007 Grand Champion sheep at the North American National Livestock Exposition. (Courtesy of Cathy Cherry.)

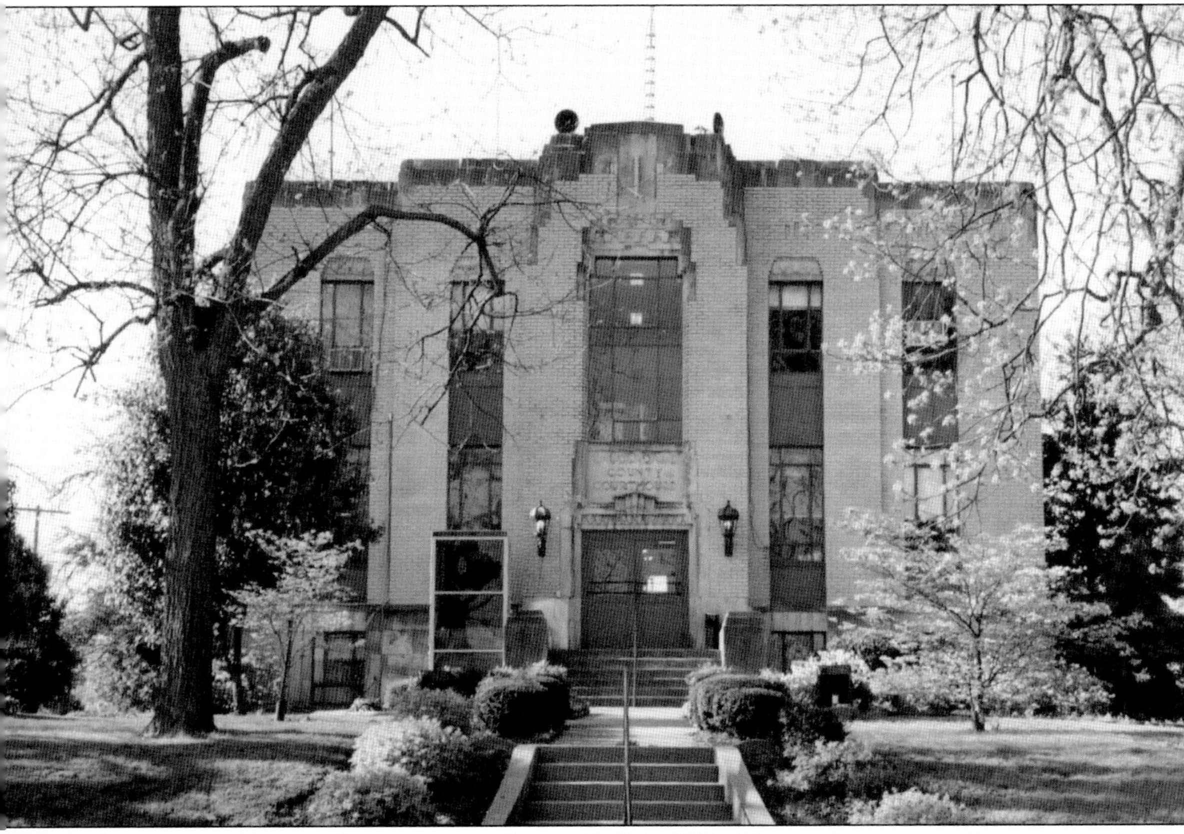

LAUDERDALE COUNTY COURTHOUSE IN RIPLEY. Built in 1936, this courthouse was unique compared to others in the area. The Art Deco style was unlike the styling used at most other courthouses in West Tennessee.

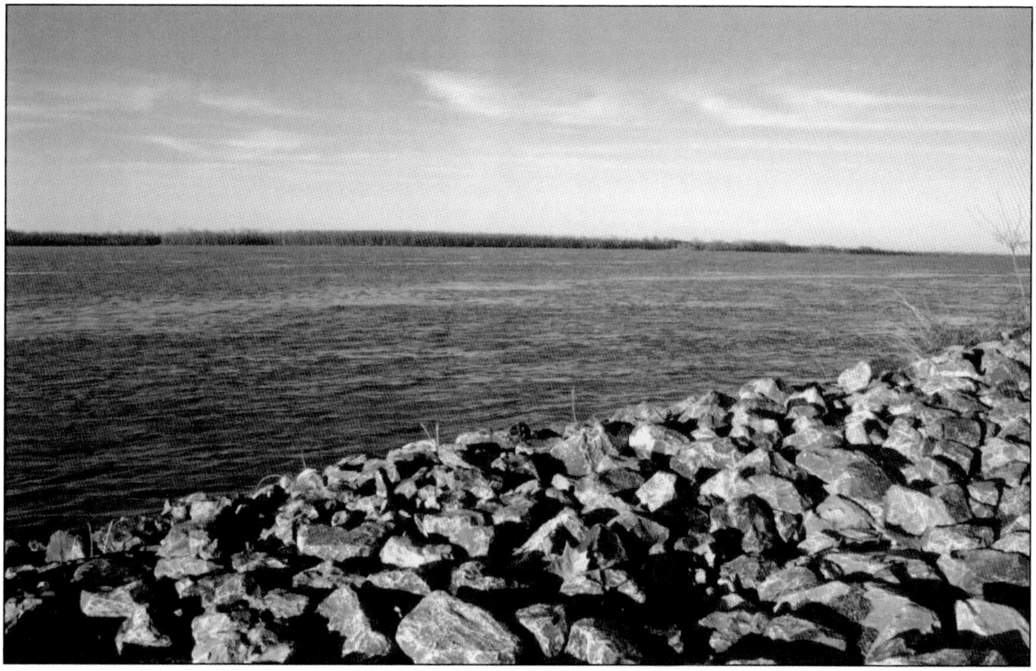

Mississippi River. The Mississippi River flows along the western border of Lauderdale County for nearly 60 miles. It provides an outdoorsman's paradise for boating, water skiing, and fishing. (Photograph by Amie Vanderford; courtesy of the author.)

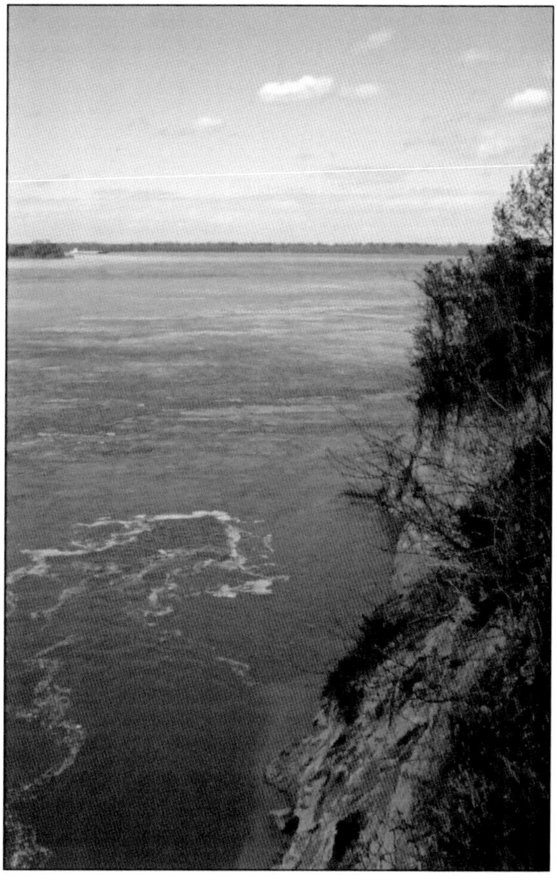

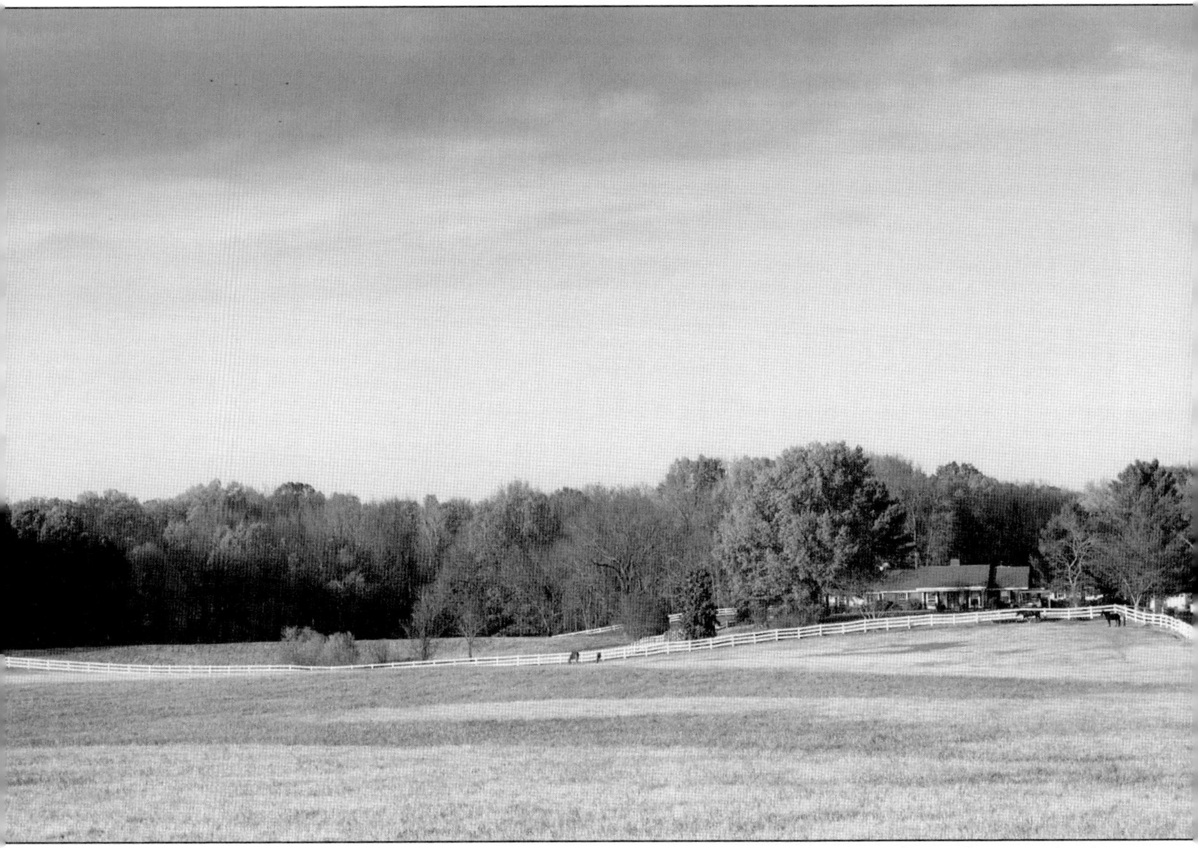

Great Oaks Farm in Ripley. This farm is owned by Bill Williams, who is known for his prizewinning Tennessee Walking horses. These rolling hills are in the Arp community. (Photograph by Grace Ferrell; courtesy of the author.)

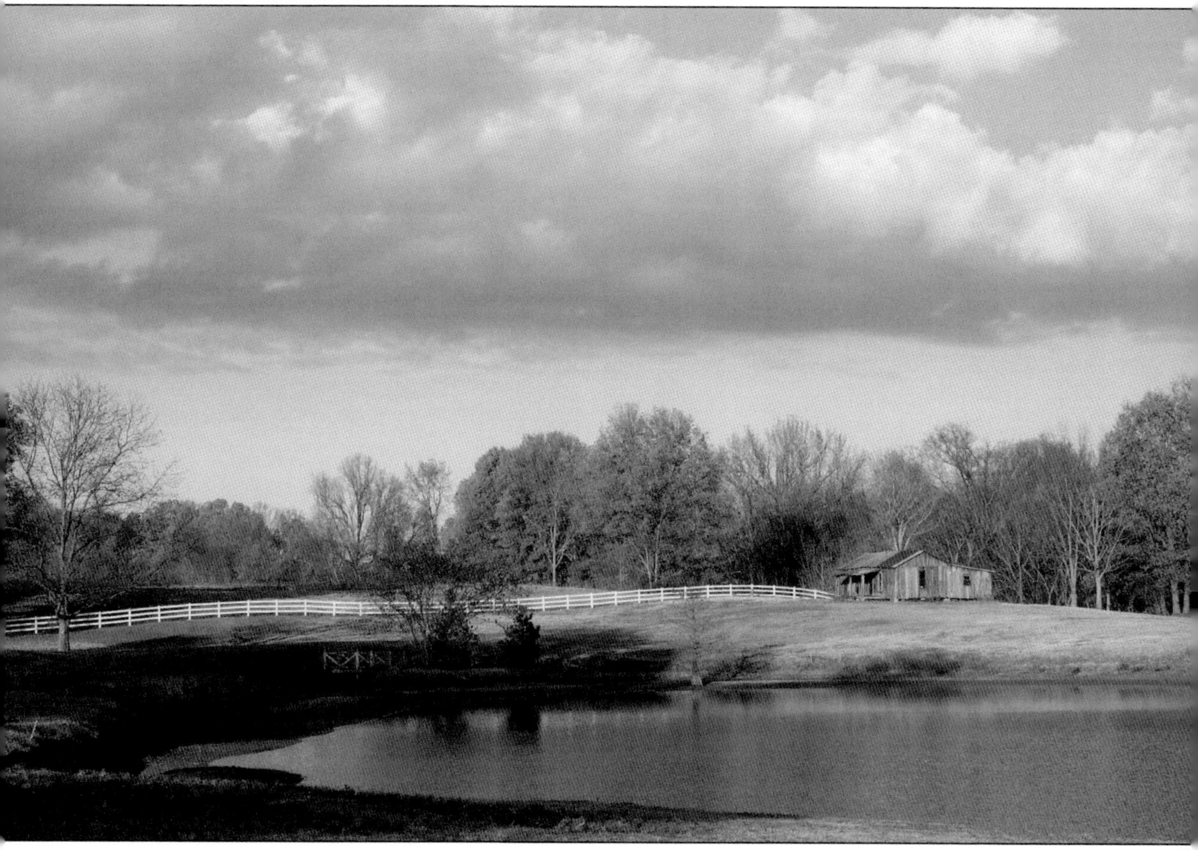

Great Oaks Farmhouse. A farmhouse is seen on a hill in the Arp community on the Great Oaks Farm. (Photograph by Grace Ferrell; courtesy of the author.)

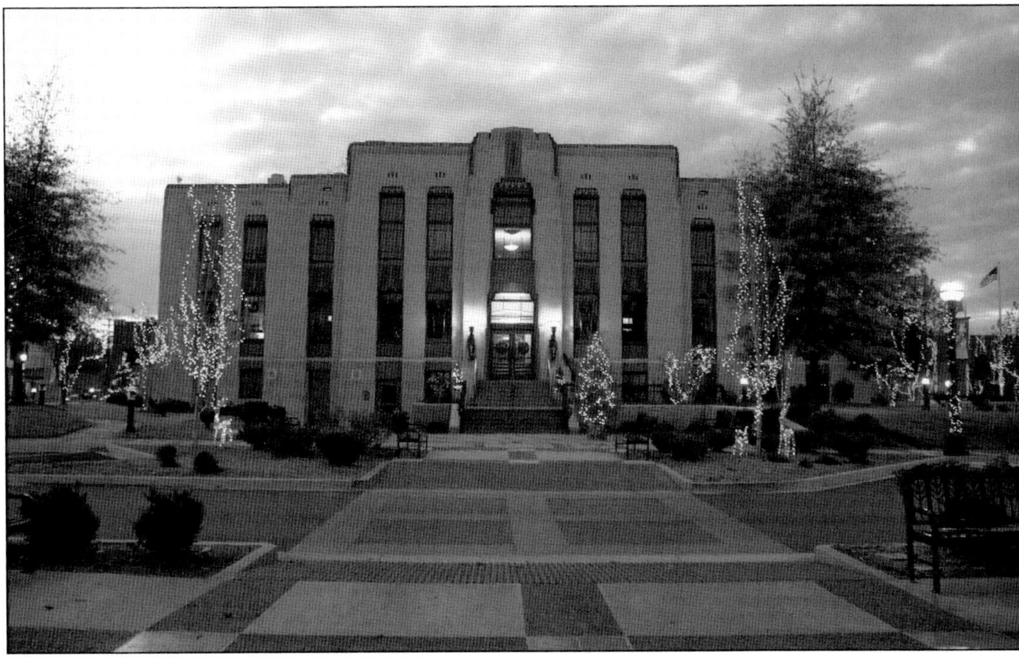

Lauderdale County Courthouse after Refurbishment, 2010. This courthouse was built in 1936. It is one of the only ones constructed in the Art Deco style and is in the National Register of Historic places. A downtown revitalization project in 2010 restored the courthouse to its current splendor. (Photograph by Grace Ferrell; courtesy of the author.)

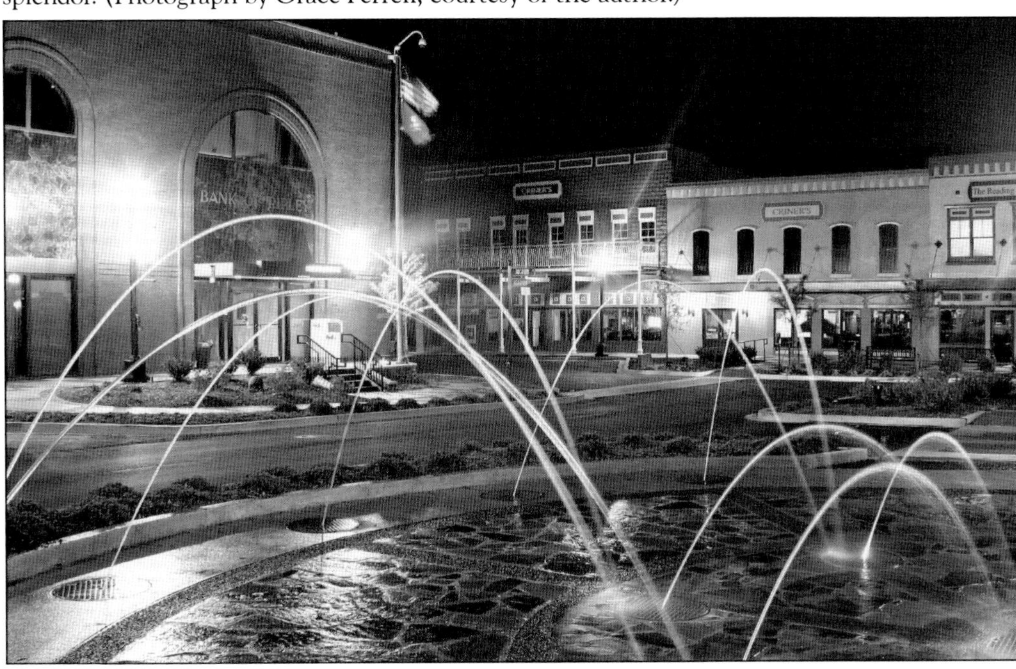

Lauderdale County Fountain. This fountain is located on the corner of the Lauderdale County Courthouse in Ripley, Tennessee. The fountain was built in 2010 during downtown renovations. The Bank of Ripley is visible in the background. (Photograph by Grace Ferrell; courtesy of the author.)

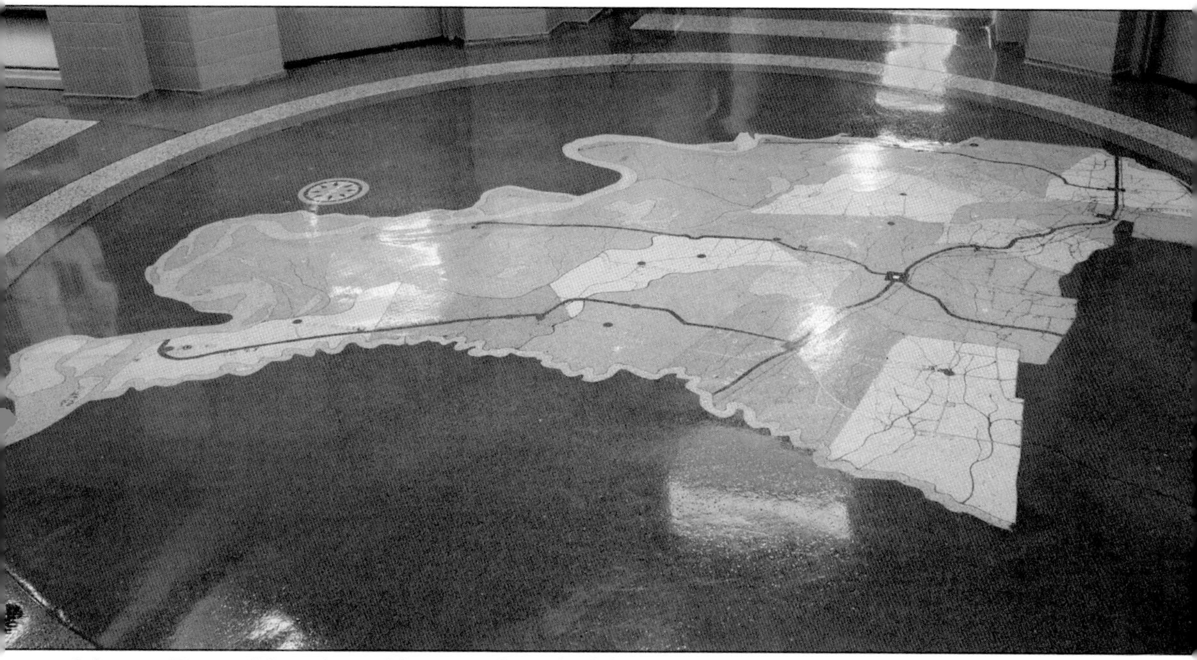

Marble Floor Map. A marble map of Lauderdale County is worked into the first floor of the Lauderdale County Courthouse, which was built in 1936. (Photograph by Grace Ferrell; courtesy of the author.)

Bibliography

Davis, Bettie. *Gates Now and Then*. Memphis, TN: 1986.

Hellums, Clarice Haynes and Kara Haynes McCauley. *Visions of Lauderdale County Past and Present*. Memphis, TN: Allan and Akin Printers, 1996.

Morris, Billie. *A Pictorial History of Lauderdale County*. Vol. I. Virginia Beach, VA: Donning Company Publishers, 2009.

Morris, Billie. *A Pictorial History of Lauderdale County*. Vol. II. Virginia Beach, VA: Donning Company Publishers, 2010.

Morris, Billie. *A Pictorial History of Lauderdale County*. Vol. III. Virginia Beach, VA: Donning Company Publishers, 2011.

Peters, Kate Johnson. *Lauderdale County From Earliest Times*. McCowt Mercer Press, Inc., 1957.

Toplovich, Ann. *The Tennessee Encyclopedia of History and Culture, Lauderdale County*. The University of Tennessee Press Online Edition.

ABOUT THE AUTHOR

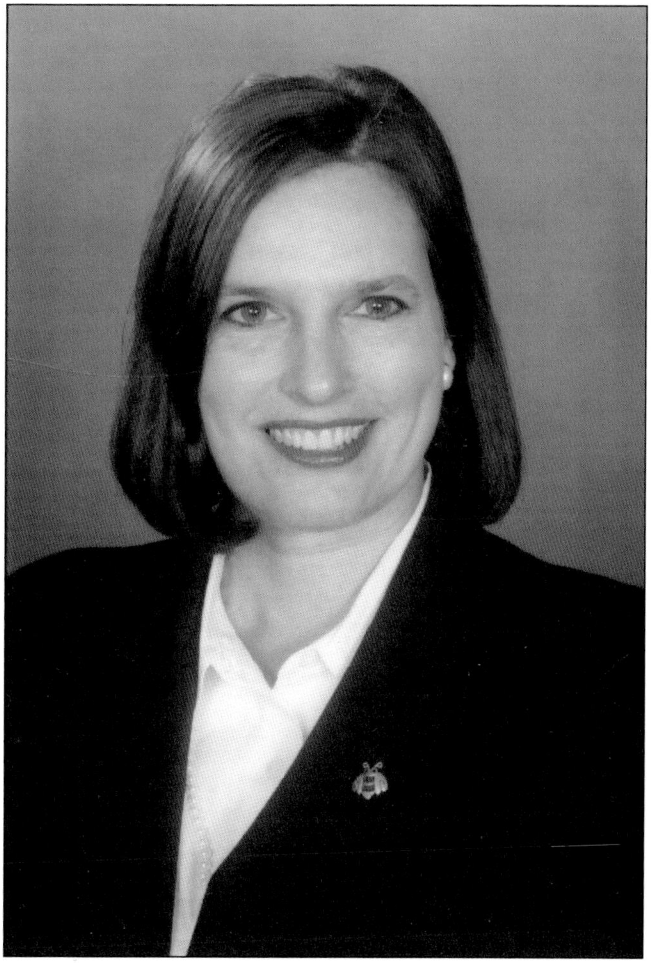

BILLIE MORRIS, AUTHOR. Billie Morris is a native of Lauderdale County. She was born in Ripley and has lived there most of her life. She is married to Joseph Morris, and they have two daughters and two granddaughters. Billie worked in Lauderdale County Industry for 30 years. She spent 25 of those years at Todd Uniform where she managed plants in Maury City, Ripley, and Henning. She is the President of Friends of the Lauderdale County Library, a former president of the Lauderdale County Historical Society, and helped with the formation of the Lauderdale County Museum. She was a longtime member and secretary-treasurer for the Ripley Rotary Club. She has served on boards for the Lauderdale County Education Foundation and Partnership Lauderdale. She was instrumental in the Lauderdale County Chamber of Commerce getting the Sugar Hill Mansion as its new home.